The VMS User's Guide

Digital Press VAX Users Series

Paul C. Anagnostopoulos
VAX/VMS: Writing Real Programs in DCL

Philip E. Bourne
UNIX for VMS Users

James F. Peters III and Patrick Holmay
The VMS User's Guide

Ronald M. Sawey and Troy T. Stokes
A Beginner's Guide to VAX/VMS Utilities and Applications

The VMS User's Guide

James F. Peters III
Patrick Holmay

Digital Press

Digital Press™ is an imprint of Butterworth–Heinemann.

Recognizing the importance of preserving what has been written, Butterworth-Heinemann prints its books on acid-free paper whenever possible.

Library of Congress Cataloging-in-Publication Data

Peters, James F.
    The VMS user's guide.

    1. VAX/VMS (Computer operating system)   I. Holmay, Patrick, 1957–
II. Title.
QA76.76.063P522   1990   005.4'44   89-23737
ISBN 1-55558-014-9

Trademarks and trademarked products mentioned in this book include: AT&T Bell Laboratories, UNIX; Digital Equipment Corporation, DCL, the Digital logo, MicroVAX, PDP-11, VAX, VAX/VMS, VMS, VK100, VT100, VT200; Microsoft Corporation, MS-DOS.

Design: Sandra Calef
Substantive editing: Christie Williams
Art: Steven Ackerman
Index: Karen Pangallo
Production and composition: Editorial Inc.
Printing and binding: Hamilton Printing Company

The publisher offers discounts on bulk orders of this book.
For information, please write:

Manager of Special Sales, Digital Press
Butterworth–Heinemann
313 Washington Street
Newton, MA 02158–1626

Order number: EY–6739E–DP

10 9 8 7 6

Printed in the United States of America

To Chota with love
Jim Peters

To my family for their patience and support
Pat Holmay

Contents

Appendixes

Index   295

Tables

Illustrations

Preface

In the world of computers, VAX computer systems enjoy celebrity status. They are widely used and have a reputation for being user-friendly. This book is about the VMS operating system from a beginning user's point-of-view. The VMS operating system is the bridge that allows you to use the power of the VAX computer. Actually, VMS is a collection of programs that provide an interface between users and a VAX computer system. VMS is responsible for the user-friendliness of VAXes.

The focus of this book is the Digital Command Language (DCL), which provides a straightforward means of issuing commands to VMS. DCL is a language that, among other things, makes it possible for users to create, name, store, and edit files. We rely on files to store information that we want to preserve on some storage medium, such as a magnetic tape or a diskette.

In addition to an extensive tour of the basic DCL commands, this book provides an introduction to two commonly used VMS editors: EDT and EVE. An editor is a program that is used in the preparation of new files or in making corrections and additions to existing files. EDT and EVE provide convenient and varied means of editing VMS files. Besides a thorough introduction to editing techniques that can be used with EDT and EVE, we also provide editing experiments you can try out at your terminal.

Experiments given in this book are self-teaching tools. They are designed to show you step-by-step use of the features of VMS. This book also provides a variety of other self-teaching tools, such as

- Aims at the beginning of every chapter—these single out what you can expect to learn
- Chapter summaries
- Quizzes at the end of each chapter
- Lists of important terms with accompanying definitions
- Chapter exercises
- Further reading lists
- User-defined DCL commands to help you customize your VMS environment
- A reference guide to selected DCL commands and utilities

This book has been designed to be useful as a textbook in courses about the VMS environment. It also provides a convenient self-teaching tool for those who want easy access to the essentials of VMS. In addition, it explains how you can customize your VMS environment to fit the way you want to work with VMS.

James F. Peters III
Patrick Holmay
September 1989

Acknowledgments

The following people reviewed various stages of this book and were very helpful in making the final result better: Paul Anagnostopoulos, Carlisle, Mass.; Jack Beidler, Department of Mathematics and Computer Science, University of Scranton; Daniel Brekke, Department of Computer Science, Moorhead State University; Fred Marsh, Digital Equipment Corporation; David Teague, Western Carolina University; Steve Thorpe, Wesley College; Andy Sadler, Digital Equipment Corporation; Hamed Sallam, Computer Science Department, Mankato State University; Ron Sawey, Department of Computer Science, Southwest Texas State University; Charles M. Shub, Computer Science Department, University of Colorado; John Stone, Department of Mathematics, Grinnell College; George Whitson, University of Texas at Tyler; Michael Wang, Department of Management and Information Science, University of Texas at Austin; Patricia Wenner, Computer Science Department, Bucknell University. We would also like to thank William Hankley, Virgil Wallentine, and Sheela Ramanna, Computing and Information Sciences Department, Kansas State University; Mike Meehan, Digital Press; Christie Williams, Westford, Mass.; and all those at Editorial Inc., Rockport, Mass., for their help and guidance during the preparation of this book. We are particularly grateful for the many improvements made by the development editor, Christie Williams, and by reviewers Paul Anagnostopoulos and Fred Marsh.

Introduction

This book is designed to give you a solid basis for working with the many features and functions of VAX computer systems using the VMS operating system. It does not cover specific applications programs that run on VAX computers but rather concentrates on the capabilities and flexibility of VMS. The book takes a hands-on approach, providing you with experiments and exercises to try out at your terminal. It also provides discussions and examples that you can use as a reference when you work with VMS on your own.

The book addresses users new to the VMS environment as well as those with VMS experience who need a reference guide. You may be in an instructor-led college class, in a company-sponsored training session, or working on your own without instructor supervision.

Before you begin to use VMS, it is helpful to have some background information about VAX computer systems and the VMS operating system. It is also useful to understand the structure of this book and how you may best use it.

The VAX/VMS Landscape

The VAX-11 computer series was introduced by Digital Equipment Corporation in 1978 as an extension of its PDP-11 series of computers. Since then, the VAX family of computer systems has grown to include systems of all sizes. The system you work with may be a free-standing MicroVAX workstation; a VAXcluster of interconnected, multiple VAX processors, or a VAX 8000 series minicomputer. Because VAX is a family of systems, however, working on one VAX system is nearly identical to working on another, and software on one system functions basically the same way on another system.

VAX is an acronym for Virtual Address eXtension, which refers to the use of virtual memory when processing programs and data. Virtual memory is computer memory, or storage, that is not physically present in the computer system. When a computer uses virtual memory, it processes programs and data in segments. Only the segments currently needed are in memory; the rest are stored on a disk or other storage device. The computer retrieves different stored segments as needed, returning unneeded segments to storage to free memory space for newly retrieved segments. The use of virtual memory allows VAX systems to support more users or larger programs than physical memory limitations would permit.

The implementation of this virtual memory scheme is made possible by a collection of programs and utilities called VMS, which stands for Virtual Memory System. VMS is an operating system that runs exclusively on VAX systems. The operating system manages and controls the resources of the computer system (such as peripheral devices and memory) and user input. Other operating systems with which you may be familiar are MS-DOS and UNIX.

One of the important features of the VMS operating system, besides its use of virtual memory, is its capability for multiprocessing. Because it can schedule system resources efficiently, many users can use a VAX computer system at the same time and yet feel that they each have exclusive use of the system. In fact, each user's tasks are being swiftly executed one at a time, with the order of processing based on need and priority.

As a user, you communicate with VMS using an interface called DCL, or the Digital Command Language. You enter into a dialogue with VMS by issuing various DCL commands. These commands are the basis for your work with VMS, and so the discussion in this book focuses on their use.

Important Considerations

A VAX computer system can comprise a variety of system components, peripheral equipment (such as terminals and printers), and applications programs. For example, you may find that your keyboard is slightly different from those illustrated in Chapter 1. (If this is the case, you can refer to your documentation or Help facility, or check with your system manager, to learn about key equivalents for your specific keyboard.) Although the system configuration may differ, VAX systems running VMS all function in basically the same way.

The experiments and examples shown in this book are current through Version 5 of VMS. If you are working with an earlier version of VMS, there may be some slight variations in your results, although there should be no major differences. Also, because the setup of each system and its software is site-specific, you may encounter slight variations in experiment results or in the availability of certain utilities.

In general, if your results differ greatly from the book's, or if you encounter problems in using features discussed in the book, check with your system manager. He or she will know the specifics of your system and be able to advise you on using the features available to you.

About This Book

This book is designed to help VMS users who are in a class or working on their own. Each chapter contains discussions, examples, experiments that demonstrate the concepts and commands, and other learning aids.

New VMS users will find it invaluable to work through each experiment step by step while at their keyboards. More experienced users may find the discussions and examples sufficient for understanding the material, or they may choose to follow the experiments. Because the experiments build on each other within each chapter, it is important to work through them from the beginning of the chapter.

In addition to the examples and experiments, each chapter contains the following learning aids and self-teaching tools:

- The summaries at the end of each chapter review important information and contain tables of the commands, symbols, special characters, and key terms used in the chapter. These tables are useful references for review or reinforcement of the material.
- Chapter exercises appear after the summaries. They reinforce the chapter's content and suggest further exploration of the capabilities of VMS.

- Each chapter contains a review quiz, which will help you to gauge how well you understand the material.
- Finally, at the end of each chapter is a list of readings designed to expand your study of VMS, DCL, and the uses of VAX computers.

The Structure of This Book

This book contains seven chapters and eight appendixes. Although the chapters follow a logical progression in presenting the material, it is not absolutely necessary to read them in order, particularly if you have some experience with VMS.

Chapter 1 explains the basics of logging in and out of the VAX and getting help through the extensive VMS Help facility. It then introduces a series of concepts, all of which are explored in detail in the chapters that follow.

Chapter 2 details the system of files and directories that VMS uses to store your information. You learn to create and manage files and work with the directory structure that helps you organize your files.

Chapter 3 introduces one of the VMS editors, EDT, which allows you to enter and edit text in files. Although not a complete word-processing application, EDT provides the commands necessary for easy text entry and manipulation.

Chapter 4 introduces a second VMS text editor, EVE. This editor provides many features similar to those of EDT as well as some unique capabilities, such as using two windows at a time.

Chapter 5 covers the Phone and Mail utilities, which allow you to communicate with other users on your system.

Chapter 6 continues with an examination of files, showing you alternative ways to create and manipulate files, sort records, merge files, and print files. In addition, it covers the creation of library files, which you use to store groups of related files.

Chapter 7 discusses the creation and use of command procedures. These procedures help you to customize VMS for maximum efficiency by allowing you to automate routine tasks.

Appendixes A through H present a guide to selected DCL commands, an ASCII character table, and information on EDT line mode commands, the editor EDT2, file protection, programming languages, ANSI mode control sequences, and terminal characteristics.

Conventions Used in This Book

Throughout the book, certain conventions are used for presenting information and representing commands and keys:

- User-typed entries, like commands and file names, appear in an uppercase "typewriter" font, for instance, the **DIRECTORY** command. In examples, the "typewriter" font is lowercase. You may use either uppercase or lowercase letters to type in command lines at the keyboard.

- In examples of interaction between VMS and the user, your entries are shown in color so that you can distinguish them from the information that VMS displays.

- Names of keys are represented in angle brackets: the <RETURN> key. When two keys are to be pressed in combination, for instance the <CTRL> (control) and <Z> keys, they are shown as <CTRL/Z>.

- Generic names that accompany commands, for instance, **PRINT** *filespec*, are shown in italic, indicating that the user is to substitute an actual file specification for the italic word.

- Optional parameters in command lines are enclosed in brackets, for example, **DIRECTORY** [*filespec*]. To indicate an unspecified number of optional parameters, [, . . .] is used.

The VMS User's Guide

Chapter 1

Discovering VMS

Intelligence . . . is the faculty of making artificial objects, especially tools to make tools, and varying the fabrication indefinitely.
—Henri Bergson, *Creative Evolution*, 1907

This chapter provides an overview of the commands, procedures, and capabilities of VMS. In doing so, it also introduces you to the topics discussed in the remaining chapters of this book. In this chapter, you will

- Explore the fundamentals of using DCL commands
- Become familiar with commonly used commands
- Explore the uses of various control keys
- Begin creating files
- Start exploring your login directory
- Experiment with the Recall, Type-ahead, and EDT buffers
- Create and implement a `LOGIN.COM` file

1.1   Introducing the Digital Command Language

The VMS operating system is a layered software system that can be thought of as a set of concentric rings, as shown in Figure 1.1.

The VMS supervisor layer provides a program called a command language interpreter (CLI), which serves as an interface between users and VMS. The

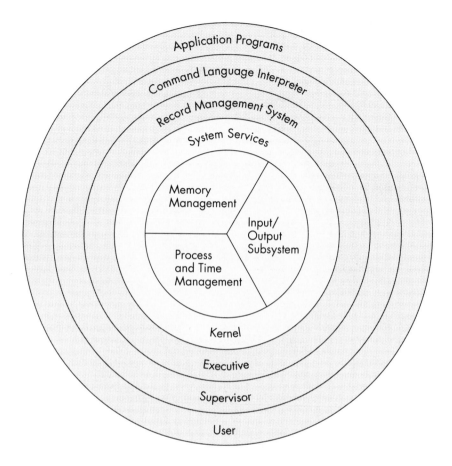

Legend

The kernel handles I/O (device drivers), schedules and controls processes, and manages memory and system services.

The executive layer provides other system services and a record management system.

The supervisor layer provides a command language interpreter, which is the interface between users and the inner layers of VMS.

The user layer provides assorted utilities, application libraries, program development tools, programming languages, and so on.

Figure 1.1 VMS Software Layers

Table 1.1 Commonly Used DCL Commands

Command	Result
CREATE	Creates a new file
DELETE	Deletes a file
DIRECTORY	Provides a list of files
EDIT	Edits (or creates) a file
HELP	Displays information about the commands on your system
LOGOUT	Logs out of the system
MAIL	Accesses the Mail utility, which you use to send and receive messages
PHONE	Accesses the Phone utility, which allows "conversations" between users
PURGE	Eliminates all but the most recent version of each file in your working directory
RENAME	Changes the name of a file
SET	Defines or changes characteristics of files and devices
SHOW	Displays information about your system, such as users, quota, and time
TYPE	Lists the contents of a file

most commonly used CLI in a VMS environment is the Digital Command Language interpreter (DCL). It is DCL that displays the $ prompt on the screen. It is also DCL that interprets each command line you type to initiate and control processes and to request various VMS services.

DCL provides over 200 commands that offer an easy-to-use interface between users and the many VMS services. Table 1.1 lists some commonly used DCL commands, or command verbs. As you can see from the table, the command verbs describe the actions resulting from the commands.

You use DCL commands by typing them in a command line. In addition to the command verb, you can include parameters and qualifiers in the command line. Figure 1.2 shows the syntax for a command line with parameters and qualifiers.

Each DCL command operates on a parameter or parameters. For example, to display information about a specific user, you enter the SHOW USERS command

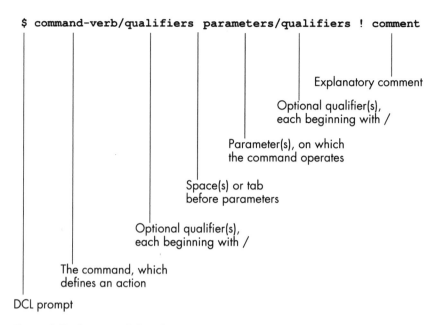

$ command-verb/qualifiers parameters/qualifiers ! comment

Explanatory comment

Optional qualifier(s),
each beginning with /

Parameter(s), on which
the command operates

Space(s) or tab
before parameters

Optional qualifier(s),
each beginning with /

The command, which
defines an action

DCL prompt

Figure 1.2 Command Line Syntax

with the *username* parameter. If *username* is Curry, you would type the following command line and press the <RETURN> key to enter it:

$ show user curry <RETURN>

The parameter indicates what you want shown, in this case, information about the user Curry.

Some commands assume a default (pre-set) parameter if you do not specify a parameter in the command line. Other commands accept or require multiple parameters. You must separate each parameter from the command verb, parameter, or qualifier before it with space(s), or tab(s).

Qualifiers may be used to further control or modify the command verb and parameters. Qualifiers narrow or broaden the scope of the requested processing. For example, to log out and, at the same time, to see how much time has elapsed while you have been using the system, you would type the command line

$ logout/full <RETURN>

The **/FULL** qualifier displays a summary of accounting statistics for the current terminal session.

Qualifiers are usually optional in DCL commands. Many commands allow you to use multiple qualifiers for a command verb or parameter. You must separate each qualifier from the command verb, parameter, or qualifier before it with a slash (/).

You can add comments to a command line by typing an exclamation point (!) and then the comment. The comment can explain what the command does or other useful information. DCL ignores any characters to the right of the exclamation point, so

```
$ show users <RETURN>
```

does the same thing as

```
$ show users ! display current users <RETURN>
```

If you are working with a hard-copy terminal, commented command lines provide you with a permanent record of explanations of new commands you have used.

When you type a DCL command line, you may use any combination of uppercase and lowercase letters, because DCL is not case-sensitive.

With its many commands, parameters, and qualifiers, DCL provides a rich selection of tools that let you use the resources of your computer system efficiently. The trick is to learn how to use these tools to fashion new tools that are tailormade to your own needs. The sections that follow introduce the topics covered in the other chapters of this book. They include the basics of working with DCL and some of the possibilities for customizing your VMS system.

1.2 The First Steps with VMS

Before you begin, take a minute to familiarize yourself with your keyboard. Figure 1.3 illustrates two common keyboard layouts.

The main keyboard contains standard typewriter keys as well as some special keys like the <CTRL> (control) key. The auxiliary, or numeric, keypad contains special function keys—<PF1> through <PF4>—and keys for entering numeric data. In some applications, these keys are used for special commands; for example, the EDT editor uses them for entering editing commands. On the VT100 keyboard, arrow keys, which you use to move the cursor, and indicators appear across the top of the keyboard. The VT200 keyboard has

VT100 Keyboard

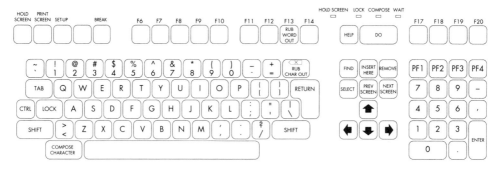

VT200 Keyboard

Figure 1.3 Keyboard Layouts for VT100 and VT200

special keys, function keys, and indicators across the top. The editing keypad contains the arrow keys and special editing keys.

The <RETURN> key on the main keyboard is particularly important. You use it to enter a line of text that you have typed in and to advance the cursor to the beginning of the next line.

Pressing the <RETURN> key tells the VMS command interpreter to start doing something with the current line you have typed. Be sure to press the <RETURN> key at the end of each command line in order to enter the command.

Also press <RETURN> to move to the login prompt when you first turn on a terminal connected to a VAX/VMS system. After you turn on your terminal and press <RETURN> one or more times, the screen displays the login prompt:

Username:

Your system manager supplies your user name, which often is your last name. When you enter your user name and press <RETURN>, the password prompt appears:

Username: curry <RETURN>
Password:

Your system manager also supplies your assigned password. For security reasons, your password is not displayed, or echoed. When you enter your password and press <RETURN>, a welcome message appears, followed by the DCL prompt, $.

If you make a mistake in entering either your user name or password, the system denies you access and displays a message. For example, if Curry's correct password is *digital* and he enters *digits* instead, the results would be

Username: curry <RETURN>
Password: digits <RETURN>
User authorization failure

If you make a mistake and you receive this message, you can restart the login procedure by pressing the <RETURN> key again.

Try logging in on your terminal, following the steps in Experiment 1.1.

Experiment 1.1   **Logging In**

1. Turn on your terminal and press <RETURN>. When you see the login prompt, enter your user name.

    <RETURN>
    Username: *your-username* <RETURN>
    Password:

2. At the password prompt, enter your password.

    Username: *your-username* <RETURN>
    Password: *your-password* <RETURN>
    Welcome to VAX/VMS Version 5.00
    Last interactive login on Tuesday 23-JAN-14-1990 14:19
    Last non-interactive login on Tuesday, 23-JAN-1990 14:10
    $

    Once you have typed your user name and password correctly, the system displays its welcome message and prints the DCL prompt, $. You can respond to the prompt with any DCL command. For example, you might want to type the LOGOUT command to tell VMS to end the current session. Log out, following the steps in Experiment 1.2.

Experiment 1.2 **Logging Out**

1. End the session by typing the LOGOUT command.

   ```
   $ logout <RETURN>
   CURRY logged out at 21-JAN-1988 11:22:36.09
   ```

2. The system displays the logout message, assuring you that the session has terminated properly. Because you want to explore other DCL commands, log in again.

   ```
   <RETURN>
   Username: your-username <RETURN>
   Password: your-password <RETURN>
   ```

It is important to log out properly at the end of each terminal session. If you fail to log out, you run the risk of someone else using your account. In addition, if you are on a pay-by-time-logged-in system, charges against your account will continue to accumulate until you log out.

1.2.1 Other Forms of Logging In and Out

The procedures for logging in and logging out that you have just explored are the most common ones. You can, however, use qualifiers to create many useful variations on these procedures.

For example, when you log in, you can specify that instead of using the default working disk you want to use a different working disk. You accomplish this by appending the /DISK qualifier to your user name when you log in. For instance, if you want to use a disk called MYDISK$ instead of the default disk, you would type

```
<RETURN>
Username: curry/disk = mydisk$ <RETURN>
Password:
```

Because of the /DISK qualifier, MYDISK$ would become the default working disk for your session.

When you log out, you may find it helpful to display the accounting statistics for the terminal session you have just completed by using the /FULL qualifier. The /FULL qualifier tells you how long your terminal session lasted, how much CPU (central processor unit) time you have used, and so on. For example,

```
$ logout/full <RETURN>
CURRY logged out at 21-JAN-1990 11:55:32.26
Accounting information:
Buffered I/O count: 128          Peak working set size: 150
Direct I/O count: 162           Peak page file size: 1490
Page faults: 28                 Mounted volumes: 0
Elapsed CPU time: 0 0000:12.02  Elapsed time: 0 00:00:28:99
```

You can get a list of the various forms of logging in, with examples, by using the HELP command. At the $ prompt, type

```
$ help login <RETURN>
```

You can also use the HELP command to list the various forms of the LOGOUT command by typing

```
$ help logout <RETURN>
```

1.2.2 *Changing Your Password*

For security reasons, VMS does not echo your password when you log in. You may be wondering if there is a DCL command that makes it possible for you to display your password. Again, for security reasons, the answer is no. In fact, if you forget your password, you will not be able to log in without your system manager's help.

Once you have logged in, it is possible to change your password by typing

```
$ set password <RETURN>
Old password: your-current-password <RETURN>
New password: your-new-password <RETURN>
Verification: your-new-password <RETURN>
$
```

The passwords entered in response to the password prompts will not be echoed on your screen.

Passwords may contain from 1 to 31 characters. It is common for system managers to set the minimum number of characters for a password at 6 or 7, in which case your password must contain at least that many characters. The following characters may be used when creating passwords:

- A through Z (uppercase or lowercase)
- 0 through 9
- $ (dollar sign)
- _ (underscore)

For example, Pascal, popcorn, catch22, catch_22, and too_much_$ are valid passwords. It is wise to change your password regularly.

NOTE: From this point on, the <RETURN> at the end of command lines in examples and experiments is omitted and should be understood.

1.3   Exploring Your System's Characteristics

Your system has a variety of characteristics, and after you have logged in, you can display these characteristics using various SHOW commands (see Table 1.2). Each SHOW command lists a particular type of information about the system. For example, to see the characteristics of your terminal, you would type

```
$ show terminal
Terminal:  _ TXG4:    Device_Type:  VT100    Owner:  YOU

   Input:    1200   LFfill:  0   Width:  80   Parity:   none
   Output:   1200   CRfill:  0   Page:   24


Terminal characteristics:
   Interactive      Echo          Type_ahead        No Escape
   No Hostsync      TTsync        Lowercase         Tab
         .             .              .                .
         .             .              .                .
         .             .              .                .
   Edit mode        DEC_CRT       Advanced_video    No Edit_mode
   No DEC_CRT2
$
```

To get a list of users currently logged into the system, you would type

```
$ show users
                     VAX/VMS Interactive Users
                     23-NOV-1990 18:01:11.51
             Total number of interactive users = 4
```

```
Username              Process Name          PID            Terminal
MAERICKSON            MOUSE             0000221C               TXD3
LJSWANKE              LJSWANKE          00001843               TXG2
YOU                   YOU               00001843               TXG2
JWILKES               JIM               00002235               TXD7
$
```

This listing tells you that three other people besides you are currently logged into the system.

In addition, like most DCL commands, many **show** commands have a variety of qualifiers. For instance, the **show users** command line has the following syntax:

show users [*username*][**/output** = *output-filespec*][**/nooutput**]

In this command, *username* is an optional parameter. It is the name of a user about whom you want information. If you omit a specific user name, a list of all interactive users is displayed. **show users** has the two optional qualifiers **/OUTPUT** and **/NOOUTPUT**. **/OUTPUT** specifies where the output from **show USERS** (the list of logged-in users) is sent. By default, the output is written to the screen or hard-copy terminal. By including a file specification with **/OUTPUT**, you can direct the output to that file. **/NOOUTPUT** inhibits the output; it is not displayed, printed, or sent to a file.

Table 1.2 Commonly Used SHOW Commands

Command	Result
SHOW DEFAULT	Displays the current default device and directory
SHOW KEY	Displays the definitions of keys created with the **DEFINE/KEY** command
SHOW QUOTA	Displays the disk quota currently authorized and currently used
SHOW SYMBOL	Displays the current symbol definitions
SHOW TERMINAL	Displays the characteristics of the terminal
SHOW TIME	Displays the current date and time
SHOW USERS	Displays information about the users currently logged into the system

Table 1.3 Commonly Used SET Commands

Command	Result
SET PASSWORD	Changes the user's password
SET PROMPT	Personalizes the VMS prompt
SET PROCESS	Defines execution characteristics of the current process
SET TERMINAL	Defines operational characteristics of a terminal

Thus, to check on the availability of a particular user, you could use a specific user name with the SHOW USERS command:

```
$ show users maerickson
                    VAX/VMS Interactive Users
                    23-NOV-1990 19:04:14.02
             Total number of interactive users = 31

Username            Process name              PID        Terminal
MAERICKSON          MOUSE                     00001EDB   TXG3
$
```

Some of the other SHOW commands also have qualifiers, allowing you to view exactly the information you need.

In addition to viewing the system characteristics, you can use the SET commands to change some of them. You have already seen that SET PASSWORD can be used to change your password. Table 1.3 lists several SET commands.

For example, by default, VMS assigns your user name to your process name. You could change your process name by using the SET PROCESS command with the /NAME qualifier. The syntax is

set process/name = *new-name*

The process name can be any string, so you could, for example, use your telephone extension or another useful string:

```
$ set process/name = ext.2788
$
```

Because the process name is displayed in the SHOW USERS listing, changing your process name in this way can convey useful information to other users.

You can modify the width of your display by using the **SET TERMINAL** command with the **/WIDTH** qualifier. For example, to change your screen width to 132 columns, you would type

```
$ set terminal/width = 132
$
```

You can explore your system and practice using the **SHOW** and **SET** commands by following Experiment 1.3. Other **SHOW** and **SET** commands are introduced throughout the rest of the chapter.

Experiment 1.3 | **Using SHOW and SET Commands**

1. To see the current date and time, use the **SHOW TIME** command.

   ```
   $ show time
   4-FEB-1990 00:05:21
   ```

2. The default system prompt is $. You can change this prompt and personalize your working environment by using the **SET PROMPT** command.

   ```
   $ set prompt = ":-)"
   :-)
   ```

   If you turn your head sideways, you can see that now your system prompt is a smile.

3. Use the **SET PROMPT** command to return to the default system prompt.

   ```
   $ set prompt = $
   $
   ```

1.4   *Getting Help*

At any point during a VMS session, you can use the **HELP** command to get information about working with your system, and with DCL commands, qualifiers, and parameters. The **HELP** command accesses the Help library, which contains information about various topics and subtopics. The command syntax is

help [*keyword*]

The optional keyword parameter is any Help topic.

If you enter the **HELP** command without a parameter, a list of topics appears along with the **Topic?** prompt. You can then type the name of a topic and press <RETURN> to see information about that topic and a list of subtopics (if any exist). You can enter a subtopic to see information about the subtopic and, possibly, a list of sub-subtopics. You can enter another subtopic or a sub-subtopic.

If you press <RETURN> without entering a subtopic, you return to the previous Help level (unless you are at the first level, in which case you exit Help). Alternatively, you can type HELP INSTRUCTIONS or HELP HINTS at the $ prompt to see instructions on using Help or hints about possible commands or topics.

If you want to see the previous screen of text, type a question mark (?). Press the <CTRL> and <Z>, or <CTRL/z>, to exit Help, or press <RETURN> to back out of the Subtopic? and Topic? prompts.

If you know the topic about which you want help, you can enter it as a parameter in the HELP command line. For example, to get help about the SET PROCESS command, type

```
$ help set process
```

1.5   A First Look at Files and Directories

Many DCL commands identify one or more files to be processed. A file is a named collection of information. Files are stored permanently on an auxiliary storage device such as a magnetic disk, diskette, or tape.

Each time you log in, VMS provides you with a login directory that lists files you own. A directory is itself a file that contains information about other files.

Chapter 2 discusses files and directories in more detail.

1.5.1   Getting a List of Files

The DIRECTORY command displays a list of files in the specified directory. To see a list of files in the current directory, type

```
$ directory
Directory DUA1:[YOURGROUP.YOU]
LOGIN.COM;1
Total of 1 file.
$
```

This form of the DIRECTORY command elicits the file names, file types, and version numbers of the files in the current directory. For example, for the file LOGIN.COM;1, the file name is LOGIN, the file type is COM, and the version number is 1. This information is part of the file specification. If there are no files in your directory, a message appears to that effect.

The /FULL qualifier may be used to see more information about the files, such as the number of blocks used, number of blocks allocated, date of create, date of last backup, file protection, and so on, for the specified file or files. For example, to see full information about the LOGIN.COM file, you would type

```
$ directory login.com/full
Directory     DUA1:[YOURGROUP.YOU]
LOGIN.COM;1                     File ID:   (149,1,0)
Size:          2/3             Owner:     [YOU]
Created:    28-APR-1990   19:17:32.84
Revised:    28-APR-1990   19:17:33.45 (1)
Expires:    <None specified>
Backup:     <No backup specified>
File organization:     Sequential
File attributes:       Allocation: 3, Extend: 0, global buffer
                             count: 0
                       No version limit
Record format:         Variable length, maximum 73 bytes
Record attributes:     Carriage return carriage control
RMS attributes:        None
Journaling enable:     None
File protection:       System: RWED, Owner: RWED, Group: RWED,
                             World, RE
Access Control List:   None
Total of 1 file, 2/3 blocks.
$
```

You can manipulate files and the information in them in many ways. For example, you can create a file using the CREATE command or by sending the results of a command line to a file. The next two sections explore these two methods of file creation.

1.5.2   ## *Saving Command Line Output as a File*

Many DCL commands that display information on the screen let you redirect that output to a file using the /OUTPUT qualifier. For example, SHOW USERS displays the list of people currently logged in. If you wanted to save that list in a file for future reference, you would type

```
$ show users/output = users.now
$
```

In this example, the file specification is USERS.NOW. The output from SHOW
USERS is redirected to the file called USERS.NOW. You can create a file in this
way by following Experiment 1.4.

Experiment 1.4   **Saving Command Line Output**

1. First use the DIRECTORY command to get a listing of the current files.

```
$ directory
Directory DUA1:[YOURGROUP.YOU]
LOGIN.COM;1
Total of 1 file.
$
```

If there are no files in the directory, a message to that effect appears.

2. Save the output from a SHOW USERS command by directing it to a file called
USERS.NOW.

```
$ show users/output = users.now
$
```

3. The /OUTPUT qualifier caused the output from the SHOW USERS command
to be written to the USERS.NOW file. To verify this, use the DIRECTORY
command again. You could type just the DIRECTORY command to get the
listing of all files. Instead, use the DIRECTORY command with the file specification and the /FULL qualifier to see the characteristics of the new
USERS.NOW file.

```
$ directory users.now/full
Directory DUA1:[YOURGROUP.YOU]
USERS.NOW;1                    File ID:   (739,5,0)
Size:        2/3               Owner:     [YOU]
Created:   24-APR-1990 10:23:05.07
        .
        .
        .
Total of 1 file, 2/3 blocks.
$
```

4. You can also verify the file's existence by using the TYPE command. TYPE
displays the contents of the specified file. If you do not specify a version
number, VMS displays the most recent version of the file.

```
$ type users.now
                    VAX/VMS Interactive Users
                     23-NOV-1990 18:01:11.51
                Total number of interactive users = 4

  Username          Process Name            PID       Terminal
  MAERICKSON          MOUSE              0000221C       TXD3
  LJSWANKE            LJSWANKE           00001E93       TXE1
  YOU                 YOU                00001843       TXG2
  JWILKES             JIM                00002235       TXD7
$
```

Many DCL commands have an /OUTPUT qualifier. Chapter 6 explores more uses of this qualifier. You can also consult Appendix A or another list of DCL commands, parameters, and qualifiers to see which commands have an /OUTPUT qualifier.

1.5.3   Creating a File

Although saving command line output as a file can be useful, you often want to create a file by typing in information. You can use the **CREATE** command to create a file of text entered from the keyboard. The **CREATE** command requires a file name as a parameter. For example, to create a file called **NOTE.TXT**, type

```
$ create note.txt
```

After you press <RETURN> at the end of the command line, the next text you enter becomes the contents of the file. Everything you input, in fact, is entered in the file until you press <CTRL/z>.

With VMS, the <CTRL> key is used together with a second key to change the meaning of the second key and tell VMS to perform a control sequence. Pressing <CTRL/z> ends a "create" session and returns you to the DCL prompt. (Other control sequences are explored in Section 1.6.)

To enter information in the **NOTE.TXT** file and complete its creation, type

```
$ create note.txt
Check the date for the poem
Jabberwocky in Lewis Carroll's
Through the Looking-Glass
<CTRL/z>
[Exit]
$
```

When entering the information in the file, press <RETURN> to move to a new line, <SPACEBAR> to enter a space, and <SHIFT> to use alternative key characters such as uppercase letters. If you need to erase a character after you have typed it, use the DELETE command by pressing the <x] key on the VT200 or the <DELETE> key on the VT100 to delete the last character entered.

Explore creating a file and entering text using these keys. Experiment 1.5 creates a file containing lines from "Jabberwocky," a poem from Lewis Carroll's *Through the Looking-Glass* (1872).

Experiment 1.5   **Creating a Sample File**

1. Use the **CREATE** command to start creating a file called **AI.TXT**.

    ```
    $ create ai.txt
    ```

2. Now enter the lines of the poem, pressing <RETURN> to move down to the next line, as necessary. Complete the process by pressing <CTRL/z>.

    ```
    'Twas brillig, and the slithy toves
       Did gyre and gimble in the wabe:
    All mimsy were the borogoves,
       And the mome raths outgrabe.
    "Beware the Jabberwock, my son!
       The jaws that bite, the claws that catch!
    Beware the Jubjub bird, and shun
       The frumious Bandersnatch!"
    He took his vorpal sword in hand:
       Long time the manxome foe he sought—
    So rested he by the Tumtum tree,
       and stood awhile in thought.
    <CTRL/z>
    [Exit]
    $
    ```

3. Thanks to the **CREATE** command, the poem is written to a file called **AI.TXT**. The <CTRL/z> terminates the input to **AI.TXT**, and the system responds with **[Exit]**. You can verify that you now have a file **AI.TXT** by using the **DIRECTORY** command.

    ```
    $ directory
    Directory DUA1:[YOURGROUP.YOU]
    AI.TXT;1      USERS.NOW;1      LOGIN.COM;1
    Total of 3 files.
    $
    ```

4. Notice that the version number, 1, indicates that this is version 1 of the AI.TXT file. At this point, there are no other versions of the file. You can view the contents of the AI.TXT file by using the TYPE command.

```
$ type ai.txt
'Twas brillig, and the slithy toves
   Did gyre and gimble in the wabe:
All mimsy were the borogoves,

   .
   .
   .

$
```

As you work with VMS files, remember that VMS file names are not case-sensitive. For example, ai.txt and AI.TXT identify the same file. Also, remember that if you do not specify a version number for a file when entering a command line, VMS will select the most recent version of the file.

1.6   Exploring Control Keys

The <CTRL/z> key sequence is one among a variety of useful control keys. The next two sections explore some of these control keys and their functions.

1.6.1   Control Keys That Control Output to the Terminal

Table 1.4 lists control keys that you can use to manage output to the terminal.

You should become comfortable with the key that suspends and resumes the flow of output to your terminal. On the VT200, this key is the <HOLD SCREEN> key; on the VT100, this key is the <NO SCROLL> key. If you press these keys while output is being displayed or printed, the display is frozen on the screen or hard-copy terminal. This gives you a chance to read a screenful of information before resuming program or command execution and the display of new output. To resume execution, press the <HOLD SCREEN> or <NO SCROLL> key again. You can press the key repeatedly, toggling it on and off.

<CTRL/o> provides another way to control the display. Pressing this key sequence stops the display of the output flowing to the terminal, that is, the output does not echo on the screen. Unlike <HOLD SCREEN> or <NO SCROLL>, <CTRL/o> does not suspend the flow of output. Even though it does not appear on the screen, the output continues flowing to the terminal. When you press <CTRL/o> a second time, a display of the *current* portion of the output

Table 1.4   Keys Used to Control Output to the Terminal

Key	Result
<CTRL/o>	Stops and starts the echoing of output
<HOLD SCREEN> or <NO SCROLL> (or <CTRL/s> or <CTRL/q>)	Suspends and continues output to the terminal

appears. In other words, <CTRL/o> makes it possible to skip past portions of output from a program or command.

Follow Experiment 1.6 to explore the <HOLD SCREEN> or <NO SCROLL> key and <CTRL/o>.

Experiment 1.6   ***Suspending and Resuming Output and the Echoing of Output***

1. Enter a **TYPE** command to see the contents of the file **AI.TXT**. As the output appears, press the <HOLD SCREEN> or <NO SCROLL> key to suspend output.

   ```
   $ type ai.txt
   'Twas brillig, and the slithy toves
      Did gyre and gimble in the wabe:
   <NO SCROLL>
   ```

2. Resume output by pressing the <HOLD SCREEN> or <NO SCROLL> key again. Then press it again to suspend output.

   ```
   <NO SCROLL>
   All mimsy were the borogoves,
      And the mome raths outgrabe.
   <NO SCROLL>
   ```

3. Resume output again. Then use <CTRL/c> to cancel the execution of the command.

   ```
   <NO SCROLL>
   "Beware the Jabberwock, my son!
   <CTRL/c>
   [Interrupt]
   ```

4. Next experiment with <CTRL/o>. Enter a **TYPE** command again and press <CTRL/o> to turn off the echoing of the output. Then press <CTRL/o> again to resume echoing of the output.

Table 1.5 Control Keys Used to Edit Command Lines

Key	Result
<CTRL/a>	Toggles the insertion or overstriking of new characters anywhere in the current command line
<CTRL/e>	Positions the cursor at the end of the current line
<CTRL/h>	Positions the cursor at the beginning of the current line or at the beginning of the preceding line if the cursor is already at the beginning of the line
<CTRL/j>	Deletes backward from the cursor position to the beginning of a word, or if the cursor is at the first character of a word, deletes the previous word
<CTRL/u>	Deletes what is to the left of the cursor on the current line

```
$ type ai.txt
'Twas brillig, and the slithy toves
   Did gyre and gimble in the wabe:
<CTRL/o>
[Output off]
<CTRL/o>
[Output on]
So rested he by the Tumtum tree,
   and stood awhile in thought.
$
```

1.6.2 Control Keys Used When Editing Command Lines

Some control keys are particularly useful when you are entering and editing command lines (see Table 1.5).

When entering or editing a command line, use <CTRL/a> to insert changes inside the command line. Use the <CTRL/e>, <CTRL/h>, <LEFT ARROW> and <RIGHT ARROW> keys to move through the command line. Using <CTRL/j> deletes the previous word from the command line. <CTRL/u> deletes what is to the left of the cursor, so if the cursor is at the end of a command line and you want to discard the command line entirely, use <CTRL/u>.

You can explore these control keys by following Experiment 1.7.

Editing a Command Line

1. Type the **DIRECTORY** command line with the **/FULL** qualifier, but leave the *i* out of *directory*. Do not press <RETURN>.

   $ `drectory/full`

2. Press <CTRL/a> and use the <LEFT ARROW> key to move the cursor over the first *r*. Type an *i* to correct the command line.

   $ `di rectory/full`

3. To position the cursor at the end of this command line, press <CTRL/e>.

4. To delete **/FULL** from this command line, press <CTRL/j> twice.

5. To position the cursor at the beginning of this command line, press <CTRL/h>.

6. Now use <CTRL/e> to position the cursor at the end of this line, and purge the current command line by pressing <CTRL/u>.

1.7

Recalling Command Lines Using the Recall Buffer

You have just used the editing control keys to edit a command line before you press <RETURN> to execute it. Many times, however, you will find that you want to edit command lines after you have executed them—to correct a mistake or add qualifiers, for instance. DCL provides you with a way to re-call previous command lines so that you can edit them.

DCL saves the last 20 commands you have entered during the session in a place in memory called the Recall buffer. The Recall buffer stores the com-mand lines as a stack, with the most recent command line on top. You can re-trieve command lines from this buffer in several different ways.

You can press either <CTRL/b> or the <UP ARROW> key to see the most re-cently entered command line. For example, suppose the last command you entered was **DIRECTORY/FULL**. To display that command line again, you would type

$ <CTRL/b>
$ `directory/full`

or

$ <UP ARROW>
$ `directory/full`

Both keys achieve the same result: the last command line is redisplayed. Once the command line is displayed, you can edit it.

If you wanted to see the command line that preceded DIRECTORY/FULL, you could press <CTRL/b> or <UP ARROW> again. By repeatedly pressing either of these keys, you can redisplay the last 20 command lines, which are stored in the Recall buffer, one at a time. Pressing the <DOWN ARROW> key displays the next, or more recent, command line. For example,

```
$  <UP  ARROW>
$  directory/full
$  <UP  ARROW>
$  show users
$  <UP  ARROW>
$  type ai.txt
$  <DOWN  ARROW>
$  show users
```

A better way to see all the command lines stored in the Recall buffer, however, is to use the RECALL command with the /ALL qualifier. The RECALL command without a qualifier redisplays the most recent command line. With the /ALL qualifier, it displays the last 20 command lines, listing the more recent command lines first. For example,

```
$  recall/all
1  directory/full
2  show users
3  type ai.txt
4  directory
5  create ai.txt
   .
   .
   .
```

The RECALL/ALL command provides you with a history of your most recent activity. It numbers the command lines, with the most recent numbered 1 and the oldest numbered 20.

You can also use the RECALL command to select a particular command line for display. Specify the command line by referring to its number in the RECALL/ALL list. For example, to display the third line in the list, you would type

```
$  recall 3
$  type ai.txt
```

Thus, you can get a list of the last 20 command lines, select the one you need to edit, and then display just that line for editing. Also, if you then need to move to the previous command line in the buffer, pressing <UP ARROW> will display that line.

Experiment 1.8 gives you practice in recalling command lines. As you follow the steps in the experiment, notice that the one command the Recall buffer does not store is the **RECALL** command.

Experiment 1.8   **Recalling Command Lines**

1. First, use **RECALL/ALL** to see the contents of the Recall buffer. (If you have just logged in, you should execute five or six commands so that the buffer contains some command lines.)

   ```
   $ recall/all
   1 type ai.txt
      .
      .
      .
   20 directory
   $
   ```

2. Use <CTRL/b>, <UP ARROW>, and <DOWN ARROW> to recall and redisplay the previous and next command lines. You can check your location in the buffer from the **RECALL/ALL** list. For example,

   ```
   $ <UP ARROW>
   $ type ai.txt
   $ <UP ARROW>
   $ directory
   $ <CTRL/b>
   $ create ai.txt
   $ <DOWN ARROW>
   $ directory
   $ <DOWN ARROW>
   $ type ai.txt
   ```

3. Next, experiment with recalling a specific command line and then moving to the previous line. For example,

   ```
   $ recall 4
   $ type users.now
   $ <UP ARROW>
   $ create ai.txt
   $ <UP ARROW>
   $ directory
   ```

4. Use **RECALL/ALL** again to see the list of command lines. Then execute a
   DIRECTORY command and use **RECALL/ALL** again.

```
$ recall/all
1 type ai.txt
  .
  .
  .
20 directory
$ directory
$ recall/all
1 directory
2 type ai.txt
  .
  .
  .
20 directory/full
```

There is yet another method for recalling a command line. You can type the
RECALL command followed by one or more of the leading characters of a previous command. For example, to see the most recent command line that begins with *sh*, you would type

```
$ recall sh
$ show users
```

These techniques offer various ways to retrieve and move backward and forward among the old command lines saved in the Recall buffer. Once you get
used to retrieving old command lines, you will probably find that the Recall
buffer is a time-saver.

1.8   Using the Type-Ahead Buffer

In addition to a Recall buffer, VMS has another buffer, the Type-ahead
buffer.

Perhaps you have noticed that you can enter new commands while VMS is
doing something else—printing a directory or listing users logged in, for example. The Type-ahead buffer stores the new keystrokes while VMS executes the other command. When VMS is finished, it acts upon the new keystrokes. For example, you can enter a **TYPE** command. While VMS is displaying the lines of the specified file, you can enter a **DIRECTORY** command. As
soon as VMS finishes the **TYPE** command, it executes the **DIRECTORY** command, which was stored in the Type-ahead buffer. If you know you have

made a typing mistake when entering commands into the Type-ahead buffer, you can clear the Type-ahead buffer by pressing <CTRL/x>. Follow Experiment 1.9 to see how this buffer works.

Experiment 1.9 **Using the Type-Ahead Buffer**

1. Enter a DIRECTORY/FULL command. While the list of file characteristics is being displayed, enter a SHOW USERS command and then a TYPE AI.TXT command.

```
$ directory/full
Directory DUA1:[YOURGROUP.YOU]
AI.TXT;1     File ID:  (14086, 53633, 0)
   .
   .
   .
```

2. Repeat step 1, but this time press <CTRL/x> after entering the TYPE command.

In the experiment, the output from DIRECTORY/FULL continued to be displayed while you entered the new command lines. The entered command lines were saved in the Type-ahead buffer. When the DIRECTORY/FULL command had finished processing, DCL fetched and executed the commands in the Type-ahead buffer. In step 2, the <CTRL/x> discards the current input line and clears the Type-ahead buffer. The size of the Type-ahead buffer varies depending on what your system administrator decided at the time your VMS system was installed.

1.9 Defining Keys

Because there are some DCL commands that you will use repeatedly, you might want to assign them to a key so that you can execute them with a single keystroke. The DCL DEFINE/KEY command makes it possible to define the function of many of your keys. You enter the command, then the name of a valid key such as <PF1>, and then the command string of the command you want to assign to the key. This command string is known as an equivalence string, and it must be enclosed in quotation marks. The syntax for this command line is

define/key *key-name* *"equivalence-string"*

For example, to define the <PF4> key on a VT100 or VT200 keyboard, you would type

```
$ define/key pf4 "show users"
DEFAULT key PF4 has been defined
%DCL-W-DEFKEY,
```

This **DEFINE/KEY** command associates the equivalence string "**show users**" with the <PF4> key. If you press the <PF4> key, the following line appears on the screen:

$ show users

The cursor appears immediately after the last character of the equivalence string displayed by pressing the <PF4> key. You must press <RETURN> to tell DCL to begin processing this command line.

To increase the usefulness of the defined key, you can use the **/TERMINATE** qualifier with the **DEFINE/KEY** command. This qualifier tells DCL to process the equivalence string command when the defined key is pressed, rather than waiting for you to press <RETURN>. In effect, the **/TERMINATE** qualifier "embeds" a <RETURN> at the end of the string associated with a key. Try defining a key by following Experiment 1.10.

Experiment 1.10 **Defining a Key**

1. Use the **DEFINE/KEY** command to define the <PF1> key so that it executes the **SHOW TIME** command.

   ```
   $ define/key pf1 "show time"
   %DCL-W-DEFKEY,DEFAULT key PF1 has been defined
   ```

2. Now press <PF1> followed by <RETURN>.

   ```
   $ <PF1> <RETURN>
   $ show time
   15-JUN-1990 15:23:14
   ```

3. By using the **/TERMINATE** qualifier in defining a <PF> key, you can eliminate the need to press <RETURN> after pressing a defined <PF> key. Use the **DEFINE/KEY** with the **/TERMINATE** qualifier to define <PF2> so that it executes the **SHOW TIME** command.

   ```
   $ define/key/terminate pf2 "show time"
   %DCL-I-DEFKEY, DEFAULT key PF2 has been defined
   ```

4. Now press <PF2> to compare the performance of this newly defined key with that of the <PF1> key from step 1.

```
$ <PF2>
$ show time
15-JUN-1990 15:26:19
```

Thus, you can define a key so that it immediately processes the command assigned to it, or so that you control execution and can add parameters or qualifiers to the command line and then press <RETURN>.

You cannot define every key on your keyboard. On VT100 and VT200 terminals, the <PF1> through <PF4> keys can be defined in this way. You can also define the 0 through 9 numeric keypad keys (use **KP0**, **KP1**, . . . **KP9** as the key names), the <LEFT ARROW> and <RIGHT ARROW> keys (use **LEFT** and **RIGHT** as the key names), and the <PERIOD>, <COMMA>, <MINUS>, and <ENTER> keys (use these names in uppercase as the key names). In addition, VT200 terminals allow you to define the <F6> through <F20> keys, the editing keypad keys, and <HELP> and <DO>.

If you want to see a list of the key assignments you have made with the **DEFINE/KEY** command, you can use the **SHOW KEY** command with the **/ALL** qualifier. For example,

```
$ show key/all
DEFAULT key definitions:
PF3 =  "directory/full"
PF4 = "show users"
```

If you only want to check the definition for a specific key, you can specify just that key. For example,

```
$ show key pf4
DEFAULT keypad definitions:
PF4 = "show users"
```

1.10   **A First Look at Using a Text Editor**

You have seen that you can use the **CREATE** command to create a short file of text. You cannot, however, use **CREATE** to edit or add to the text. In general, when you are writing a text file or you want to edit text in a file, you use a text editor. Text editors are programs that provide specific commands and procedures for editing, manipulating, and moving around the text within a new or existing file.

VMS provides several text editors, among them EDT and EVE. Chapters 3 and 4 discuss in EDT and EVE in detail. This section provides a brief introduction to working with a text editor, focusing on EDT.

The **EDIT** command with the editor's qualifier is used to access a text editor. The syntax for the **EDIT** command that accesses EDT is

edit/edt *filespec*

The file specification can be for a new or existing file. For example, to begin using the EDT editor to change the contents of the existing file **AI.TXT**, you would type

```
$ edit/edt ai.txt
```

If your system is set up so that EDT begins in keypad mode, this command line displays the file's text. If your system is set up so that EDT begins in line mode, the command line produces the following results:

```
$ edit/edt ai.txt
1 'Twas brillig, and the slithy toves
*
```

To move to keypad mode, enter the **CHANGE** command at the asterisk prompt. Then the file's text appears.

In keypad mode, whatever you type on the keyboard is entered into the file being edited, and you can use the numeric keypad on the right-hand side of the keyboard to perform a variety of editing functions.

The **[EOB]** printed at the end of the file being edited stands for end-of-buffer. Behind the scenes, VMS has transferred a copy of the file being edited to a buffer, or temporary storage area, in memory.

You can move around the lines of the file using the arrow keys. To add a new line, move to the beginning or end of a line and press <RETURN>. Once you finish editing the file, press <CTRL/z> and then type **EXIT** to terminate the editing session.

Try using the EDT editor by following Experiment 1.11. In this experiment, you create and edit a **LOGIN.COM** file. Each time you log in, VMS checks for a **LOGIN.COM** file and, if it finds one, executes any commands in that file. In the experiment, you add several commands to **LOGIN.COM**.

1. Although you can use EDT to create a new file, in this experiment first use **CREATE** to create a **LOGIN.COM** file with a single comment line.

   ```
   $ create login.com
   $ ! commands executed each time you log in
   <CTRL/z>
   [Exit]
   $
   ```

   Notice that **$** is the first character you enter in the newly created **LOGIN.COM** file.

2. Move to the EDT editor, specifying **LOGIN.COM** as the file to edit. (If necessary, enter the **CHANGE** command at the asterisk prompt to move to keypad mode.)

   ```
   $ edit/edt login.com
   $ ! commands executed each time you log in
   [EOB]
   ```

   or

   ```
   $ edit/edt login.com
   1 $ ! commands executed each time you log in
   * change
   $ ! commands executed each time you log in
   [EOB]
   ```

3. Use the <DOWN ARROW> key to move the cursor down to the [EOB] line. Open up a blank line by pressing <RETURN>.

   ```
   $ ! commands executed each time you log in

   [EOB]
   ```

4. Use the <UP ARROW> key to move the cursor up to the blank line and add two command lines, **SHOW USERS** and **SHOW QUOTA**. Remember to include **$** at the beginning of each line.

   ```
   $ ! commands executed each time you log in
   $ show users
   $ show quota
   [EOB]
   ```

5. You are finished editing the file, so press <CTRL/z> and type **EXIT** to leave the editor.

```
<CTRL/z>
* exit
$
```

6. To see the results of this sample editing session, use the TYPE command.

```
$ type login.com
$ ! commands executed each time you log in
$ show users
$ show quota
$
```

7. You now have two versions of your LOGIN.COM file. Use the DIRECTORY command to verify this.

```
$ directory
Directory DUA1:[YOURGROUP.YOU]
AI.TXT;1    LOGIN.COM;2    LOGIN.COM;1    USERS.NOW;1
Total of 4 files.
$
```

When you log in, VMS uses the most recent version of LOGIN.COM.

Each time you exit from the editor with <CTRL/z> and EXIT, a new version of the file you are working on is created. You may not want this to happen. For instance, if you have made mistakes, you may not want to save the edited file. You can use the QUIT command to exit from the editor without saving the changes to the file. After you press <CTRL/z>, type QUIT instead of EXIT. In effect, QUIT aborts an editing session.

Challenge Problem

Try using the EDT editor to add the following additional command lines to your LOGIN.COM file:

```
$ show time
$ directory/full
```

1.11   **Logging In with the New LOGIN.COM File**

There is a bonus from the sample editing session in the previous section. The LOGIN.COM file you built has a special purpose. Each time you log in, VMS executes the commands in the LOGIN.COM file; so now, more information will appear during the login procedure, as Experiment 1.12 demonstrates.

1. First, log out of the system.

   $ logout

2. Now log back in.

   Username: *your-username*
   Password: *your-password*

   At this point, VMS executes the commands in your **LOGIN.COM** file.

1.12 Summary

A user communicates with VMS through the system command language interpreter, or CLI. A CLI is a program that provides an interface between the various operating system programs and system users. The most commonly used VMS command language interpreter is DCL, the Digital Command Language.

Command lines begin with command verbs and can include parameters and qualifiers. A command verb identifies a VMS service and, once executed, performs a task according to your specifications. You can enter, recall, and edit command lines.

A file is a named collection of information. Much of what you do with VMS involves some form of file handling. VMS provides a wide variety of tools for managing files.

Tables 1.6–1.8 give an overview of the commands, special characters, and important terms used in this chapter.

1.13 Exercises

1. Make a list of uses of optional qualifiers for the following commands: **DIRECTORY, RECALL.**

2. Which key is used most often? Why?

3. Give a command line that would cause **Happy New Year!** to be printed on your screen.

4. Perform the following steps:

Table 1.6   DCL Commands

Command	Result
CREATE	Establishes a new file
DEFINE/KEY	Defines the function of a key
DIRECTORY	Displays the specified directory or directories
/FULL	Displays additional information about the files
EDIT	Accesses a text editor so you can edit a file
/EDT	Accesses the EDT editor
HELP	Displays information about commands and procedures
LOGOUT	Logs out of the system
/FULL	Displays a summary of accounting statistics when logging out
RECALL	Displays old command lines stacked in the recall buffer
/ALL	Displays the last 20 command lines
SET PASSWORD	Changes your password
SET PROCESS	Changes characteristics associated with a process
/NAME	Changes the process name
SET TERMINAL	Changes characteristics of the terminal
/WIDTH	Changes the width of the display
SHOW KEY	Displays the function of the specified defined key
/ALL	Displays the functions of all defined keys
SHOW TERMINAL	Displays the characteristics of the terminal
SHOW USERS	Displays information about the users currently logged in to the system
/OUTPUT	Redirects the information to a file
TYPE	Displays the contents of specified file(s)

a. Create a JOHN.LTR file that contains the first line of a letter.

b. Repeat step (a) but type in the next line of the same letter. The preceding line of the letter will be in the earlier version of the JOHN.LTR file.

c. Execute a DIRECTORY command to check on the number of versions of the JOHN.LTR file in your current directory.

d. Repeat steps (b) and (c) at least ten times. Explain what you find.

Table 1.7 Special Characters

Character	Meaning
\<CTRL\>	Control key
[EOB]	End-of-buffer for the editor
Space	Delimits the parts of a command line
$	DCL prompt
!	Begins a command line comment
" "	Encloses a character string
/	Precedes a command qualifier

Table 1.8 Important Terms

Term	Definition
Buffer	Temporary storage area
CLI	Command language interpreter, a program that processes command lines
Command	Instruction specifying an action for the system to perform
Command line	Instruction consisting of a verb plus optional parameters and qualifiers
Current directory	Directory currently being used
DCL	Digital Command Language, a CLI
Directory	File containing the names of files
Editor	Program that makes it possible to modify the contents of a file
File	Named collection of information
Login directory	Directory assigned by VMS to you when you log in
Recall buffer	Buffer used to store up to 20 old command lines
Type-ahead buffer	Buffer used for temporary storage of command lines typed during execution of other commands

5. Give the command lines to define the following keys:

    a. \<PF1\> to print a list of current users

    b. \<PF2\> to list the contents of your login directory

    c. \<PF3\> to print the date and time

    d. \<PF4\> to recall all the command lines in the Recall buffer

6. List three ways to retrieve a previous command line.

7. How does the Type-ahead buffer differ from the Recall buffer?

8. Execute a **RECALL/ALL** command and use <CTRL/b> and **RECALL** instead of the <UP ARROW> and <DOWN ARROW> keys to recall command lines.

9. Give a listing of the new **LOGIN.COM** file that was created in the Challenge Problem at the end of Section 1.10.

1.14   *Review Quiz*

Indicate whether the following statements are true or false:

1. The Recall and Type-ahead buffers are both used to hold command lines.

2. You can flush out your Recall buffer by pressing <CTRL/x>.

3. The <CTRL/b> and <UP ARROW> keys can both be used to recall a previous command line.

4. A directory is a file.

5. Pressing <CTRL/o> and pressing <HOLD SCREEN> or <NO SCROLL> do the same thing during the execution of a program that is sending output to the screen.

6. DCL is an interpreter.

7. Your CLI is a program.

1.15   *Further Reading*

Baer, R. M. *The Digital Villain*. Reading, Mass.: Addison-Wesley, 1972.

DEC VAX-11/785 Manual and User's Guide. Collegeville, Minn.: Academic Computing Services, 1985. *Address*: John Muggli, Academic Computing Center, St. John's University, Collegeville, MN 56321.

Introduction to the VAX/VMS System CCRM-11. Austin, Texas: University of Texas at Austin Computation Center, 1983. *Address*: Editor, Computation Center, University of Texas, Austin, TX 78712.

Kenah, L. J., R. E. Goldenberg, S. F. Bate. *VAX/VMS Internals and Data Structures*. Bedford, Mass.: Digital Press, 1988.

Levy, H. M., and R. H. Eckhouse. *Computer Programming and Architecture: The VAX-11*. Bedford, Mass.: Digital Press, 1980.

Peters, J. F. *The Art of Assembly Language Programming VAX-11*. Englewood Cliffs, N. J.: Reston Publishing Co., 1985.

Sawey, R. M., and T. T. Stokes. *A Beginner's Guide to VAX/VMS Utilities and Applications*. Bedford, Mass.: Digital Press, 1989.

Order from Digital Equipment Corporation, POB CS2008, Nashua, NH 03061:

VMS DCL Concepts Manual. Order no. AA-LA/OA-TE.

VMS DCL Dictionary. Order no. AA-LA12A-TE.

VMS General User's Manual. Order no. AA-LA98A-TE.

Chapter 2

A Beginner's Guide
to VMS File Management

Information reaching long-term memory must be filed, and this process depends on the context.
                              —James L. Adams, *Conceptual Blockbusting*, 1979

VMS provides several methods for creating, manipulating, and organizing files. In this chapter, you will

- Obtain an overview of VMS files
- Become familiar with various forms of file specifications
- Begin using wildcards in file specifications
- Survey commonly used file management tools
- Explore the uses of the /LOG qualifier with various file-handling commands
- Distinguish between purging and deleting files
- Experiment with the /CONFIRM qualifier when purging and deleting files
- Begin exploring the VMS directory system
- Begin creating and using subdirectories

2.1   Files and Directories

Many VMS command lines identify one or more files to be processed. A file is a named, organized collection of components that is stored on media such as magnetic disks and tapes, diskettes, or cassettes. Files are comparable to

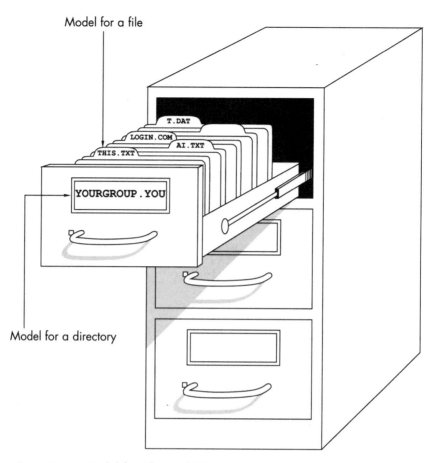

Model for a file

YOURGROUP.YOU

Model for a directory

Figure 2.1 A Model for Files and Directories

the file folders in a filing cabinet, as shown in Figure 2.1. Each holds a collection of related information.

Files are useful because they allow you to permanently store and manage information. For example, you can type

```
$ ! See Kenah, Goldenberg, & Bate, p. 625, on logical names
```

This information would be lost, however, when you press the <RETURN> key. To make a permanent record of this reference, you would type

```
$ create logical.nms
See Kenah, Goldenberg, & Bate, p. 625, on logical names
<CTRL/Z>
[Exit]
$
```

This stores the information in a file.

Once the information is in a file, you can retrieve it in a variety of ways. For example, you can use the **TYPE** command to display the file's contents. It is also easy to update a file, refining an old piece of information, or adding new information, using an editor like EDT or EVE.

In addition, files make information sharing possible. Files can be exchanged between users on the same system or across computer networks. For example, VMS has a Mail utility that you can use to send files to other users. For instance, you could send the file **LOGICAL.NMS** to another person on your system by typing

```
$ mail logical.nms jmuggli
```

In this case, jmuggli is the other person's user name. When you press the <RETURN> key at the end of this command line, a copy of the **LOGICAL.NMS** file is sent to jmuggli.

Files also make it possible to work with massive segments of information that are too large to be brought into primary memory at one time but that you want to keep together as a single logical entity. For example, suppose the system on which you are working limits your workspace to 4 million bytes, and you need to save birth records for a large city, which requires 20 million bytes. You can take advantage of the typically large storage capacities of volumes like 300-million-byte disks to build these large files. Then VMS will bring chunks of the large files into memory when you need that information.

Every file you own is listed in a directory. A directory is a file containing information about other files. When you log in, VMS makes your default, or login, directory available to you. The names of the files you have created are maintained by VMS in this login directory and possibly in other directories and subdirectories.

To check the directories you have available to you, type

```
$ directory *.dir
```

This command line uses the wildcard ∗ to specify all files with a DIR extension, which is the file type of directory files. Wildcards are discussed in Section 2.1.2.

If you wanted to see only the name of your login directory, which is the default directory unless you have changed the default, you would type

```
$ show default
```

Using directories helps you to organize and keep track of your files. Directories also provide an enormously valuable means of information sharing. Section 2.3 discusses directories in detail.

2.1.1   VMS File Specifications

Each file on a VMS system has a file specification that uniquely identifies the file to the system. The complete specification for a file has the following syntax:

pathname filename.type;version

For example, Figure 2.2 shows the file specification for a file on an MIT network, and Figure 2.3 shows the pathname for this file. The sample pathname consists of a network node name, a device name, and directory and subdirectory names.

The network node name identifies the specific computer system in the network. Network node names have from one to six characters and end with a

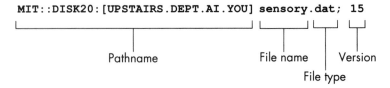

Figure 2.2 Sample File Specification

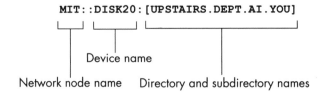

Figure 2.3 Sample Pathname

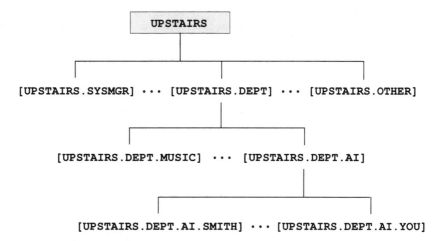

Figure 2.4 Hierarchy of Directories

double colon (::). If the system is not a node on a network, the file specification does not have a node name.

The device name indicates the physical device (such as a disk drive) that contains the files and directories. Device names can have up to 15 alphanumeric characters, and they end with a single colon (:).

Directory names are listed in hierarchical order. They are separated by a period (.) and enclosed in brackets ([ ]) or angle brackets (< >). In the example in Figure 2.3, the **UPSTAIRS** directory is a directory for the system and contains the **DEPT** directory. The **DEPT** directory is a directory for all departments and contains the **AI** directory. The **AI** directory contains all files and directories for the AI department including the **YOU** directory. The **YOU** directory contains your files and directories. In effect, this sample file specification identifies the hierarchy of directories shown in Figure 2.4.

For the sake of simplicity, you can identify a file in your current default directory by referring only to its file name and file type. For example, to see the contents of the file specified in Figure 2.2, you would type

```
$ type sensory.dat
```

A file name can have up to 39 alphanumeric characters. It is generally best to use a file name that helps you remember the contents of the file. The file name is separated from the file type by a period (.).

The file type indicates the type of information in the file. The file type can also consist of up to 39 alphanumeric characters, but certain three-character file types are commonly used, such as DAT for data files, COM for command procedure files, and so on.

File version numbers are one- to five-digit numbers that the system assigns to the file. Each time you change the file or create another version of it, the file version number increases by 1. You may specify a specific version number instead.

You can use file version numbers to select earlier versions of a file—after various editing sessions, for example. For instance, instead of version 15, you can inspect version 14 (if you still have it) by typing

```
$ type sensory.dat;14
```

To economize on the use of disk space, system managers typically limit the number of versions of a file that are kept.

If you want to see the pathname for your files, and their file names, file types, and version numbers, use the DIRECTORY command. For example,

```
$ directory
Directory DUA1:[YOURGROUP.YOU]
AI.TXT;1  LOGIN.COM;2   LOGIN.COM;1   USERS.NOW;1
Total of 4 files.
$
```

The pathname for the files in your default directory is the first line displayed by the DIRECTORY command. In this example, DUA1 identifies the disk drive being used to store the files. If your VAX is part of a network, the pathname will include its network node name. The files are listed in the next line.

To see the pathname of a specific file and a list of all the file's versions, enter the file name and file type after the DIRECTORY command. For example, to see the pathname of the LOGIN.COM file, you would type

```
$ directory login.com
Directory DUA1:[YOURGROUP.YOU]
LOGIN.COM;2   LOGIN.COM;1
Total of 2 files.
$
```

The pathname for LOGIN.COM appears in the first line of the output, and the two versions of LOGIN.COM are listed below it.

There are many ways to select collections of files with the DIRECTORY command and with other commands. Before you explore further, create some new files by following Experiment 2.1.

Experiment 2.1   **Creating Some New Files**

1. Use the CREATE command to create four new files with the file type DAT. These files will contain information about various kinds of books.

```
$ create sfbks.dat
Isaac Asimov, I, Robot
<CTRL/z>
[Exit]
$ create csbks.dat
Brinch Hansen  The Architecture of Concurrent Programs.
Englewood Cliffs, NJ: Prentice-Hall, 1977.
Stroustrop, B.  The C++ Programming Language. Reading,
MA: Addison-Wesley, 1986.
<CTRL/z>
[Exit]
$ create vaxbks.dat
Kenah, L.J. Goldenberg, R.E. Bate, S.F. VAX/VMS
Internals and Data Structures. Bedford, MA:
Digital Press, 1988.
<CTRL/z>
[Exit]
$ create vaxman.dat
VAX C Run_Time Library Reference Manual.
Maynard, MA: Digital Equipment Corporation,
March 1987.
<CTRL/z>
[Exit]
$
```

2. Now create a file with definitions of some VMS terms. The file type should be TXT.

```
$ create vaxdef.txt
A wildcard char. can specify more than one file.
CLI stands for Command Language Interpreter.
A file is a named piece of information.
*.*;* specifies all files in your default directory.
<CTRL/z>
[Exit]
$
```

3. Finally, create two files containing very simple Pascal programs. The file type should be **PAS**.

```
$ create doesnothing.pas
program doesnothing;
begin
end.
<CTRL/z>
[Exit]
$ create sayshello.pas
program sayshello(output);
begin
  writeln('Hello, world!')
end.
<CTRL/z>
[Exit]
$
```

4. In addition to these files, you might also have the single version of **AI.TXT** and **USERS.NOW** and two versions of the **LOGIN.COM** files created in Chapter 1. Get a directory listing of your current files.

```
$ directory
Directory DUA1:[YOURGROUP.YOU]
AI.TXT;1        CSBKS.DAT;1      DOESNOTHING.PAS;1   LOGIN.COM;1
LOGIN.COM;1     SAYSHELLO.PAS;1  SFBKS.DAT;1         USERS.NOW;1
VAXBKS.DAT;1    VAXDEF.TXT;1     VAXMAN.DAT;1
Total of 11 files.
$
```

2.1.2   *Using Wildcards to Specify Files*

Wildcards are special characters used in the file specifications in command lines to identify zero or more files. Wildcards save you time and keystrokes because they let you enter a single command to process multiple files. There are two types of wildcards used to specify file names, file types, and versions:

- Use an asterisk (*) to match 0 to 39 characters in the file name, file type, or version number.

- Use a percent sign (%) to match exactly one character in the file name or file type.

The * and % wildcards can be used in a variety of ways to specify groups of files. You can explore some of the possibilities in Experiments 2.2 and 2.3.

Using * to Select Files

1. Use the **DIRECTORY** command and a * wildcard to display the names of all files of type **DAT** in your current directory. To do this, enter * instead of a specific file name.

```
$ directory *.dat
Directory DUA1:[YOURGROUP.YOU]
CSBKS.DAT;1    SFBKS.DAT;1    VAXBKS.DAT;1    VAXMAN.DAT;1
Total of 4 files.
$
```

2. Next, to select all your version-2 files, use * in place of both the file name and file type.

```
$ directory *.*;2
Directory DUA1:[YOURGROUP.YOU]
LOGIN.COM;2
Total of 1 file.
$
```

3. Finally, list all versions of your files of type **COM**.

```
$ directory *.com;*
Directory DUA1:[YOURGROUP.YOU]
LOGIN.COM;2    LOGIN.COM;1
Total of 2 files.
$
```

There is another, more concise, way to accomplish step 3 in Experiment 2.2:

```
$ directory *.com
```

In this command line, all versions of your files of type **COM** are selected by *.**COM** by default. Similarly, you can specify all your files in the default directory by entering either of the following command lines:

```
$ directory *.*;*
```

or

```
$ directory
```

When you want to match a single character, use the **%** wildcard. For example, you could specify all files with names beginning with **VAX** followed by a single letter by entering

```
$ directory vax%.*
```

If you do not have files that meet this specification, no list of files appears. To specify files with names beginning with **vax** followed by three letters, you would type

```
$ directory vax%%%.*
Directory DUA1:[YOURGROUP.YOU]
VAXBKS.DAT;1    VAXDEF.TXT;1    VAXMAN.DAT;1
Total of 3 files.
$
```

Because * matches multiple characters, you could specify all files with file names beginning with **vax** by entering

```
$ directory vax*.*
Directory DUA1:[YOURGROUP.YOU]
VAXBKS.DAT;1    VAXDEF.TXT;1    VAXMAN.DAT;1
Total of 3 files.
$
```

Try using the % wildcard by performing Experiment 2.3.

Experiment 2.3   **Using % to Select Files**

1. First create two new files, **VAX1.TXT** and **A.TXT**.

```
$ create vax1.txt
Models:   VAX-11/780, VAX-11/785
<CTRL/z>
[Exit]
$ create a.txt
rhyming words: aha, amoeba, amnesia
<CTRL/z>
[Exit]
```

2. Now get a directory listing of the **TXT** files with four letter names beginning with **vax**.

```
$ directory vax%.txt
Directory DUA1:[YOURGROUP.YOU]
VAX1.TXT;1
Total of 1 file.
$
```

3. Get a directory listing of the **TXT** files with single-letter names.

```
$ directory %.txt
Directory DUA1:[YOURGROUP.YOU]
A.TXT;1
Total of 1 file.
$
```

In this last step, notice that **%.TXT** does not include **AI.TXT** in its specification. Can you see why?

So far, you have used the * and % wildcards only with the **DIRECTORY** command, but you can use them with many DCL commands. As you continue exploring, you will see just how widespread the use of wildcards can be in a typical working session on a VAX/VMS system. For example, you might want to display the contents of files of type **TXT** and so would enter

```
$ type *.txt
```

Or perhaps you want to print copies of your files with names beginning with **VAX** using the **PRINT** command, which queues specified files for printing. Then you would type

```
$ print vax*.*
```

2.2 Managing Files

As you have seen, you can use the **DIRECTORY** command to obtain information about VMS files. VMS also provides other commands that help you manage files. Table 2.1 presents some commonly used file management commands. The following sections discuss these commands.

2.2.1 Copying Files

The **COPY** command makes it possible to copy a file. You can copy a file into a new file, thus creating the new file; or you can copy a file into an existing file, adding the copied file's contents to those of the existing file. This file management command has the following syntax:

copy *input-filespec* [, . . .] *output-filespec*

The *input-filespec* is the file to be copied, [, . . .] represents optional additional input file specifications, and the *output-filespec* is the copy's destination file.

Experiment with the **COPY** command by following Experiment 2.4.

Experiment 2.4 **Using the COPY Command**

1. Make a copy of the **SFBKS.DAT** file to begin a new, separate file containing a list of Isaac Asimov's books. Call the new file **SFASIMOV.DAT**.

```
$ copy sfbks.dat sfasimov.dat
$
```

Table 2.1   Selected File Management Commands

Command	Result
APPEND	Appends the contents of one file to another file
COPY	Copies the contents of a file to a new file
CREATE	Creates a new file
DELETE	Removes a file
DIFFERENCES	Compares files, flagging any differences
PRINT	Sends a copy of the file to the printer queue
PURGE	Removes all but the latest version of a file or files
RENAME	Gives a file a new name
TYPE	Lists the contents of a file or files

2. Use the **DIRECTORY** command to verify that the new file was created.

```
$ directory sf*.dat
Directory DUA1:[YOURGROUP.YOU]
SFASIMOV.DAT;1     SFBKS.DAT;1
Total of 2 files.
$
```

You can use the **COPY** command to concatenate, or string together, several input files that you want copied to a specified output file. When specifying more than one input file with the **COPY** command, place a comma (,) between the input file names. For example, to copy two files into a third file, you could type

```
$ copy vaxbks.dat,vaxman.dat vaxpubs.dat
```

This form of the **COPY** command copies the first specified input file, **VAXBKS.DAT**, to the new file named **VAXPUBS.DAT** and then appends the remaining input file(s) you have specified (**VAXMAN.DAT**, in this example) to the output file. You could use the **TYPE** command to see the contents of the new file created by the example:

```
$ type vaxpubs.dat
Kenah, L.J. Goldenberg, R.E. Bate, S.F. VAX/VMS
Internals and Data Structures. Bedford, MA:
Digital Press, 1988.
VAX C Run_Time Library Reference Manual.
Maynard, MA: Digital Equipment Corporation,
March 1987.
$
```

You can also use wildcards in the input file specification of a COPY command line. For instance, to collect all your files of type DAT inside a single output file, you would type

```
$ copy *.dat all.dat
```

You can also use wildcards in specifying multiple output files to be created by the COPY command. To make a copy of your files of type TXT in new files of type LTR using the same file names, you could enter

```
$ copy ai.txt;1,vaxdef.txt;1 *.ltr
```

To see the results of this form of the COPY command, type

```
$ directory *.ltr
Directory DUA1:[YOURGROUP.YOU]
AI.LTR;1      VAXDEF.LTR;1
Total of 2 files.
$
```

Challenge Problem

What new files would be created by the following uses of the COPY command when used with the following files: SFBKS.DAT, CSBKS.DAT, VAXBKS.DAT, VAXMAN.DAT, VAXDEF.TXT, DOESNOTHING.PAS, SAYSHELLO.PAS, and LOGIN.COM?

1. `$ copy *.dat;1 *.ltr`

2. `$ copy login.com;1 *.old`

There are a variety of qualifiers for the COPY command. You can find out more about the COPY command by entering

```
$ help copy
```

Of the many available qualifiers for the COPY command, you will probably find the /LOG qualifier most helpful right away. The /LOG qualifier causes the COPY command to describe each of its actions line by line. For example,

```
$ copy/log login.com;1 login.old
%COPY-S-COPIED, DUA1:[YOURGROUP.YOU]LOGIN.COM;1
copied to DUA1:[YOURGROUP.YOU]LOGIN.OLD;1 (1 block)
$
```

In this example, the /LOG qualifier displays a line indicating that LOGIN.COM;1 was copied to LOGIN.OLD;1.

You can try this form of the COPY command to verify your answers to the challenge problem.

2.2.2 Appending Files

The **APPEND** command makes it possible to attach the contents of one or more files to another file. You can append a file to an existing file, or you can append a file to a new file, thus creating the new file. The **APPEND** command has the following syntax:

append *input-filespec* [, . . .] *output-filespec*

The *input-filespec* is the file to be appended, [, . . .] represents optional additional input file specifications, and the *output-filespec* is the file to which the input files are appended.

The **APPEND** command is a time-saver because you can add information from one file to another file quickly. Experiment 2.5 shows how the **APPEND** command is used in its simplest form.

Experiment 2.5 **Using the APPEND Command**

1. Create a file containing a short letter. Call the file **MAX.LTR**.

   ```
   $ create max.ltr
   Hi, Max!
   I've appended to this letter the list of books I told
   you about earlier.
   Sue
   <CTRL/z>
   [Exit]
   $
   ```

2. Append the **VAXBKS.DAT** file to **MAX.LTR**.

   ```
   $ append vaxbks.dat max.ltr
   $
   ```

3. Now the **MAX.LTR** file has the contents of the **VAXBKS.DAT** file appended to it. Use the **DIRECTORY** command, asking to see all versions of both **MAX.LTR** and **VAXBKS.DAT**.

   ```
   $ directory max.ltr, vaxbks.dat
   Directory DUA1:[YOURGROUP.YOU]
   MAX.LTR;1      VAXBKS.DAT;1
   Total of 2 files.
   $
   ```

   Notice that, by default, the version number of a file does not change as a result of an append operation.

Like the COPY command, the APPEND command has a /LOG qualifier. It allows you to trace the actions performed by the APPEND command. For example, to see the actions performed in Experiment 2.5, type

```
$ append/log vaxbks.dat max.ltr
%APPEND-S-APPENDED, DUA1:[YOURGROUP.YOU]VAXBKS.DAT;1
appended to DUA1:[YOURGROUP.YOU]MAX.LTR;1 (2 records)
$
```

If the output file you specify in an APPEND command line does not exist, you must use the /NEW_VERSION qualifier with the APPEND command to create a new file. So, for example, if you do not have a LETTER.BOX file in your default directory, the following command line will create a new file with that name and append the contents of MAX.LTR to it:

```
$ append/new_version/log max.ltr letter.box
%APPEND-I-CREATED, DUA1:[YOURGROUP.YOU]LETTER.BOX;1
created
%APPEND-S-COPIED, DUA1:[YOURGROUP.YOU]MAX.LTR;1
copied to DUA1:[YOURGROUP.YOU]LETTER.BOX;1 (1 block)
$
```

Besides helping you with file management, the APPEND command is useful for many routine tasks. For example, suppose you have a file you want to mail to someone else on your system. You can create a short letter explaining the file you are mailing, append the file to the letter, and then use the VMS Mail utility to send the letter with the appended file.

2.2.3   *Purging Files*

You have started to accumulate quite a few files, some of which you may not need any longer. VMS has DELETE and PURGE commands, which make it possible to eliminate files. The PURGE command completely erases the files from the disk. It is useful if you have multiple versions of the same file and you need to keep only selected versions. The PURGE command has the following syntax:

purge [*filespec* [, . . .]]

The *filespec* specifies one or more files to be purged. The simplest form of this command eliminates all but the most recent version of every file in your current directory:

```
$ purge
```

You can also use the PURGE command more selectively by specifying particular files in the command line. For example, you may have more than one version of the `LOGIN.COM` file, and you only need the most recent version of this file. To purge all but the most recent version of this file, you would type

```
$ purge login.com
```

You can also use wildcards in the directory, file name, and file type fields with the `PURGE` command. For example, to purge all but the most recent versions of files of type `DAT` in your default directory, you would type

```
$ purge *.dat
```

You cannot specify version numbers when entering file specifications in the `PURGE` command line. If you want to keep more than the most recent version of a file, you must use the `/KEEP` qualifier, specifying the number of versions to be retained. This form of the `PURGE` command has the following syntax:

purge/keep = *number-of-versions* [*filespec* [, . . .]]

For example, suppose you have been editing the `LOGIN.COM` file repeatedly and have accumulated five versions of it. To keep the two most recent versions of the `LOGIN.COM` file, you would type

```
$ purge/keep = 2 login.com
```

To explore using the `PURGE` command, try Experiment 2.6.

Using the PURGE Command with the /KEEP Qualifier

1. Create four new versions of the `MAX.LTR` file by using EDT to add text to the file, as follows. Add the text shown in color, using the arrow keys to move around the file and the <RETURN> key to add a new line. (Remember to enter the `CHANGE` command at the asterisk prompt to move to keypad mode if necessary.)

```
$ edit/edt max.ltr
Hi Maxwell!
I've appended to this letter the list of books I told
you about earlier.
Sue
Kenah, L.J. Goldenberg, R.E. Bate, S.F. VAX/VMS
Internals and Data Structures. Bedford, MA:
Digital Press, 1988.
<CTRL/z>
* exit
$

$ edit/edt max.ltr
Hi Maxwell!
```

```
I've appended to this letter the list of books I told
you about earlier.
Hope this is helpful.
Sue
Kenah, L.J. Goldenberg, R.E. Bate, S.F. VAX/VMS
Internals and Data Structures. Bedford, MA:
Digital Press, 1988.
<CTRL/z>
* exit
$


$ edit/edt max.ltr
Hi Maxwell!
I've appended to this letter the list of books I told
you about earlier.
Hope this is helpful. Call me if you need more info.
Sue
Kenah, L.J. Goldenberg, R.E. Bate, S.F. VAX/VMS
Internals and Data Structures. Bedford, MA:
Digital Press, 1988.
<CTRL/z>
* exit
$


$ edit/edt max.ltr
Hi Maxwell!
I've appended to this letter the list of books I told
you about earlier.
Hope this is helpful. Call me if you need more info.
Sue Reed
Kenah, L.J. Goldenberg, R.E. Bate, S.F. VAX/VMS
Internals and Data Structures. Bedford, MA:
Digital Press, 1988.
<CTRL/z>
* exit
$
```

2. Check how many versions of **MAX.LTR** you have.

```
$ directory max.ltr
Directory DUA1:[YOURGROUP.YOU]
MAX.LTR;5    MAX.LTR;4    MAX.LTR;3    MAX.LTR;2
MAX.LTR;1
Total of 5 files.
$
```

3. Now purge all but the last four versions.

```
$ purge/keep = 4 max.ltr
$
```

4. Check the versions you have.

```
$ directory max.ltr
Directory DUA1:[YOURGROUP.YOU]
MAX.LTR;5     MAX.LTR;4     MAX.LTR;3     MAX.LTR;2
Total of 4 files.
$
```

5. Purge all but the last two versions. This time use the /LOG qualifier to see the file specifications of the files as they are purged.

```
$ purge/keep = 2/log max.ltr
%PURGE-I-FILPURG, DUA1:[YOURGROUP.YOU]MAX.LTR;2
deleted (3 blocks)
%PURGE-I-FILPURG, DUA1:[YOURGROUP.YOU]MAX.LTR;3
deleted (3 blocks)
$
```

One useful application of the PURGE command is to enter it in your LOGIN.COM file, specifying the number of versions you want kept. Then, each time you log in, VMS will purge all but that many versions of each file or of the specified files. For example, if you enter the following command line in your LOGIN.COM file, all but the two most recent versions of your files of type COM will be purged:

```
$ purge/keep = 2 *.com
```

You probably have guessed that it may be dangerous to use the PURGE command with a file specification containing a wildcard. For example, you might not want to purge all but the most recent version of *all* your files of type COM. In such a case, you will find the /CONFIRM qualifier useful. This qualifier causes the PURGE command to check that you want a file purged. You respond with either Y (yes) to confirm or N (no) to stop the purging of that file. Here is the syntax for this form of the PURGE command:

purge/confirm [*filespec* [, . . .]]

For example, you can confirm the purging of all files of type COM and type DAT by entering

```
$ purge/confirm *.com, *.dat
DELETE DUA1:[YOURGROUP.YOU]LOGIN.COM;1? [N]
```

Then, if you want the file purged, type **y** at the prompt. To keep the file from being purged, type **n**. VMS will ask about each file before the file is purged.

2.2.4 Deleting Files

You can selectively delete unwanted files by using the **DELETE** command. **DELETE** differs from **PURGE** because it requires you to specify file version numbers as well as the directory, file name, and file type. This command has the following syntax:

delete *filespec* [, . . .]

You must always specify a version number for the files you want to delete. For example, to delete version 1 of your **LOGIN.COM**, you would enter

```
$ delete login.com;1
$
```

You can also use a wildcard in place of a specific version number or in the directory, file name, and file type fields when using the **DELETE** command. Experiment 2.7 explores using the * wildcard to delete all versions of a file.

Experiment 2.7

Deleting All Versions of a File

1. Because this experiment deletes all versions of the **MAX.LTR** file, you should first make a copy of the most recent version of this file, giving the copy a new name.

   ```
   $ copy max.ltr copymax.ltr
   ```

2. Now use the * wildcard to delete all versions of **MAX.LTR**.

   ```
   $ delete max.ltr;*
   ```

3. You can also use * to delete all files of a certain type. Because **DELETE** requires a version number, you must specify a number or use a wildcard as a version number. Try deleting all **LTR** files.

   ```
   $ delete *.ltr;*
   ```

It is easy to accidentally delete files you need to keep. Remember the danger in using the **DELETE** command with a file specification that has a wildcard.

Like the other file management commands, the **DELETE** command has several useful qualifiers. You can see the effects of executing the **DELETE** command by using the **/LOG** qualifier. For example,

```
$ delete/log *.ltr;*
%DELETE-I-FILDEL, DUA1:[YOURGROUP.YOU]MAX.LTR;5
deleted (3 blocks)
%DELETE-I-FILDEL, DUA1;[YOURGROUP.YOU]COPYMAX.LTR;1
deleted (3 blocks)
%DELETE-I-TOTAL, 2 files deleted (6 blocks)
$
```

With the **/LOG** qualifier, you can at least see which files are deleted. Better still, the **DELETE** command also has a **/CONFIRM** qualifier, which lets you control which files are deleted by typing **y** or **n** at the prompt before the file is deleted. For example,

```
$ delete/confirm *.txt;*
DELETE DUA1:[YOURGROUP.YOU]AI.TXT;1? [N]:y
DELETE DUA1:[YOURGROUP.YOU]VAXDEF.TXT;1? [N]:n
  .
  .
  .
```

In this example, only **AI.TXT** was deleted; **VAXDEF.TXT** was retained by entering **n** at the prompt. You should get used to using the **/CONFIRM** qualifier with the **DELETE** command to avoid unintentional losses of valued files.

2.2.5   *Renaming Files*

At times, you may need to change a file's name. You can give new names to existing files using the **RENAME** command. This command has the following syntax:

rename *input-filespec* [, . . .] *output-filespec*

The *input-filespec* is the current file name or names and the *output-filespec* is the new name of the files.

The **RENAME** command is both versatile and easy to use. For example, to rename the **VAXDEF.TXT** file, enter

```
$ rename vaxdef.txt decdefs
$
```

The **VAXDEF.TXT;1** file is now renamed **DECDEFS;1**. After being renamed, **VAXDEF.TXT;1** no longer exists in the directory.

As with other file management commands, the **/LOG** qualifier lets you trace the results of the **RENAME** command. Experiment 2.8 uses the **RENAME** command with /LOG at the same time as it explores another feature of all DCL commands, automatic prompts.

When you are entering a command line, you might forget all the required specifications. If you press the <RETURN> key before entering all the required information, DCL prompts you for the missing information. These automatic prompts guide you through the requirements of the command.

Experiment 2.8   **Using the RENAME Command and Exploring DCL Automatic Prompts**

1. Begin by entering the **RENAME** command with the /LOG qualifier. Instead of specifying the file to be renamed, press the <RETURN> key.

```
$ rename/log
_From:
```

2. DCL prompts you for the name of the input file. Fill in the name and press the <RETURN> key again.

```
_From: sayshello.pas
_To:
```

3. Now you are prompted for the new name of the file. When you enter the name, the **RENAME** command completes its task. Because of the /LOG qualifier, you can trace the results of the command.

```
_To: hello
%RENAME-I-RENAMED, DUA1:[YOURGROUP.YOU]SAYSHELLO.PAS;1
renamed to DUA1:[YOURGROUP.YOU]HELLO.PAS;1
$
```

2.2.6   *Checking the Differences Between Files*

The **DIFFERENCES** command compares the contents of two files and lists the nonmatching portions of the compared files. It has the following syntax:

differences *input1-filespec* [*input2-filespec*]

This command lists the differences between the first input file and the second input file. If you do not specify a second input file, the **DIFFERENCES** command compares the first input file with the next lower version of that file. For example, to compare the two highest versions of your **LOGIN.COM** file, you would type

```
$ differences login.com
************
File DUA1:[YOURGROUP.YOU]LOGIN.COM;2
    2 $ show users
    3 $ show quota
******
File DUA1:[YOURGROUP.YOU]LOGIN.COM;1
************

Number of difference sections found: 1
Number of difference records found: 2

DIFFERENCES /IGNORE = <>/MERGED = 1
    DUA1:[YOURGROUP.YOU]LOGIN.COM;2
    DUA1:[YOURGROUP.YOU]LOGIN.COM;1
```

To compare versions 5 and 1 of your LOGIN.COM file, you would type

```
$ differences login.com;5 login.com;1
```

You cannot use wildcards in either of the file specifications in a DIFFER-ENCES command line.

Try Experiment 2.9 to see how the DIFFERENCES command works.

Experiment 2.9   ***Comparing the Differences Between Two Files***

1. First use the EDT editor to edit the HELLO.PAS file to create two new ver-sions of the file. Change the lines of the file as indicated by the text in color. The first change produces HELLO.PAS;2, and the second change pro-duces HELLO.PAS;3. Use the arrow keys to move through the text and the <DELETE> key or the <x] key to erase text as necessary. (Remember to enter the CHANGE command at the asterisk prompt to move to keypad mode if necessary.)

```
$ edit/edt hello.pas
program sayshello(output);
begin
writeln ('Hello, Your name!')
end.
[EOB]
<CTRL/z>
* exit
$

$ edit/edt hello.pas
program sayshello(output);
begin
```

```
writeln('Hello, world, again!')
end.
[EOB]
<CTRL/z>
* exit
$
```

2. Now use the **DIFFERENCES** command to compare the two most recent versions of **HELLO.PAS**.

```
$ differences hello.pas
************
File DUA1:[YOURGROUP.YOU]HELLO.PAS;3
   3 writeln('Hello, world, again!')
   4 end.
******
File DUA1:[YOURGROUP.YOU]HELLO.PAS;2
   3 writeln('Hello, Your name!')
   4 end.
************

Number of difference sections found:1
Number of difference records found:1

DIFFERENCES /IGNORE = <>/MERGED = 1
    DUA1:[YOURGROUP.YOU]HELLO.PAS;3
    DUA1:[YOURGROUP.YOU]HELLO.PAS;2
```

3. Finally, compare versions 3 and 1 of **HELLO.PAS**.

```
$ differences hello.pas;3 hello.pas;1
************
File DUA1:[YOURGROUP.YOU]HELLO.PAS;3
   3 writeln('Hello, world, again!')
   4 end.
  ******
File DUA1:[YOURGROUP.YOU]HELLO.PAS;1
   3 writeln('Hello, world!')
   4 end.
************

Number of difference sections found:1
Number of difference records found:1

DIFFERENCES /IGNORE = <>/MERGED = 1
    DUA1:[YOURGROUP.YOU]HELLO.PAS;3
    DUA1:[YOURGROUP.YOU]HELLO.PAS;1
```

When you examined the pathname of the file specification, you saw how the directory names are listed in hierarchical order. A subdirectory is a directory that is cataloged in another, higher-level directory. In specifications, the different directory levels are separated by a period (.).

For example, so far, the experiments have assumed that your login directory, **YOU**, is a subdirectory of a group's or department's directory, **YOURGROUP**. The directory specification for your files, then, is [YOURGROUP.YOU].

Another directory specification might be **DUA1:[UPSTAIRS.AI.YOU]**. In this imaginary situation, **YOU** is a subdirectory of **AI**; the **AI** directory is itself a subdirectory of the **UPSTAIRS** directory, which might be a directory of all departments.

When referring to a subdirectory of your working, or default, directory, you can specify either the full directory specification or just the subdirectory. For example, the following both specify the subdirectory **VMS**:

    [.VMS]

    [YOURGROUP.YOU.VMS]

Subdirectories, like directories, are files of type **DIR**.

2.3.1   *Creating a Subdirectory*

You use the **CREATE** command with the **/DIRECTORY** qualifier to establish a new subdirectory. The **CREATE/DIRECTORY** command has the following syntax:

create/directory *directory-specification* [, . . .]

When you create a subdirectory, VMS assigns a **DIR** extension to it. To list the files contained in a subdirectory, you must specify the name of that subdirectory. For example, to see the files in the **TEXTS** subdirectory, you would type

    $ directory [.texts]

Try Experiment 2.10 to explore working with subdirectories.

Creating a Subdirectory

1. Use the **CREATE/DIRECTORY** command to create a **VMS** subdirectory.

   ```
   $ create/directory [.vms]
   ```

2. To verify that the subdirectory now exists, use the **DIRECTORY** command to list all subdirectories.

   ```
   $ directory *.dir
   Directory DUA1:[YOURGROUP.YOU]
   VMS.DIR;1
   Total of 1 file.
   $
   ```

3. This **VMS** subdirectory is empty. Add some files to it by copying files from the default directory.

   ```
   $ copy vax*.* [.vms]
   ```

4. Now get a directory listing for the **VMS** subdirectory.

   ```
   $ directory [.vms]
   Directory DUA1:[YOURGROUP.YOU.VMS]
   VAX1.TXT      VAXBKS.DAT;1      VAXDEF.TXT;1
   VAXMAN.DAT;1
   Total of 4 files.
   $
   ```

If you wanted to display the contents of the **VAXBKS.DAT** file in the **VMS** subdirectory, you could use one of the following versions of the **TYPE** command:

```
$ type [.vms]vaxbks.dat
$ type [yourgroup.you.vms]vaxbks.dat
```

By default, VMS considers a file name without a specified directory name to be in the default directory.

To get more experience with establishing new subdirectories, perform Experiment 2.11.

Creating More Subdirectories

1. Create two new subdirectories: **PASCAL** and **TEXTS**. You can use the **/LOG** qualifier after the **/DIRECTORY** qualifier to trace the procedure.

   ```
   $ create/directory/log [.pascal]
   %CREATE-I-CREATED, DUA1:[YOURGROUP.YOU.PASCAL] created
   ```

```
$ create/directory/log [.texts]
%CREATE-I-CREATED, DUA1:[YOURGROUP.YOU.TEXTS] created
$
```

2. Now check the size of the subdirectories by using the DIRECTORY command with the /SIZE qualifier.

```
$ directory/size *.dir
Directory DUA1:[YOURGROUP.YOU]
PASCAL.DIR;1          1
TEXTS.DIR;1          1
VMS.DIR;1            1
```

3. Copy the files of type PAS to the PASCAL subdirectory and the files of type TXT to the TEXTS subdirectory. Again, use /LOG to trace the procedure.

```
$ copy/log *.pas [.pascal]
%COPY-S-COPIED, DUA1:[YOURGROUP.YOU]DOESNOTHING.PAS;1
copied to DUA1:[YOURGROUP.YOU.PASCAL]DOESNOTHING.PAS;1 (1
block)
%COPY-S-COPIED, DUA1:[YOURGROUP.YOU]HELLO.PAS;3 copied to
DUA1:[YOURGROUP.YOU.PASCAL]HELLO.PAS;3 (1 block)
%COPY-S-NEWFILES, 2 files created
$
```

```
$ copy/log *.txt [.texts]
%COPY-S-COPIED, DUA1:[YOURGROUP.YOU]A.TXT;1 copied to
DUA1:[YOURGROUP.YOU.TEXTS]A.TXT;1 (1 block)
%COPY-S-COPIED, DUA1:[YOURGROUP.YOU]AI.TXT;1 copied to
DUA1:[YOURGROUP.YOU.TEXTS]AI.TXT;1 (1 block)
%COPY-S-COPIED, DUA1:[YOURGROUP.YOU]VAX1.TXT;1 copied to
DUA1:[YOURGROUP.YOU.TEXTS]VAX1.TXT;1 (1 block)
%COPY-S-COPIED, DUA1:[YOURGROUP.YOU]VAXDEF.TXT;1 copied to
DUA1:[YOURGROUP.YOU.TEXTS]VAXDEF.TXT;1 (1 block)
%COPY-S-NEWFILES, 4 files created
$
```

4. Use the DIRECTORY command to get a listing of the contents of each new directory.

```
$ directory [.pascal]
Directory DUA1:[YOURGROUP.YOU.PASCAL]
DOESNOTHING.PAS;1    HELLO.PAS;3
Total of 2 files.
$
```

```
$ directory [.texts]
Directory DUA1:[YOURGROUP.YOU.TEXTS]
A.TXT;1    AI.TXT;1    VAX1.TXT;1    VAXDEF.TXT;1
Total of 4 files.
$
```

You can create more than one directory with a single command line by entering the directory names separated by commas. For example,

```
$ create/directory [.PASCAL],[.TEXTS]
```

2.3.2   *Changing the Default Directory*

The directory in which you are working is called your working, or default, directory. By default, your login directory is your default directory each time you log into a VAX system. Any files you create automatically become part of your default directory. You can change your default directory with the SET DEFAULT command, which has the following syntax:

set default *directory-specification*

For example, if you are working primarily with the files in the **VMS** subdirectory, you can make that directory the default directory. To change the default directory from your login directory to the **VMS** subdirectory, you would type

```
$ set default [.vms]
$
```

You can check which directory is the default directory with the SHOW DEFAULT command:

```
$ show default
DUA1:[YOURGROUP.YOU.VMS]
$
```

You can change back to your login directory with the SET DEFAULT command and the hyphen (-) directory-searching wildcard character. In general, this wildcard changes you from one directory to the next higher directory. For example, to change from the **VMS** subdirectory back to the **YOU** subdirectory (your login directory), you would type

```
$ set default [-]
```

Using SET DEFAULT and the [-] wildcard, you can move up the path of directories above your login directory on your system. To explore moving through the directories, try Experiment 2.12.

Move down directory tree by typing

```
$ set default [.ai.you]
```

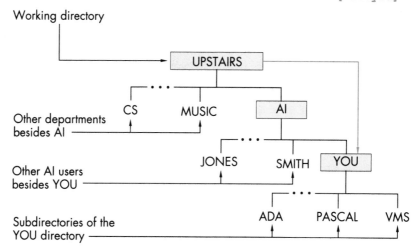

Figure 2.5 **Moving Up and Down a Directory Tree**

Experiment 2.12 ***Moving Around Your Directory Tree***

1. Use **SHOW DEFAULT** to make sure you are in your login directory.

   ```
   $ show default
   DUA1:[YOURGROUP.YOU]
   ```

2. Now move up one level in your directory tree, and check the new default directory with **SHOW DEFAULT**.

   ```
   $ set default [-]
   $ show default
   DUA1:[YOURGROUP]
   ```

   This step may produce an error message, depending on what your system manager has done in setting up the directory one level above your login directory. That is, you may not have sufficient privilege to list the contents of the directories above your login directory. Check whether this is the case.

   ```
   $ directory
   ```

3. Finally, move back to your login directory. (Remember to replace **DUA1:[YOURGROUP.YOU]** with your directory specification.)

   ```
   $ set default dua1:[yourgroup.you]
   ```

As you move up the directory tree above your login directory, you may find you are not able to list the contents of any subdirectories above your login directory because you do not have sufficient privilege. VMS has an elaborate scheme for protecting files against unauthorized access. An explanation of how this protection scheme works is given in Appendix E.

By moving up the directory tree of your system in Experiment 2.12, you can get a feel for the overall directory structure. This movement up and down a directory tree is shown in Figure 2.5.

Notice in Figure 2.5 what you must type to return to the login directory if you are more than two levels above this directory. For example, if your working directory is [UPSTAIRS], then to move down the directory tree to your login directory, you would type

```
$ set default [.ai.you]
```

2.3.3   *Organizing Files with Subdirectories*

By creating subdirectories, you can organize your files into logically related groups. In effect, a subdirectory is like a drawer in a file cabinet, with each file being a file folder.

As you work with subdirectories, consider the following tips for setting up a system of subdirectories:

1. Decide what logical groups of files you should have. For example, for the set of files that you have created so far, the logical groups and their corresponding subdirectories might be

Logical Group of Files	Subdirectory
SAYHELLO.PAS;1 DONOTHING.PAS;1	Pascal files
SFBKS.DAT;1 VAXBKS.DAT;1 VAXMAN.DAT;1	Bibliographies
VAXDEF.DAT;1	Definitions
VAXBKS.DAT;1 VAXDEF.TXT;1 VAXMAN.DAT;1	VAX/VMS ideas

2. Once you have identified a logical group, you can check for possible logical subgroups. These subgroups can become subdirectories of the logical group's subdirectory. In the sample logical groups, here are some possible subgroups and their corresponding subdirectories.

Logical Groups and Subgroups	Subdirectory
Bibliographies	
SFBKS.DAT;1	Science fiction
VAXBKS.DAT;1	VAX/VMS publications
VAXMAN.DAT;1	
VAX/VMS ideas	
VAXDEF.TXT;1	VAX/VMS definitions
VAXBKS.DAT;1	VAX/VMS books
VAXMAN.DAT;1	VAX/VMS manuals

3. When creating subdirectories, it is important to choose meaningful subdirectory names. Then you are less likely to forget what a subdirectory contains.

For example, to see how to set up a directory system for the VAX/VMS files you have created in this chapter, perform Experiment 2.13.

Experiment 2.13 **Establishing a System of Subdirectories**

1. Use SET DEFAULT to change to your login directory, if necessary.

2. Create a master VAX/VMS subdirectory. Use the /LOG qualifier to trace the procedure.

```
$ create/directory/log [.vaxideas]
%CREATE-I-CREATED, DUA1:[YOURGROUP.YOU.VAXIDEAS] created
$
```

3. Next create three subdirectories of VAXIDEAS.

```
$ create/directory/log [.vaxideas.books]
%CREATE-I-CREATED, DUA1:[YOURGROUP.YOU.VAXIDEAS.BOOKS]
created
$ create/directory/log [.vaxideas.manuals]
%CREATE-I-CREATED, DUA1:[YOURGROUP.YOU.VAXIDEAS.MANUALS]
created
$ create/directory/log [.vaxideas.definitions]
%CREATE-I-CREATED, DUA1:[YOURGROUP.YOU.VAXIDEAS.DEFINITIONS]
created
```

4. Now install the appropriate files in the new subdirectories of your VAXIDEAS subdirectory.

```
$ copy/log vaxbks.dat [.vaxideas.books]
%COPY-S-COPIED, DUA1:[YOURGROUP.YOU]VAXBKS.DAT;1 copied to
DUA1:[YOURGROUP.YOU.VAXIDEAS.BOOKS]VAXBKS.DAT;1 (1 block)
$ copy/log vaxman.dat [.vaxideas.manuals]
%COPY-S-COPIED, DUA1:[YOURGROUP.YOU]VAXMAN.DAT;1 copied to
DUA1:[YOURGROUP.YOU.VAXIDEAS.MANUALS]VAXMAN.DAT;1 (1 block)
$ copy/log vaxdef.txt [.vaxideas.definitions]
%COPY-S-COPIED, DUA1:[YOURGROUP.YOU]VAXDEF.TXT;1 copied to
DUA1:[YOURGROUP.YOU.VAXIDEAS.DEFINITIONS]VAXDEF.TXT;1
(1 block)
```

2.4 Short Forms for DCL Commands

Most DCL commands have an abbreviated form that you may use rather than
typing the whole command. For example, to use the DIRECTORY command,
you may type DIR rather than DIRECTORY. The short form of a command is its
first four characters; you may use fewer than four characters as long as the
abbreviation uniquely identifies the command.

Because these short forms are composed of fewer characters, they save you
time. As you work with VMS and become familiar with its commands, you
will probably start to use the short forms. Be aware when using abbreviations, however, that an abbreviation unique in one version of VMS might not
be unique in the next version.

2.5 Summary

With the VMS file-handling tools you have seen so far, various approaches
to files are possible, as seen in Table 2.2. As you master these file-handling
tools, you will also want to consider various means of creating and organizing your files and directories.

Tables 2.3–2.5 give an overview of the commands, special characters, and
important terms used in this chapter.

2.6 Exercises

1. What is the pathname for the files in your login directory?

   Exercises 2, 3, and 4 reference the following files:

   SFBKS.DAT;30 SFBKS.DAT;29 SFBKS.DAT;28

   SFASIMOV.DAT;5

Table 2.2 Approaches to VMS Files

Approach	DCL Command	Result
File creation	COPY	Duplicates a file or files
	CREATE	Creates a new file
	EDIT	Creates (and possibly changes) a file
File inspection	DIRECTORY	Displays a list of files
	TYPE	Displays the contents of a file or files
File management	APPEND	Appends a copy of a file to a file
	DELETE	Removes a file or files
	DIFFERENCES	Compares a pair of files
	PRINT	Sends a file to the printer queue
	PURGE	Removes a version or versions of a file
	RENAME	Gives a file a new name
Directory management	CREATE /DIRECTORY	Establishes a new subdirectory
	SET DEFAULT	Changes the default directory
	SHOW DEFAULT	Displays the current default directory

```
SFHOYLE.DAT;7  SFHOYLE.DAT;6

SFDEF.TXT;1  SFDEF.TXT;2

VAXDEF.TXT;9  VAXDEF.TXT;8

VMSBKS.DAT;9  XENIX.TXT;5
```

2. List the files in the preceding list that are indicated by the following file specifications:

   a. `sf%.dat;*`

   b. `sf%%.dat;*`

   c. `sf%%%.dat;*`

   d. `sf*.*;*`

   e. `sf*.txt;*`

Table 2.3 DCL Commands

Command	Result
APPEND	Attaches one or more files to a named file
/LOG	Displays the **APPEND** command's actions
/NEW_VERSION	Creates a new output file
COPY	Makes a copy of a file
/LOG	Displays the **COPY** command's actions
CREATE	Establishes a new file
/DIRECTORY	Establishes a new subdirectory
/LOG	Displays the **CREATE** command's actions
DELETE	Deletes a specified file or files
/CONFIRM	Issues a request to confirm before *each* deletion
/LOG	Displays the **DELETE** command's actions
DIFFERENCES	Compares the contents of two files
PURGE	Removes the specified versions or all versions of the specified file or files
/CONFIRM	Issues a request to confirm before *each* purge
/KEEP=N	Purge all but the *n* most recent file versions
/LOG	Displays the **PURGE** command's actions
RENAME	Renames a file or files
/LOG	Displays the **RENAME** command's actions
SET DEFAULT	Changes the default directory to be another directory
SET DEFAULT [-]	Moves the default directory to be the directory up one level
SHOW DEFAULT	Displays the current default directory

  f. `v*.*;9`

  g. `s*.*;*`

3. Give a single file specification for each of the following:

  a. All files whose names begin with **VAX**

  b. All files of type **TXT**

  c. All version-1 files

  d. All files with **HOYLE** in the file name

Table 2.4 Special Characters

Character	Meaning
%	Wildcard representing any single character
*	Wildcard representing one or more characters
[-]	Represents the name of the directory one level above the default directory
[.*name*]	Subdirectory name
[.*name*] *filename*	Subdirectory file's file name

    e. All files having a type that begins with **D**

    f. All files with file names having six letters that begin with **v** and end with **s**

4. In terms of the preceding list of files, give command lines that perform the following:

    a. Append all files whose names begin with **SF** to an **SFIDEAS.DAT** file.

    b. Copy all the files to a list of files of type **YES**.

5. Without using wildcards, give four ways to specify a file named **VAXBKS.DAT** in a **VAXIDEAS** subdirectory of your login directory.

6. For your system, what is the full file specification for the **SFBKS.DAT** file (created in Experiment 2.1, Section 2.1.1)?

7. Give two ways to specify the directory at the level above your login directory on your system.

8. Give a single command line that tells VMS to display the contents of all your files of type **TXT**.

9. Give command lines to do the following:

    a. Create a **LETTERS** subdirectory of your login directory

    b. Create a sample letter that ends with P.S.

    c. Append all the files of type **TXT** to the letter created in (b).

    d. Put a copy of the letter from (b) into your **LETTERS** subdirectory.

10. Give a single command line that creates three subdirectories named **YES1**, **YES2**, and **YES3**.

Table 2.5   Important Terms

Terms	Definition
Default directory	Directory currently being used
Directory	File containing names of files
Login directory	Directory assigned by VMS to you when you log in
Subdirectory	Any directory whose name appears in your default directory and that is "below" your default directory
Wildcard	Special character used in a file name to specify a collection of related files
Working directory	The same as the default directory

11. Using the files created in Experiment 2.1 (Section 2.1.1), give command lines that accomplish the following:

   a.   Append the files of type **TXT** to **ALL.TXT**.

   b.   Create a **PROGRAMS** subdirectory.

   c.   Copy all files of type **PAS** to the **PROGRAMS** subdirectory.

12. Give a new version of your **LOGIN.COM** file that produces a list of the subdirectories of your login directory each time you log in.

Review Quiz

Indicate whether the following statements are true or false:

1. The following command line references only version-1 files in your current directory:

   ```
   $ directory *.*;1
   ```

2. The **%** wildcard can be used in a file specification to specify version numbers.

3. The ***.COM** file specification specifies *all* versions of your files of type **COM**.

4. The ***.DAT** and ***.DAT;*** file specifications identify the same group of files.

5. A **COPY** command line specifies one or more files to be created.

6. The **PURGE** and **DELETE** commands can both be used to eliminate files.

7. You must give the version number of a file you wish to delete.

8. It is possible to have version 39 and version 1 of the same file and *no* other versions of that file.

9. The type specification for a subdirectory is DIR.

10. The following command line will move down exactly one directory level:

```
$ set default [-]
```

2.8   *Further Reading*

Adams, J. L. *Conceptual Blockbusting: A Guide to Better Ideas*. New York: W. W. Norton, 1979.

DEC VAX-11/785 Manual and User's Guide. Collegeville, Minn.: Academic Computing Services, 1985. *Address*: John Muggli, Academic Computing Center, St. John's University, Collegeville, MN 56321.

Order from Digital Equipment Corporation, POB CS2008, Nashua, NH 03061:

VMS DCL Concepts Manual. Order no. AA-OA-TE.

VMS DCL Dictionary. Order no. AA-LA12A-TE.

VMS General User's Manual. Order no. AA-LA98A-TE.

Chapter 3

Full-Screen Editing with EDT

*Poetry should surprise by a fine excess, and not by singularity. It should strike
the reader as a wording of his own highest thoughts, and appear almost as a
remembrance.*

—John Keats, Letter to John Taylor, 1818

VMS provides several different text editors, which you can use to create and
edit text files. This chapter explores the text editor EDT. In this chapter, you
will

- Learn how to use EDT keypad mode
- Learn how EDT stores a text file
- Explore commonly used EDT keypad commands
- Experiment with various methods of moving the cursor
- Explore various ways to locate text
- Examine different ways to recover from system interruptions

3.1   About EDT

EDT is one of the full-screen editors offered by VMS. It allows you to create
and modify text files, which are files of characters and include such things as
source programs, command files, and memoranda. EDT is called a full-
screen editor because text can be edited anywhere on the screen.

EDT has three separate modes—line, nokeypad, and keypad—which can be used in combination with one another. Line mode allows you to manipulate a range of one or more lines of text. It is most frequently used on hard-copy, or printing, terminals. In nokeypad mode, English words and abbreviations are used to manipulate text on the screen.

Keypad mode provides easy manipulation of text using simple keystrokes. Using the keys on the numeric keypad, to the right of the main keyboard, you can work with characters as well as with larger portions of text. Cursor position determines how text will be affected by the EDT commands, and you can move the cursor through a file in a variety of ways. In keypad mode, the keypad commands make it possible to delete, find, insert, substitute, or move text in a file with a single keystroke.

In addition, EDT provides the following features to make your editing easier:

- An on-line Help facility, which can be used at any time during an editing session without affecting the work in progress
- A fail-safe mechanism called a Journal facility, which allows retrieval of lost files after a system crash
- Several methods of searching for text rapidly
- Multiple cursor movement functions

This chapter emphasizes editing in keypad mode. Occasionally, line mode commands that are essential to the editing process are discussed. A more detailed treatment of line mode commands is given in Appendix C. Before you explore EDT, follow Experiment 3.1, which uses the DCL CREATE command to set up a file. The text in this file is a familiar verse from Augustus De Morgan's *A Budget of Paradoxes* (c. 1850). You will use this file during experiments in this chapter.

Experiment 3.1   **Creating the Initial File**

1. Use the DCL CREATE command to create the file FLEAS.TXT.

   ```
   $ create fleas.txt
   ```

2. Type the following text, which has a missing line. Use the <TAB> key to indent the appropriate lines.

```
        upon their backs to bite 'em,
And little fleas have lesser fleas,
    and so ad infinitum.
And the great fleas themselves, in turn,
    have greater fleas to go on;
While these again have greater still,
    and greater still, and so on.
```

3. Exit by pressing <CTRL/z>.

```
<CTRL/z>
[Exit]
$
```

3.2   Getting Started with EDT

To activate EDT, use the DCL **EDIT** command with the **/EDT** qualifier:

```
$ edit/edt filename
```

On some systems, EDT is the default editor. When this is the case, you do not need to use the **/EDT** qualifier but can simply enter the **EDIT** command. Because the command to activate EDT varies somewhat from place to place, you will need to find out how to activate EDT on your system.

In addition, you can enter the **EDIT** command with or without the file name. If you do not enter the file name with the command, DCL prompts you for the file name. For example,

```
$ edit/edt
_File:
```

Then enter the file name and press <RETURN>.

Once you have entered the **EDIT** command and the file name, you have activated EDT. On some systems, EDT will be in line mode and the first line of the file appears followed by the line mode prompt, an asterisk. For example,

```
$ edit/edt test.txt
    1 First line of file appears
*
```

To move from line mode to keypad mode, type **CHANGE** at the line mode prompt and press <RETURN>. Then the first 22 lines of the file appear on the screen.

On other systems, a special file called an initialization file (`EDTINI.EDT`) has been created. It contains the line mode command `SET MODE CHANGE`, which shifts EDT automatically into keypad mode. This file may exist in your user directory or in one of the systemwide directories. If it exists, EDT goes directly into keypad mode, and the first 22 lines of the file appear on the screen. In this case, you do not need to enter the `CHANGE` command.

Whether EDT activates in line mode or keypad mode, it places a copy of the file in a workspace called the Main buffer, where you can manipulate the text. In addition, EDT keeps track of each keystroke you make during an EDT session in a special file called a journal file. When you end an editing session normally, by typing `EXIT` or `QUIT`, EDT discards the journal file. If the editing session ends abruptly because of system interruption, however, the journal file is saved, and you can use it to restore almost all your lost editing work.

Try activating EDT by following Experiment 3.2.

Experiment 3.2   **Activating EDT**

1. Activate EDT by entering the `EDIT` command and the file name on one line. Retrieve the file `FLEAS.TXT`, which you created in Experiment 3.1.

    ```
    $ edit/edt fleas.txt
    ```

    EDT either is in line mode and displays the first line of the file and the line mode asterisk prompt, as shown below, or it is in keypad mode and displays all seven lines of the file and the `[EOB]` symbol, which signifies end-of-buffer, as shown in Figure 3.1.

    ```
    $ edit/edt fleas.txt
        1 upon their backs to bite 'em,
    *
    ```

2. If EDT is in line mode, use the `CHANGE` command to move to keypad mode.

    ```
    $ edit/edt fleas.txt
        1 upon their backs to bite 'em,
    * change
    ```

    Once EDT finishes painting the screen with text, the cursor appears in the upper left-hand corner and the `[EOB]` symbol, or end-of-buffer marker, flags the end of the file, as seen in Figure 3.1. Behind the scenes, a copy of `FLEAS.TXT` has been put into the Main buffer, as shown in Figure 3.2.

```
▌ upon their backs to bite 'em,
And little fleas have lesser fleas,
   and so ad infinitum.
And the great fleas themselves, in turn,
   have greater fleas to go on;
While these again have greater still,
   and greater still, and so on.
[EOB]
```

Figure 3.1 Keypad Mode's Full-Screen Display

An Overview of the EDT Keypad

The EDT keypad includes the standard numeric keypad, shown in Figure 3.3, and the cursor movement keys.

The keys on the numeric keypad are assigned different functions, or commands. With the exception of the <GOLD> key (which is the <PF1> key) and the <HELP> key, each key is assigned two commands. For instance, key number 4 on the numeric keypad is assigned the ADVANCE and BOTTOM commands (see Figure 3.3). To issue the upper command on a key, press the key. To issue the lower, or alternative, command on a key, hold down <GOLD> and press the key. For instance, press the <4> key to issue the ADVANCE command. Press <GOLD> and the <4> key, or <GOLD/4>, to issue the BOTTOM command.

In addition, EDT makes use of the auxiliary keypad on VT200 keyboards and the arrow keys on VT100 keyboards.

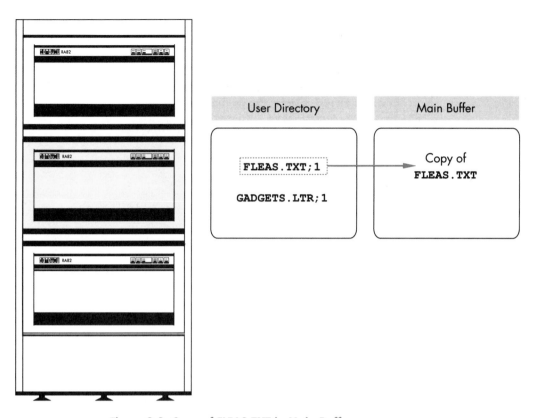

Figure 3.2 Copy of FLEAS.TXT in Main Buffer

Entering and Editing Text

When you work in EDT, you use keypad commands to modify and manipulate text. Some of the commands move the cursor to particular places in the text, and using the arrow keys will move the cursor as well.

3.4.1 Moving Around the File

The cursor is positioned at the beginning of the file when you enter keypad mode. You can move the cursor through the file using the arrow keys. The <LEFT ARROW> and <RIGHT ARROW> keys move the cursor one character to the left and right, respectively. The <UP ARROW> and <DOWN ARROW> keys move the cursor up and down one line. When using these keys, you cannot move past the beginning of the file or the top of the buffer, nor can you move past the end of the file or the end of the buffer.

Figure 3.3 The EDT Keypad

When you want to move directly to the top or bottom of the buffer, you can use the TOP and BOTTOM commands. Both of these commands are the lower, or alternative, commands on their respective keys, so you must first hold down <GOLD> and then press the appropriate key for the command: <5> for the TOP command, or <4> for the BOTTOM command. These keys are particularly useful when you are working with large files.

There is also a quick way to move to the end of the current line of text: issuing the EOL (end-of-line) command by pressing the <2> key. Since EOL is the upper command on its key (see Figure 3.3), no <GOLD> key press is needed.

To move to the beginning of the current line, press <F12> on the VT200 keyboard or <BACKSPACE> on the VT100 keyboard. To move to the beginning of the next line, use the LINE command by pressing the <0> key.

Experiment with these cursor movement keys and commands by following the steps in Experiment 3.3. Consult Figure 3.3 to become familiar with the commands associated with the various numeric keypad keys.

Exploring Some Cursor Movement Keys and Commands

1. Try using the arrow keys to move around the file.

2. Issue the TOP command (<GOLD/5>) to move to the top of the buffer; and issue the BOTTOM command (<GOLD/4>) to move to the bottom of the buffer.

3. Move to the top of the buffer and then press the <UP ARROW> key. Notice the message that appears. The bell and the message are EDT's way of telling you that the cursor cannot be moved past the beginning of the file. You would get a similar response if you tried to move past the end of the file.

4. Use the EOL command (<2>), the LINE command (<0>), and <F12> on the VT200 or <BACKSPACE> on the VT100 to move to the end and beginning of lines of text.

5. When you are finished experimenting, move to the top of the buffer.

There are several other ways to move around a file. They are discussed in later sections of this chapter.

3.4.2   Inserting Text

You can add text to a file by moving the cursor to the place where the text should be added and typing the text. As you type each character, EDT pushes the cursor and any text to the right of the cursor further right. You can insert from a single character to many lines of text. The characters are always inserted to the left of the cursor.

When you want to break a line of text, use <RETURN> or the OPEN LINE command (<GOLD/0>). To use <RETURN>, position the cursor *on* the character that should be the first character of the new line and press <RETURN>. To use the OPEN LINE command, position the cursor *before* the character that should be the first character of the new line and press <GOLD/0>.

The text file that you created in Experiment 3.1 is missing the first line. To practice using the EDT editor to make insertions, insert this line by following the steps in Experiment 3.4.

```
Great fleas have little flees█ upon their backs to bite 'em,
And little fleas have lesser fleas,
    and so ad infinitum.
And the great fleas themselves, in turn,
    have greater fleas to go on;
While these again have greater still,
    and greater still, and so on.
[EOB]
```

Figure 3.4 Entering a Line

Experiment 3.4   **Inserting Text**

1. The cursor should be at the top of the buffer. Type the missing line as shown in Figure 3.4. Make sure to misspell the last word as shown.

2. Now break the line by pressing <RETURN>. This enters a line terminator and moves the character the cursor is on plus the text to the right of the cursor to the next line, as shown in Figure 3.5.

3. Next try using the OPEN LINE command to break a line. In preparation, you should delete the line terminator, and so move the new second line back to the end of the first, by pressing the <x] key on the VT200 or <DELETE> on the VT100.

4. Use the OPEN LINE command to break the line. First press <GOLD> and then <0>. Notice that the text has been moved down a line. This time, however, the cursor remains at the end of the first line, as shown in Figure 3.6.

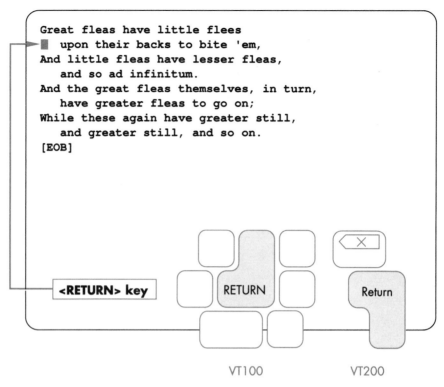

```
Great fleas have little flees
■  upon their backs to bite 'em,
And little fleas have lesser fleas,
    and so ad infinitum.
And the great fleas themselves, in turn,
    have greater fleas to go on;
While these again have greater still,
    and greater still, and so on.
[EOB]
```

<RETURN> key

RETURN

Return

VT100   VT200

Figure 3.5 Using RETURN to Break a Line

3.4.3   *Deleting Text*

With EDT, you can delete text by the character, word, or line. There are two methods of deleting characters. You can use the DELETE command by pressing the <x] key on the VT200 or <DELETE> on the VT100, which deletes the character to the left of the cursor; or you can use the DEL C (delete character) command, which deletes the character at the cursor position, by pressing the numeric keypad <COMMA> key.

To delete a word, position the cursor on the word and issue the DEL W (delete word) command by pressing the numeric keypad <MINUS> key.

To delete a line of text, position the cursor at the beginning of the line and use the DEL L (delete line) command by pressing the <PF4> key. Alternatively, you can use the DEL EOL command (<GOLD/2>). It differs from the DEL L command because it does not delete the line terminator and so leaves a blank line on the screen. Both the DEL L and DEL EOL commands delete

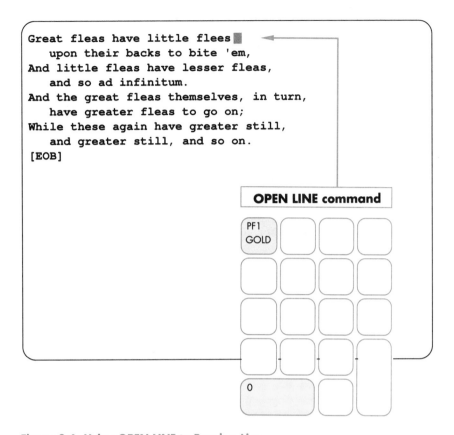

```
Great fleas have little flees▊      ◄──────────┐
   upon their backs to bite 'em,                │
And little fleas have lesser fleas,             │
   and so ad infinitum.                         │
And the great fleas themselves, in turn,        │
   have greater fleas to go on;                 │
While these again have greater still,           │
   and greater still, and so on.                │
[EOB]                                           │
```

OPEN LINE command

PF1
GOLD

0

Figure 3.6 Using OPEN LINE to Break a Line

from the cursor position to the end of the line, so you can use them to delete just part of a line as well.

Explore the use of these commands by following Experiment 3.5.

Experiment 3.5   **Deleting Text**

1. The first text you need to delete is the misspelling in the word *fleas.* The cursor is at the end of the line containing this error. Press the <x] key or <DELETE> twice to delete the last two characters of the line. Then type **as** to correct the spelling.

2. Move to the beginning of the second line and issue the DEL C command by pressing <COMMA> to delete the tab character and the *u* in *upon.*

3. Move to the beginning of the third line and issue the DEL W command by pressing <MINUS> to delete the first word, *And.*

4. Move to the beginning of the fourth line and use the DEL L command (<PF4>) to delete the line. Notice that the lines below the deleted line move up.

5. The cursor is at the beginning of the fifth line of text (*And the great fleas . . .*). Use the DEL EOL command (<GOLD/2>) to delete to the end of that line. Notice that although the text disappears, a blank line remains, as shown in Figure 3.7.

When you delete text with these commands, EDT stores the text in buffers. The Character buffer stores the most recently deleted character, the Word buffer stores the most recently deleted word, and the Line buffer stores the most recently deleted line. You can use the contents of these buffers to restore the most recent character, word, or line that you have deleted.

3.4.4   Undeleting Text

The undelete commands are used to restore deleted text that was stored in buffers. The UND L (undelete line) command (<GOLD/PF4>) restores the most recently deleted line. The UND W (undelete word) command (<GOLD/MINUS>) restores the most recently deleted word, and the UND C command (<GOLD/COMMA>) restores the most recently deleted character.

Use these functions to restore the text you deleted in Experiment 3.5.

Experiment 3.6   **Undeleting Text**

1. The cursor is at the beginning of the fourth line, which is blank (see Figure 3.7). Use the UND L command (<GOLD/PF4>) to restore the line.

2. You also deleted the line *and so ad infinitum*, but because the line buffer holds only the most recently deleted line, this line cannot be restored using the UND L command. Instead, open a line with the OPEN LINE command (<GOLD/0>) and retype the line of text.

3. Next move to the *p* in *pon* and use the UND C command (<GOLD/COMMA>) to restore the *u*. Then add a tab character to indent the line, as shown in Figure 3.8.

4. If you want to work more with deleting and undeleting text, add several lines to the bottom of the file and work with the commands on the new text. When you are finished, delete the extra text from the file.

```
Great fleas have little fleas
pon their backs to bite 'em,
little fleas have lesser fleas,
▓
   have greater fleas to go on;
While these again have greater still,
   and greater still, and so on.
[EOB]
```

Figure 3.7 Results of the Deletions

3.5 **Leaving an EDT Editing Session**

You have finished editing this file of text, so you need to leave the EDT editing session and save the completed poem in **FLEAS.TXT**. To save the results
of an editing session, you can use the COMMAND command (<GOLD/7>) to
remain in keypad mode but cause EDT to prompt for a line mode command,
as shown in Figure 3.9. You can then enter the line mode command **EXIT** and
press <ENTER>.

Alternatively, you can move from keypad mode to line mode by pressing
<CTRL/Z>. The line mode prompt * appears. Then enter the **EXIT** command
and press either <RETURN> or <ENTER>.

In either case, the **EXIT** command copies the contents of the Main buffer to a
file in your user directory. The file has the same name but a higher version
number, as illustrated in Figure 3.10.

You can also exit an EDT editing session and save the contents of the Main
buffer in a file having a different name. To do this, type the new file name

```
Great fleas have little fleas
   upon their backs to bite 'em,
And little fleas have lesser fleas,
   and so ad infinitum.
And the great fleas themselves, in turn,
   have greater fleas to go on;
While these again have greater still,
   and greater still, and so on.
[EOB]
```

Figure 3.8 Results of Undeleting Text

after the **EXIT** command. For example, to save the **FLEAS.TXT** file under a new name, type

Command: `exit newfleas.txt`

Remember to press <ENTER> (and not <RETURN>) when using COMMAND to exit.

There may come a time when you realize that you are editing the wrong file or you have accidentally deleted information that you need. You can leave an EDT editing session without saving the file in the Main buffer by using the **QUIT** command rather than the **EXIT** command.

Experiment 3.7 demonstrates various methods of leaving an EDT editing session.

Experiment 3.7 **Leaving an EDT Editing Session**

1. First, try leaving the EDT editing session and saving the changes to the file under the same name. Move to line mode by pressing <CTRL/Z>.

```
Great fleas have little fleas
    upon their backs to bite 'em,
And little fleas have lesser fleas,
    and so ad infinitum.
And the great fleas themselves, in turn,
    have greater fleas to go on;
While these again have greater still,
    and greater still, and so on.
[EOB]
```

PF1
GOLD

7

Command:

COMMAND command

Figure 3.9 Using COMMAND

2. At the line mode asterisk prompt, type the **EXIT** command and press
    <RETURN>.

3. You are back at the DCL prompt, **$**. The changes to the file are now saved
    in a new version of **FLEAS.TXT**. You can verify this by using the
    DIRECTORY command to get a listing of files. Notice the higher version
    number for **FLEAS.TXT**.

    ```
    $ directory fleas.txt
    Directory DUA1:[YOURGROUP.YOU]
    FLEAS.TXT;2     FLEAS.TXT;1
    Total of 2 files.
    $
    ```

4. Now return to EDT as if you were going to edit **FLEAS.TXT**.

    ```
    $ edit/edt fleas.txt
    ```

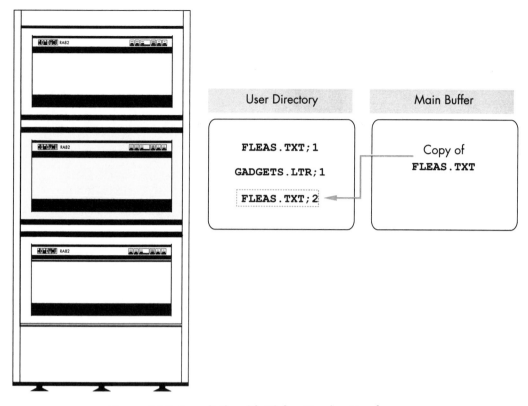

Figure 3.10 Saved File with Higher Version Number

5. If EDT moves automatically to keypad mode, press <CTRL/z> to change to line mode. Otherwise, remain in line mode at the * prompt.

6. Try exiting the EDT session and saving the file with a new name, **FLEAS1.TXT**.

7. The file is now saved under **FLEAS1.TXT**. Check this by using the **DIRECTORY** command to see all files beginning with **FLEAS** and having the **TXT** extension.

```
$ directory fleas*.txt
Directory DUA1:[YOURGROUP.YOU]
FLEAS.TXT;2      FLEAS.TXT;1      FLEAS1.TXT;1
Total of 3 files.
$
```

8. Once again, return to EDT as if you were going to edit **FLEAS.TXT**. If you need to, move to keypad mode.

```
$ edit/edt fleas.txt
```

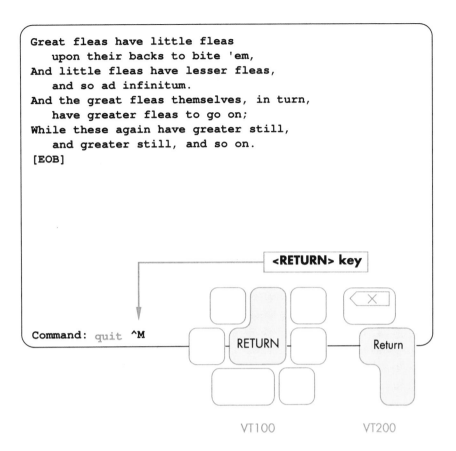

```
Great fleas have little fleas
   upon their backs to bite 'em,
And little fleas have lesser fleas,
   and so ad infinitum.
And the great fleas themselves, in turn,
   have greater fleas to go on;
While these again have greater still,
   and greater still, and so on.
[EOB]
```

<RETURN> key

Command: quit ^M

RETURN

Return

VT100   VT200

Figure 3.11 Results from Pressing RETURN

9. Try using the COMMAND command (<GOLD/7>) to see the line mode *
   prompt while running in keypad mode. At the **COMMAND**: prompt, enter the
   QUIT command rather than **EXIT**. Then press <RETURN>. Because
   <RETURN> is not the correct key for processing with the COMMAND
   command, **^M** appears, as shown in Figure 3.11.

10. Delete **^M** and press <ENTER> to enter the **QUIT** command.

11. With **QUIT**, the contents of the buffer are not saved in a file. Use the **DIREC-**
    TORY command to check that a new version of **FLEAS.TXT** has not been
    saved.

```
$ directory fleas.txt
Directory DUA1:[YOURGROUP.YOU]
FLEAS.TXT;2      FLEAS.TXT;1
Total of 2 files.
$
```

Creating a File with EDT

You used the DCL **CREATE** command to create the **FLEAS.TXT** file and then moved to EDT to make changes to that file. You can also create a new file from EDT by specifying a new file name when you enter the **EDIT/EDT** command.

Follow Experiment 3.8 to create a new file, which contains a Pascal procedure to do a bubblesort. (The bubblesort procedure enables a small set of data to be manipulated easily, by comparing pairs of elements in a list. As the sort moves down the list, elements are compared, and the smaller data items eventually "float" to one end, while the larger data items move to the other end.)

Experiment 3.8   **Creating a New File with EDT**

1. Activate EDT using the file name **BUBBLE.PAS**.

```
$ edit/edt bubble.pas
[EOB]
Input file does not exist
```

Because EDT cannot locate the file **BUBBLE.PAS** in your user account, it displays a message and an end-of-buffer symbol and, possibly, the line mode asterisk prompt.

2. If necessary, use the **CHANGE** command to change from line mode to keypad mode.

3. Enter the following text exactly as it appears. Remember to press <RETURN> to start a new line. Notice that as you enter more than 21 lines of text, the text scrolls off the top of the screen.

```
const
     max = 512;
     ListMax = 10000;
type
     KeyType = integer;
     OtherInfo = packed array[1..max] of char;
     ItemType = record
          bytes: OtherInfo
          key: KeyType
          end; (*ItemType*)
     ListType = array[1..ListMax] of ItemType;
```

```
procedure BubbleSort (var list: ListType;
                          ListSize: integer);

var SwapMade: Boolean;      (*to detect if swap was made*)
    index:   integer;       (*array index*)

begin
    SwapMade := true;

    while (ListSize >  1 and SwapMade do begin
        ListSize := ListSize - 1;
        SwapMade := false;

        for index := 1 to ListSize do
            if list[index].key >  list[index + 1].key then

            begin
                swap(list, index); (*hidden procedure*)
                SwapMade := true    (*signal swap was made*)
            end
        end
end; (*BubbleSort*)
```

4. Use the TOP command (<GOLD/5>) to return to the beginning of the file.

3.7

Getting Help with EDT Commands

There will come a time when you will forget a specific EDT command or need additional information on it. EDT has a built-in Help facility that allows you to obtain information on keypad and line mode commands during an editing session.

To get help while in keypad mode, use the HELP command (<HELP> on the VT200; <PF2> on the VT100). A help screen appears. You can then press any key to obtain help about that command.

To get help while in line mode, type **HELP** at the asterisk prompt and press <RETURN>. A help screen appears. You can also type **HELP** and the name of a command to obtain help about that command. For example, you could type **HELP COPY** to see information about the **COPY** command. Explore the Help facility by following the steps in Experiment 3.9.

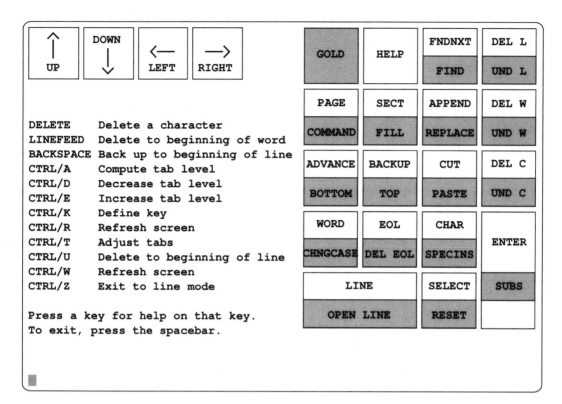

```
  ┌───┐ ┌─────┐ ┌─────┐ ┌─────┐        ┌─────┐ ┌─────┐ ┌───────┐ ┌─────┐
  │ ↑ │ │DOWN │ │ ←── │ │ ──→ │        │GOLD │ │HELP │ │FNDNXT │ │DEL L│
  │   │ │  │  │ │     │ │     │        │     │ │     │ ├───────┤ ├─────┤
  │UP │ │  ↓  │ │LEFT │ │RIGHT│        │     │ │     │ │ FIND  │ │UND L│
  └───┘ └─────┘ └─────┘ └─────┘        └─────┘ └─────┘ └───────┘ └─────┘
```

DELETE   Delete a character
LINEFEED Delete to beginning of word
BACKSPACE Back up to beginning of line
CTRL/A   Compute tab level
CTRL/D   Decrease tab level
CTRL/E   Increase tab level
CTRL/K   Define key
CTRL/R   Refresh screen
CTRL/T   Adjust tabs
CTRL/U   Delete to beginning of line
CTRL/W   Refresh screen
CTRL/Z   Exit to line mode

Press a key for help on that key.
To exit, press the spacebar.

Figure 3.12 Keypad Mode Help

Experiment 3.9   **Getting Help**

1. You should be in EDT keypad mode to begin. If you have been following the experiments, the file BUBBLE.PAS will be on the screen. Use <HELP> or <PF2> to move to the help screen, which should resemble Figure 3.12.

2. Read the instructions on the screen. Press any of the numeric keypad keys to see information about that key's commands.

3. Once you have finished reading the help text, return to the editing session by pressing <SPACEBAR>.

4. Shift into line mode by pressing <CTRL/z>. The line mode asterisk prompt should appear on the screen.

5. Type HELP and press <RETURN>. The screen should resemble Figure 3.13.

6. Read the instructions on the screen. You can now obtain information about a particular command or topic. Enter text to explore a topic, for example, HELP COPY.

```
        HELP topic subtopic subsubtopic...

A topic can have one of the following forms:

    1. An alphanumeric string (e.g. a command name, option, etc.)
    2. The match-all or wildcard symbol (*)

Examples:  HELP SUBSTITUTE NEXT
           HELP CHANGE SUBCOMMAND
           HELP CH

If a topic is abbreviated, HELP displays the text for all topics that
match the abbreviation.


Additional information available:

CHANGE        CLEAR     COPY       DEFINE     DELETE       EXIT      FILL
FIND          HELP      INCLUDE    INSERT     JOURNAL      KEYPAD    MOVE
PRINT         QUIT      RANGE      REPLACE    RESEQUENCE   SET       SHOW
SUBSTITUTE    TAB       TYPE       WRITE

*
```

Figure 3.13 Line Mode Help

7. Once you have finished reading the help text, return to the keypad mode editing session by typing **CHANGE** and <RETURN> at the asterisk prompt.

3.8   More Editing Commands

EDT provides many useful editing commands in keypad mode. You can change the editing direction, search for text strings, cut and paste portions of text, and so on. The following sections introduce these commands.

3.8.1   Changing the Editing Direction

By default, movement through the text in a file is forward, or toward the end of the file. For example, when you use DEL W, the word following the cursor is deleted; or when you use FIND to search for a text string, the search advances from the cursor toward the end of the file.

You can change this editing direction by using the BACKUP command (<5>) and the ADVANCE command (<4>). After you select BACKUP, movement through the file will be back toward the beginning of the file. To return to forward movement, you must select ADVANCE.

Being able to control the editing direction is advantageous when working with many EDT functions, as you will see in the sections that follow.

3.8.2   *Other Ways of Moving the Cursor*

Up to this point, you have been moving the cursor around the screen by the character or line, or by moving to the top or bottom of the file. Exploring EDT further, you will find that there are other cursor movement commands available.

You can use the CHAR (character) command (<3>) to move one character at a time. The CHAR command can be used as an alternative to the <LEFT ARROW> and <RIGHT ARROW> keys. Use the WORD command (<1>) to move one word at a time. A word is any group of characters bounded by a space, horizontal tab, line feed, vertical tab, form feed, or carriage return.

The direction the cursor moves depends on the editing direction. If BACKUP is in effect, the cursor moves to the previous character or word. If ADVANCE is in effect, the cursor moves to the next character or word. Explore these cursor movement options by following Experiment 3.10.

Experiment 3.10   ***More Cursor Movement Options***

1. Move to the beginning of a line of text and use the CHAR command (<3>) several times. The default editing direction is forward, so the cursor moves forward along the line.

2. Use the BACKUP command (<5>) to change the editing direction. Then use the CHAR command several times. The cursor moves back toward the beginning of the file.

3. Now use the WORD command (<1>) several times. Because BACKUP is still in effect, the cursor moves to the previous word.

4. Use the ADVANCE command (<4>) to change the editing direction. Use the WORD command again. Now the cursor moves forward through the file.

You can also move the cursor in increments of 16 lines at a time using the SECT (section) command (<8>). This command brings a different section of text into view with a single keystroke. The direction of movement depends on the editing direction. Follow Experiment 3.11 to try out the SECT command.

Experiment 3.11 **Viewing Sections of Text**

1. First, use the BOTTOM command (<GOLD/4>) to move to the end of the file.

2. Reverse the editing direction using the BACKUP command (<5>).

3. Use the SECT command (<8>) to move 16 lines from the [EOB] marker up toward the beginning of the file.

4. Use the ADVANCE (<4>) command to set the editing direction forward and then use the SECT command again to move the cursor back to its original position.

3.8.3 ## Dividing the Text into Pages

When you are working with long files, it is sometimes useful to divide the text into pages. You can then speed up movement through the text by moving page by page.

To divide the text into pages, enter a page marker. The default page marker is the form feed character, <FF>, which is accepted by many printers as an end-of-page delimiter. Insert this character by holding down the <CTRL> key and pressing the <L> key.

Once page markers are set, you can use the PAGE command (<7>) to move to the markers. The direction in which the cursor moves depends on the editing direction. If no page markers are set, the PAGE command moves the cursor to the top or bottom of the file. Follow the steps in Experiment 3.12 to see how this command works.

Experiment 3.12 **Defining Page Boundaries**

1. Move the cursor to the blank line that appears after the following line in your BUBBLE.PAS file:

    ```
    ListType = array[1..ListMax] of ItemType;
    ```

```
   KeyType = integer;
   OtherInfo = packed array[1..max] of char;
   ItemType = record
      bytes: OtherInfo
      key: KeyType
      end;   (*ItemType*)
   ListType = array[1..ListMax] of ItemType;
<FF>▊
procedure BubbleSort (var list: ListType;
                          ListSize: integer);

var SwapMade: Boolean;      (*to detect if swap was made*)
    index: integer;        (*array index*)

begin
   SwapMade := true;

   while (ListSize > 1) and SwapMade do begin
      ListSize := ListSize - 1;
      SwapMade := false;

      for index := 1 to ListSize do
```

Figure 3.14 The Form Feed Character

2. Enter a page marker by pressing the <CTRL> key and then the <L> key. The form feed character <FF> appears, as shown in Figure 3.14.

3. Move the cursor to the beginning of the file using the TOP command (<GOLD/5>).

4. Use the PAGE command (<7>) to move to the first page marker.

3.8.4   A Simple Method of Locating Text

Up to this point, you have located text by moving the cursor through the file. Using this method on small files is tedious but tolerable. On larger files, however, it would not be tolerable.

Using the FIND command (<GOLD/PF3>) and the FNDNXT (find next) command (<PF3>), you can move directly to a specified text string. When you use FIND, EDT prompts for the text string to search for, or search string. You type the search string and press <ENTER>. EDT searches for the string and moves the cursor to the first occurrence of the search string that it encounters. The direction of the search depends on the current editing direction.

If you want to find the next occurrence of the search string, use FNDNXT. EDT moves the cursor to the next occurrence.

This method of locating text can save a considerable amount of time when searching for a sequence of characters within a lengthy document. Keep in mind, when searching for text, it is important to make the search string unique. You should try to include in the search string as many landmarks surrounding the text as possible so that EDT can locate the text on the first attempt.

It is possible for EDT not to be able to locate a search string and to give a message to that effect. This happens when a search string is mistyped, a string does not exist, or the direction of the search is moving away from the string in the text. In the last case, you can switch the editing direction to search in the opposite direction.

Try using the FIND and FNDNXT commands by following Experiment 3.13.

Experiment 3.13   **Using FIND and FNDNXT to Locate Text**

1. Move the cursor to the beginning of the **BUBBLE.PAS** file. The editing direction is set forward.

2. Use the FIND command (<GOLD/PF3>). EDT prompts you for the search string, as shown in Figure 3.15.

3. Type **begin** and press <ENTER>. EDT searches toward the end of the file for the first occurrence of *begin*.

4. Search for the next occurrence by using the FNDNXT command (<PF3>). EDT moves to the next occurrence of *begin*. Use FNDNXT again, to find the next occurrence.

5. Use FNDNXT again. EDT did not find another occurrence of the search string and so displays a message, as shown in Figure 3.16.

6. Use BACKUP (<5>) to change the editing direction. Then use FNDNXT (<PF3>) again. Now EDT searches backward through the file for the search string.

7. Finally, use ADVANCE (<4>) to reset the editing direction to forward.

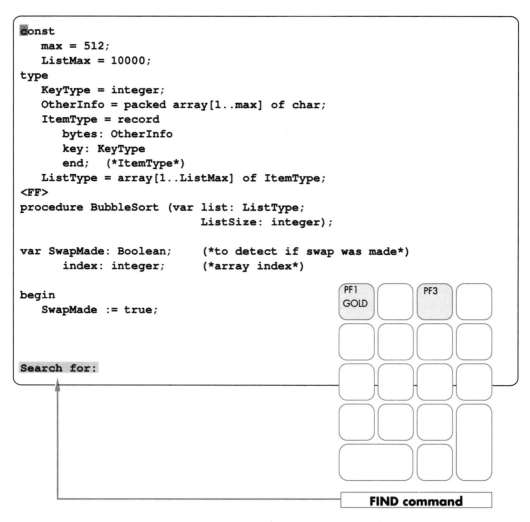

```
const
    max = 512;
    ListMax = 10000;
type
    KeyType = integer;
    OtherInfo = packed array[1..max] of char;
    ItemType = record
        bytes: OtherInfo
        key: KeyType
        end;   (*ItemType*)
    ListType = array[1..ListMax] of ItemType;
<FF>
procedure BubbleSort (var list: ListType;
                         ListSize: integer);

var SwapMade: Boolean;    (*to detect if swap was made*)
    index: integer;       (*array index*)

begin
    SwapMade := true;
```

`Search for:`

PF1 GOLD   PF3

FIND command

Figure 3.15 The Search Prompt

3.9 *Working with a Selected Range of Text*

As you have seen, EDT has a great deal of editing capability. You have explored various methods of moving the cursor around the screen and manipulating small portions of text. However, EDT has several other features that enhance its editing abilities. In particular, EDT allows you to select a larger portion of text, which you can then manipulate as a unit, moving it, reformatting it, replacing it, and so on.

```
procedure BubbleSort (var list: ListType;
                          ListSize: integer);

var SwapMade: Boolean;      (*to detect if swap was made*)
    index: integer;       (*array index*)

begin
   SwapMade := true;

   while (ListSize > 1) and SwapMade do begin
      ListSize := ListSize - 1;
      SwapMade := false;

      for index := 1 to ListSize do
         if list[index].key > list[index + 1].key then

            begin
               swap(list,index);      (*hidden procedure*)
               SwapMade := true       (*signal swap was made*)
            end

      end
end; (*BubbleSort*)
[EOB]

String was not found
```

Figure 3.16 String-Not-Found Message

3.9.1   *Selecting a Range of Text*

You can use the SELECT command (<PERIOD> on the numeric keypad) to select a range of text. Move to the beginning of the range, issue SELECT, and then use any of the cursor movement keys to highlight the appropriate text. For example, you can use the arrow keys to extend the highlight up or down a line, or left or right, or you can use the WORD command <1> to highlight the next word. To highlight in the opposite direction, change the editing direction.

If you decide that portions of the selected text should not be included in the selected range, you can move the cursor back until you exclude any un-wanted text. EDT also provides a RESET command (<GOLD/PERIOD>), which allows you to cancel an active selected range at any time. (RESET also resets the editing direction to forward.) A selected range stays active until you either use the RESET command or execute a function or command that uses the selected range.

Practice selecting ranges of text by following Experiment 3.14.

Experiment 3.14 **Selecting a Range of Text**

1. In the experiments in this section, work with the **FLEAS.TXT** file. Retrieve that file by exiting EDT and then reactivating EDT specifying the **FLEAS.TXT** file. If necessary, move to keypad mode.

2. Select the first four lines of text by using SELECT (<PERIOD>) and then use the LINE command (<0>) to move the cursor down to the beginning of the fifth line. As you move the cursor down, EDT extends the highlight, as shown in Figure 3.17.

3. All the highlighted text is selected. You could now use other commands to manipulate the selected range. If you decide you do not want to work with this range, cancel the selection with RESET (<GOLD/PERIOD>).

3.9.2   *Changing the Case of a Range of Text*

One of the changes you can make to a range of text is to change its case. The CHNGCASE command (<GOLD/1>) switches lowercase letters to uppercase or uppercase letters to lowercase. You may use CHNGCASE for individual letters or for all text in the selected range. To see how this works, try Experiment 3.15.

Experiment 3.15 **Changing the Case of a Range of Text**

1. Move the cursor to the beginning of the file.

2. Use the SELECT command (<PERIOD>) to mark the beginning of the selected range.

3. Move the cursor to the end of the file with the BOTTOM command (<GOLD/4>).

4. Use the CHNGCASE command (<GOLD/1>) to change the case of the selected range. Notice that the uppercase letters become lowercase, and vice versa.

5. Repeat steps 1 through 4 to return the text to its previous state.

```
Great fleas have little fleas
    upon their backs to bite 'em,
And little fleas have lesser fleas,
    and so ad infinitum.
And the great fleas themselves, in turn,
    have greater fleas to go on;
While these again have greater still,
    and greater still, and so on.
[EOB]
```

Figure 3.17 Selecting a Range of Text

3.9.3   *Cutting and Pasting a Range of Text*

In previous experiments, you worked with commands that deleted text by the character, word, or line. EDT also has a command, CUT (<6>), that lets you delete the text in the selected range. Using this method, you can choose large sections of text to be cut with a single keystroke.

Like the delete commands discussed previously, the CUT command saves deleted text in a special storage area, called the Paste buffer. The text stored in the Paste buffer can be pasted back into the file using the PASTE command (<GOLD/6>), a keystroke combination similar to the UND C, UND W, UND L commands. The contents of the Paste buffer remain until you execute another CUT command or end the EDT session.

You can see how CUT and PASTE work by following Experiment 3.16.

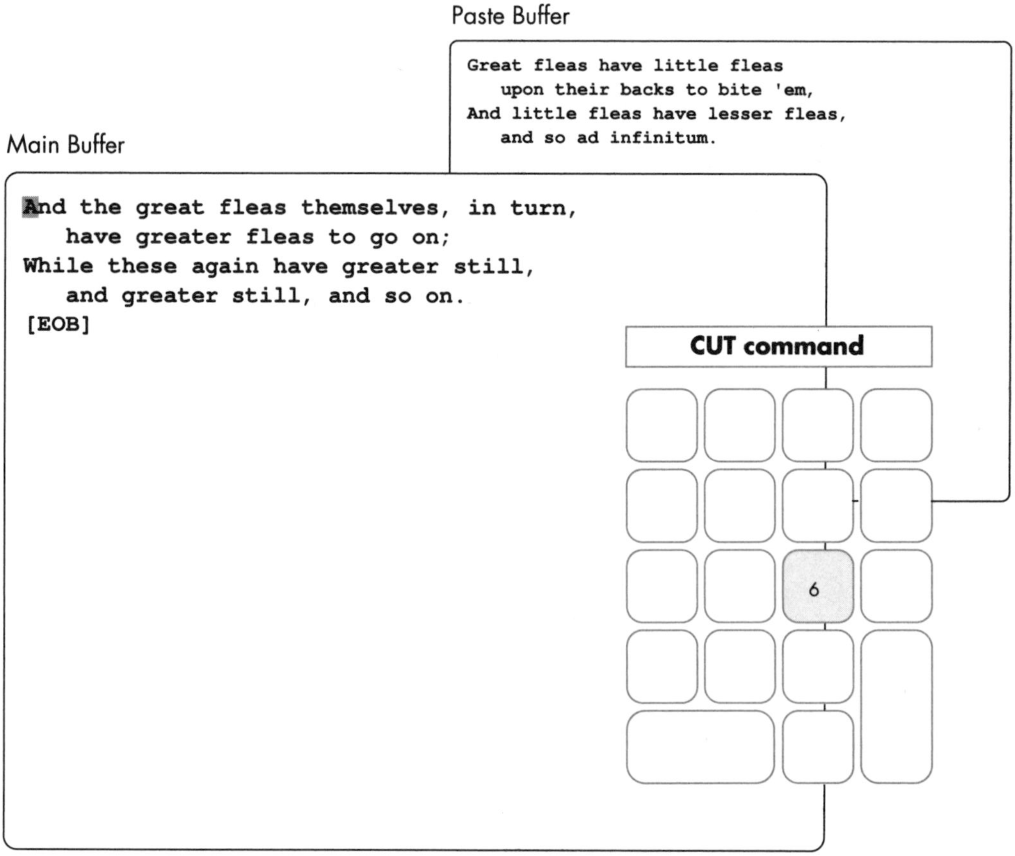

Paste Buffer

```
Great fleas have little fleas
    upon their backs to bite 'em,
And little fleas have lesser fleas,
    and so ad infinitum.
```

Main Buffer

```
And the great fleas themselves, in turn,
    have greater fleas to go on;
While these again have greater still,
    and greater still, and so on.
[EOB]
```

CUT command

6

Figure 3.18 The Paste Buffer

Experiment 3.16 **Cutting and Pasting Text**

1. Move the cursor to the beginning of the file.

2. Use the SELECT command (<PERIOD>) and move the cursor to the beginning of the fifth line.

3. Use CUT (<6>) to cut the selected text (the first four lines) from the file. The selected text is now in the Paste buffer, as seen in Figure 3.18.

4. To restore the cut portion of text, you can paste it back into its previous location, or if you want to paste it elsewhere, you can move the cursor to the new location. Move the cursor to the beginning of the third line (*While these . . .*), and use PASTE (<GOLD/6>) to paste the contents of the Paste buffer into the file.

3.9.4   *Using the Paste Buffer to Replace Text*

You can use the Paste buffer to temporarily store text that you want to use to replace other text. The REPLACE command (<GOLD/9>) deletes a selected range of text and replaces it with the contents of the Paste buffer. Follow Experiment 3.17 to replace the first two lines of text with the contents of the Paste buffer.

Experiment 3.17   **Replacing a Selected Range of Text**

1. The Paste buffer still contains the first four lines of the poem. Use SELECT (<PERIOD>) to establish a selected range containing the current third and fourth lines of text in the file, or Main buffer (*Great fleas . . . to bite 'em*).

2. Use REPLACE (<GOLD/9>) to replace these two lines with the contents of the Paste buffer, as shown in Figure 3.19.

3.9.5   *Finding and Replacing Text*

There is another way to select and replace text. You can use the FIND command (<GOLD/PF3>) to establish which text should be replaced with the contents of the Paste buffer, and then use the SUBS (substitute) command (<GOLD/ENTER>) to replace that text with the contents of the Paste buffer. This method is useful when you have numerous occurrences of text that need to be replaced, because once you find and replace the first occurrence you can continue finding and replacing other occurrences just by using SUBS. Follow Experiment 3.18 to see how this works.

Experiment 3.18   **Finding and Replacing Text**

1. Move the cursor to the top of the file.

2. You want to replace **fleas** with **FLEAS**. First, type **FLEAS**. Then move to the beginning of the word and use the SELECT command (<PERIOD>) to select **FLEAS**. Use the CUT command (<6>) to move **FLEAS** to the Paste buffer.

3. Use the FIND command (<GOLD/PF3>), entering **fleas** as the search string and pressing <ENTER>.

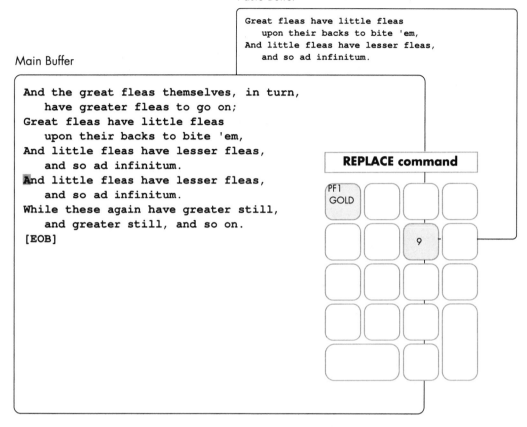

Paste Buffer

```
Great fleas have little fleas
    upon their backs to bite 'em,
And little fleas have lesser fleas,
    and so ad infinitum.
```

Main Buffer

```
And the great fleas themselves, in turn,
    have greater fleas to go on;
Great fleas have little fleas
    upon their backs to bite 'em,
And little fleas have lesser fleas,
    and so ad infinitum.
And little fleas have lesser fleas,
    and so ad infinitum.
While these again have greater still,
    and greater still, and so on.
[EOB]
```

REPLACE command

PF1 GOLD

9

Figure 3.19 Using REPLACE

4. Use the SUBS command (<GOLD/ENTER>) to replace the first occurrence of **fleas**, and move to the next occurrence. Use SUBS to replace each remaining occurrence.

5. Restore the word **fleas** by following steps 1 through 4 and using **fleas** to replace **FLEAS**.

3.9.6   *Adding to the Paste Buffer*

The contents of the Paste buffer remain intact until you cut more text or end the EDT session. Sometimes, however, you want to add more text to the Paste buffer without destroying its current contents. You can add selected text to the Paste buffer using the APPEND command (<9>).

APPEND removes the selected text from the Main buffer and adds it to the end of the Paste buffer. It is particularly useful for correcting the order of text, as Experiment 3.19 demonstrates.

Experiment 3.19 **Using APPEND to Add to the Paste Buffer**

1. The lines of the poem are out of sequence. Using CUT and APPEND, you can reassemble them in the paste buffer in the proper order. First, move to the beginning of the current third line of the file (*Great fleas . . .*).

2. Use the SELECT command (<PERIOD>) to select the third through the sixth lines.

3. Use the CUT command (<6>) to remove those lines and place them in the Paste buffer.

4. Move to the current first line of the file (*And the great fleas . . .*), and use the SELECT command to select the first and second lines.

5. Now use the APPEND command (<9>) to append these lines to the contents of the Paste buffer.

6. Move to the fifth line (*While these . . .*), and use the SELECT command to select the fifth and sixth lines.

7. Use the APPEND command to append these two lines to the contents of the Paste buffer.

8. Move to the beginning of the first line, and use the SELECT command to select the remaining lines on the screen. Then use the REPLACE command (<GOLD/9>) to replace this selected text with the contents of the Paste buffer.

3.9.7   Reformatting a Paragraph

When EDT is first activated, it establishes the margin boundaries at columns 1 and 80. Though these default values are set, they do not affect the length of text that can be typed on each line. To readjust text (within a paragraph) that extends beyond 80 columns, use the FILL command (<GOLD/8>).

The FILL command allows you to reformat a selected range of text neatly between the pre-established margins. It is particularly useful when you have added and deleted text in an existing document paragraph, creating short lines within the paragraph. Follow the steps in Experiment 3.20 to see how the FILL command works.

Readjusting Document Paragraphs

1. Exit EDT and then reactivate it using the file name **LET.TXT**. If necessary, change from line mode to keypad mode.

```
$ edit/edt let.txt
[EOB]
Input file does not exist
```

2. Enter the following text exactly as it appears. Remember to press <RETURN> to start each new line as shown.

```
                                          -----date-----
Gentlemen:
We are in the process of contacting firms or individuals
who have sent information for which we
have no interest.
Attached is the label from such a mailing list sent by
you.
We request that you please remove us from your mailing list.
Should you have any question regarding
this, please feel free to contact me.

Sincerely,
-----signature-----
```

3. Position the cursor at the beginning of the first *We*.

4. Use the SELECT command (<PERIOD>) to mark the beginning of the selected range.

5. Move the cursor to the end of the paragraph using any of the cursor movement functions.

6. Use the FILL command (<GOLD/8>) to reformat the paragraph.

3.10 Discovering Some of EDT's Special Features

EDT has special features that are not apparent until you begin to explore further. Two of these are introduced in the following sections.

3.10.1 Repeating a Keystroke Automatically

When you know you want to repeat a keypad editing command a certain number of times, you can use the <GOLD> Repeat function. As its name suggests, this function repeats a keystroke the number of times that you specify.

To use this function, first press the <GOLD> key and then press a keyboard number key or keys to indicate the number of times you want the next keystroke repeated. Note that this is the number key on the regular keyboard, not the numeric keypad. EDT displays the number in the lower portion of the screen, and the next keystroke you make will be repeated as many times as you have specified. To try this, follow the steps in Experiment 3.21.

Experiment 3.21 **Repeating Keystrokes**

1. Suppose you want to move the cursor two words to the right. Press <GOLD> and type **2** on the regular keyboard. The number 2 appears in the lower left-hand corner of the screen. Now use the WORD command (<1>). The cursor moves right past the next two words.

2. You can use this function to repeat characters as well. Move the cursor to the end of the file. Press <GOLD> and then type **6**. Now type the keyboard period character. The last line of **LETTER.TXT** now contains six periods.

3.10.2   Inserting Special Characters

Another EDT feature is the SPECINS command (<GOLD/3>). This command allows you to insert into text any character from the DEC Multinational Character Set, ranging from ASCII control characters to letters with accent marks. To enter a character, press <GOLD>, type the decimal value of the ASCII character, and then use the SPECINS command. Table B.1 in Appendix B lists these decimal values.

3.11   Recovering from Interruptions

The four most common circumstances that can interrupt or end your editing session without your consent are

1. Noise in a communication channel, which may cause extraneous characters to appear on the screen during an editing session

2. Accidentally pressing <CTRL/y>, which interrupts command processing

3. A system crash without warning

4. Exceeding your disk quota

The methods that allow you to recover from such misfortunes are discussed in the sections that follow.

3.11.1 Deleting Extraneous Characters

During an editing session, you may receive broadcast messages, or messages indicating that you have received electronic mail. In other instances, garbage characters may mysteriously float across the screen while you are using a dial-up modem to access the computer system.

To purge uninvited characters or messages, hold down <CTRL> and press <W>. This clears and redraws the screen. Using <CTRL/w> is especially important when foreign characters appear on the screen, because it will ensure that the cursor is in the correct position.

If the garbage characters actually get inserted into a file, you can delete them using any of the delete commands.

3.11.2 Resuming an Interrupted Editing Session

Imagine that you have just spent the last two hours typing a computer program or important document into an EDT file. As you are typing, you accidentally press <CTRL/y>. Panic sets in when you realize you do not have a backup copy of your work.

This has happened to most of us at one time or another. Luckily there is a simple solution. By typing CONTINUE at the DCL $ prompt, you can return to the EDT session. Follow Experiment 3.22 to see how this works.

Experiment 3.22 **Interrupting an Editing Session with CTRL/Y**

1. Exit EDT and reactivate it using the FLEAS.TXT file. Change into keypad mode if necessary.

2. Interrupt the editing session by pressing <CTRL/y>.

3. Locate the DCL $ prompt and the cursor. Enter the CONTINUE command and press <RETURN>.

4. You are back in EDT. Now press <CTRL/w> to restore the screen to its state before the interruption.

3.11.3 Recovering a Lost Session

Suppose your system has just crashed. On some computers this would mean that the contents of the file you were editing would be lost forever. Not so with EDT; you can recover text lost because of a system failure.

EDT has a Journal facility that keeps track of each keystroke you make during your editing session, in a special file called a journal file. If your editing session should end abruptly because of a system crash, EDT saves the journal file. Even though the text of your editing work has been lost, the keystrokes you used are saved; so, using the journal file, EDT can restore almost all your editing work. However, sometimes the last few commands you typed or the last few keystrokes you made may not have been recorded in the journal file at the time of the interruption.

The journal file is normally stored in the current directory with the same file name as the file you were working on and **JOU** as the file type. When you next activate EDT, you use the **/RECOVER** qualifier and specify the name of the file you want to recover.

When EDT begins the recovery process, do not touch the keyboard until the file is restored. EDT reproduces the editing session, reading the commands from the journal file and executing them on the screen. EDT will re-edit your file in exactly the same fashion and sequence as you did prior to the interruption.

Once EDT has finished processing all the command information and keystrokes stored in the journal file, it will continue to use the same journal file during your editing session. If you are able to end your editing session successfully, using the **EXIT** or **QUIT** commands, EDT discards the journal file from your directory. (However, if you find journal files in your directory that you do not plan to use, simply delete them.)

To simulate a system crash, try Experiment 3.23.

Experiment 3.23   **Simulating a Crash and Recovering**

1. Enter several new lines to the **FLEAS.TXT** file. For instance, you can add a copy of the last three lines of the poem.

2. Simulate a system crash by pressing <CTRL/y> and then logging out of the system.

3. Log back into the system.

4. Activate EDT to edit **FLEAS.TXT** but include the **/RECOVER** qualifier before the file name.

```
$ edit/edt/recover fleas.txt
```

Sit back and watch as EDT re-edits the file.

There are two important things to remember when you recover an interrupted EDT session. First, you must use the same type of terminal you used during the original editing session. In fact, the terminal should be identical in all characteristics. Do not start a recovery operation on a hard-copy terminal when you were working on a VT200 or VT100 terminal. Second, you should never modify the file you were editing before you attempt its recovery.

3.11.4   *Exceeding Your Disk Quota*

There are essentially two ways you can exceed your disk quota while using EDT. Your disk storage might be full prior to activating EDT, or there may be disk storage available in your user account but not enough to store the contents of the Main buffer. These two events occur more often than you would think, especially in environments in which disk storage is limited and the compilation of programs is frequent.

When you exceed your disk quota prior to activating EDT, a message similar to the following appears:

```
Error opening DUA1:[USER]TOTAL.TXT as output
ACP file extend failed
Disk quota exceeded
```

To solve this problem, you can purge or delete files to recover space on the disk, or you may need to request additional disk space.

When you exceed your disk quota while exiting EDT and saving a file, a message similar to the following appears:

```
Output file could not be created
Filename: DUA1:[USER]LIST.TXT
ACP file create failed
Disk quota exceeded
Press Return to continue
```

To solve this problem, press <RETURN> and then <CTRL/z> to return to line mode. Then enter a QUIT/SAVE command. The QUIT/SAVE command does not save the contents of the file you were working on, but it does save the journal file for later use.

Once out of EDT, you can purge or delete obsolete files to free a minimum number of blocks of disk storage equal to the size of the file you are working on plus a little extra to allow for growth. In some instances, you may have to request additional disk space.

To start editing your file again, type the same command line used to begin the original editing session, but include the /RECOVER qualifier so that EDT can reconstruct your editing session. For example, to recover a file called BUBBLE.PAS, you would type

```
$ edit/edt/recover bubble.pas
```

3.12   *Summary*

EDT is an interactive text editor with three distinct editing modes: keypad, line, and nokeypad. Both the keypad and nokeypad modes are screen editors. Line mode can be used on any type of terminal—hard-copy or screen.

With the EDT editor, you can create and edit text files. When you are editing a file, you can add or delete text, move or copy text from one place to another, and save or discard your editing work. To activate the EDT editor, enter the DCL EDIT command and the name of the file.

If the file does not exist, EDT displays the [EOB] marker and a message that the file does not exist. If the file exists in your user directory, EDT puts a copy of the file into the Main buffer and displays a portion of it on the screen. The next step in either case is to insert and edit text using one of the three editing modes.

In some systems, EDT will start in line mode and you can change to keypad mode. In other systems, EDT begins in keypad mode.

You can use EDT's on-line Help facility any time during your editing session. The line mode HELP command supplies general information on EDT as well as details on line mode and nokeypad mode commands. The HELP command by itself provides information on using the Help facility and a list of topics on which you can get help. For help on a specific topic, type the HELP command followed by the name of the topic.

When you are in keypad mode, press <HELP> on the VT200 or <PF2> on the VT100. EDT displays a diagram of the keypad and a list of other keypad commands and tells you to press the key for which you want help.

EDT's Journal facility keeps track of each keystroke you make during an EDT session in a special file called the journal file. When you finish your editing session using the **EXIT** or **QUIT** commands, EDT normally discards the journal file. If your editing session ends abruptly because of a system interruption, the journal file is saved even though your editing work has been lost. Using the journal file, EDT can restore almost all your editing work.

This chapter has only scratched the surface when it comes to the editing capabilities of EDT. However, it describes and demonstrates the most commonly used editing features. Features not discussed in this chapter, such as defining keys and creating macros and initialization files, can be explored on your own and used to expand EDT's editing capabilities further.

Tables 3.1–3.5 summarize the functions, commands, special characters, and important terms discussed in this chapter.

Table 3.1   EDT Keypad Commands and Functions

Command/Function	Key	Result
ADVANCE	<4>	Sets the editing direction to forward
APPEND	<9>	Deletes the selected range from the current buffer and appends it to the end of the Paste buffer
BACKUP	<5>	Sets the editing direction to backward
BOTTOM	<GOLD/4>	Moves the cursor to the end of the current buffer
CHAR	<3>	Moves the cursor one character in the current editing direction
CHNGCASE	<GOLD/1>	Changes the case of all letters in the selected range or at the current cursor position

Table 3.1 EDT Keypad Commands and Functions *(continued)*

Command/Function	Key	Result
COMMAND	<GOLD/7>	Accesses line mode commands while in keypad mode
CUT	<6>	Deletes the selected range of text and places it in the Paste buffer
DEL C	<COMMA>	Deletes the character that the cursor is on
DEL EOL	<GOLD/2>	Deletes the text from the cursor to the end of the line
DEL L	<PF4>	Deletes the text from the cursor to the beginning of the next line, deleting the line terminator
DEL W	<MINUS>	Deletes characters from the cursor to the beginning of the next word
ENTER	<ENTER>	Sends a command or search to EDT for processing
EOL	<2>	Moves the cursor to the next line terminator in the current editing direction
FILL	<GOLD/8>	Reformats the text in the selected range so that as many whole words as possible are included in the lines, within the current margins
FIND	<GOLD/PF3>	Locates the search string that you specified when EDT displayed the **Search for:** prompt
FNDNXT	<PF3>	Locates the next occurrence of the current search string in the current editing direction
Gold	<PF1>	Accesses the alternative keypad commands
HELP	<PF2>	Provides information on keypad mode editing keys

Table 3.1   EDT Keypad Commands and Functions *(continued)*

Command/Function	Key	Result
LINE	<0>	Moves the cursor to the beginning of the next line in the current editing direction
OPEN LINE	<GOLD/0>	Adds a line terminator to the right of the cursor, which does not move
PAGE	<7>	Moves the cursor to the next EDT page boundary in the current editing direction or, if no page boundary is present, moves the cursor to the top or bottom of the buffer
PASTE	<GOLD/6>	Inserts the contents of the Paste buffer to the left of the cursor
REPLACE	<GOLD/9>	Deletes the selected range of text and replaces it with the contents of the Paste buffer
RESET	<GOLD/PERIOD>	Cancels the selected range and sets the editing direction to forward
SECT	<8>	Moves the cursor 16 lines in the current editing direction
SELECT	<PERIOD>	Marks one end of a selected range
SPECINS	<GOLD/3>	Allows you to insert any character from the DEC Multinational Character Set into your text by entering the decimal value for that character
SUBS	<GOLD/ENTER>	Replaces the next occurrence of the current search string with the contents of the Paste buffer
TOP	<GOLD/5>	Moves the cursor to the beginning of the current buffer

Table 3.1 EDT Keypad Commands and Functions *(continued)*

Command/Function	Key	Result
UND C	<GOLD/COMMA>	Inserts the contents of the delete character buffer to the left of the cursor
UND L	<GOLD/PF4>	Inserts the contents of the delete line buffer to the left of the cursor
UND W	<GOLD/MINUS>	Inserts the contents of the delete word buffer to the left of the cursor
WORD	<1>	Moves the cursor to the beginning of the next word in the current editing direction

Table 3.2 Keyboard Key Functions

Key	Result
<BACKSPACE> or <F12>	Moves the cursor to the beginning of the current line or to the previous line
<CTRL/ l>	Inserts a form feed character in text
<CTRL/w>	Clears and redraws the screen
<CTRL/z>	Shifts from keypad mode to line mode
<DELETE> or <x]	Deletes the character to the left of the cursor
<DOWN ARROW>	Moves the cursor down to the next line
<LEFT ARROW>	Moves the cursor one character to the left
<RETURN>	Inserts a line terminator in the text and moves the cursor to the beginning of the new line
<RIGHT ARROW>	Moves the cursor one character to the right
<UP ARROW>	Moves the cursor up to the previous line

Table 3.3   DCL and Line Mode Commands

Command	Short Form[a]	Result
CHANGE	**C**	Shifts EDT to keypad mode
CREATE	**CR**	Establishes a new file
EDIT		Activates the EDT editor
/RECOVER		Instructs EDT to use the journal file to restore a file after a system interruption
EXIT	**EX**	Ends the EDT session, saving a copy of the Main buffer text to an external file
HELP	**H**	Activates the line mode Help facility
QUIT	**QU**	Ends the EDT session without saving a copy of your editing work
QUIT/SAVE		Ends the EDT session without saving a copy of your editing work but does save the journal file

a.   Short forms of commands can only be used in line mode. Using the short form while in keypad mode (with the COMMAND command) causes an error.

Table 3.4   Special Characters

Character	Meaning
Command:	COMMAND function prompt
[EOB]	Designates the end of a buffer (or file)
<FF>	EDT symbol designating a form feed
_File:	EDT input file prompt
JOU	Identifies an EDT journal file
Search for:	FIND command prompt
^M	ASCII control character for a carriage return
★	Line mode editing prompt
$	DCL prompt

Table 3.5 Important Terms

Term	Definition
Alternative command	Secondary command sequence executed by a key on the numeric keypad
Buffer	Temporary workspace in EDT specifically for manipulating text
Character	Letter or symbol
Command	Instruction specifying an action for EDT to perform
Cursor	Used by EDT to indicate the current editing position
Editor	Application software package used to create and modify text files
EDT	VMS full-screen editor
Journal file	File containing commands from the current editing session
Main buffer	Space containing an input file while changes and additions take place during an EDT editing session
Numeric keypad	Group of keys located on the far right-hand side of the keyboard
Paste buffer	Storage area used in conjunction with the CUT command
Primary command	Principal command sequence executed by a key on the numeric keypad
Screen editor	Text editor that allows you to view the contents of a file on the screen
Scrolling	Movement of lines of text up or down the screen
Searching	Looking for specified text within a text file
Selected range	Portion of text that has been flagged to be manipulated by an EDT command
String	Group of characters
Text file	File containing ASCII characters
Word	Group of characters bounded by a space, horizontal tab, line feed, vertical tab, form feed, or carriage return

1. Name the three EDT editing modes.

2. What is the difference between the CUT and APPEND commands?

3. Make a list of all the EDT keypad commands that only work with a selected range of text.

4. Which of the commands in question 3 use the Paste buffer to manipulate text within the Main buffer?

5. Use the SPECINS command to create an ASCII character chart.

6. Find out how to redefine or relocate preset keypad editing keys.

7. What is the maximum number of characters that can be typed on one line during an EDT editing session?

8. Determine the minimum amount of disk storage required to create the journal file when you activate EDT.

9. Define the key sequence <GOLD/e> to locate a semicolon (;) and delete to end-of-line.

10. Describe all the ways you can change the case of two letters preceding the cursor.

11. What are two ways of inserting a form feed into a text file?

12. Create a directory of terms (acronyms, DCL commands, special symbols, and so on) that you have encountered so far. Use the following format when creating your table:

    Term   Meaning   Example

13. While in EDT, interrupt your editing session using <CTRL/y>. Once out of EDT, type the following DCL commands: **DIRECTORY, SHOW PROCESS, MAIL**. Now try to reinstate your editing session using the **CONTINUE** command. Did it work? How can you resume the session?

14. In question 13, you entered DCL commands before reinstating your interrupted EDT session. This time, execute a command file such as **LOGIN.COM**, and then enter the **CONTINUE** command.

15. Name all the possible methods of searching for text within a file.

16. Exit from an EDT session saving the contents of the Main buffer to a subdirectory in your user account.

17. Try saving a file to another user directory. Explain what happens.

18. Explain the result of the following experiment:

    a. Activate EDT using any text file stored in your user directory.

    b. Move the cursor to the end of the third line.

    c. Use the EOL command and watch what happens.

    d. Set the editing direction to backward.

    e. Repeat step (c).

19. Modify question 18 using the <BACKSPACE> key instead of the EOL command.

20. Try the following experiment:

    a. Activate EDT using any text file stored in your user directory.

    b. Set the line width to 132 columns.

    c. Use the SELECT command.

    d. Move the cursor to the end of the file.

    e. Use the FILL command.

21. Try using the CUT command without selecting a range of text first. What happened?

22. Try the following experiment:

    a. Activate EDT using any text file stored in your user directory.

    b. Move the cursor to the beginning of the third line.

    c. Set the editing direction to backward.

    d. Use the LINE command.

    What happened?

3.14   Review Quiz

Indicate whether the following statements are true or false:

1. The contents of the Main buffer can only be saved to the file specified at the time you activated EDT.

2. The SHIFT command is used to move from line mode to keypad mode.

3. There are two ways of specifying an input file name when you activate EDT.

4. The default editing direction when you first enter EDT is backward.

5. The file stored in the Main buffer is only a copy of the original file.

6. The <DELETE> key deletes one character to the right of the cursor.

7. To process a line mode command using the COMMAND command, you need to press <RETURN>.

8. Searches using the FIND command can only occur in the forward direction.

9. The CHARACTER command can be used as an alternative to using the <LEFT ARROW> and <RIGHT ARROW> keys.

10. The PAGE command moves the cursor in increments of 16 lines at a time.

11. The REPLACE command exchanges a selected range of text, established using the FIND command, with the contents of the Paste buffer.

12. The <GOLD> Repeat function allows you to repeat a keypad editing function a specific number of times.

13. <CTRL/x> allows you to clear and redraw the screen.

14. You can start a recovery operation after a system crash on a hard-copy terminal when you were working on a VT200 or VT100 terminal.

15. EDT will not activate successfully if there is not enough disk storage to create the journal file.

16. The QUIT/SAVE command sequence saves the contents of the Main buffer even though there is not enough disk storage.

3.15   Further Reading

Introduction to EDT. Digital Equipment Corporation, 1989. Educational Services BUO/E55-193, 12 Crosby Drive, Bedford, MA 01730-9964.

Order from Digital Equipment Corporation, POB CS2008, Nashua, NH 03061:

VAX EDT Reference Manual. Order no. AA-LA16A-TE.

VMS General User's Manual. Order no. AA-LA98A-TE.

VMS Mini-Reference. Order no. AA-LA96A-TE.

Chapter 4

Full-Screen Editing with EVE

*The form or law of thought . . . is detected when we watch the machine in oper-
ation without attending to the matter operated on.*
—Augustus De Morgan, *On the Syllogism, and Other Logical Writings,* 1860

VMS provides several different text editors, which you can use to create and
edit text files. This chapter introduces the text editor EVE (Extensible VAX
editor). In this chapter, you will

- Learn how to use EVE keypad mode
- Learn how EVE stores a text file
- Explore commonly used EVE keypad and line commands
- Experiment with various methods of moving the cursor
- Explore various ways to locate text
- Experiment with multiple editing windows
- Examine different ways to recover from system interruptions

4.1   About EVE

As a full-screen editor, EVE incorporates many of the same features that the
EDT editor has. What makes EVE unique, however, is its flexibility in allowing you to adapt it for your specific editing needs. EVE can be used to edit or
create new files such as letters, memos, or complex computer programs.

EVE is written in VAXTPU, which is a high-performance, programmable, text-processing utility. The EVE editor can only be activated on an ANSI standard terminal like the VT100 or VT200.

The keyboard on an ANSI standard terminal provides an editing keypad and some additional keys that EVE uses to perform editing functions. The <CTRL> key can be used with several main keyboard keys to perform specific editing functions. In addition, EVE uses some of the function keys on the VT200 for editing.

EVE allows you to edit text in one of two ways. The first method is editing in keypad mode. With keypad mode, you use various keypad and function keys on the keyboard. The second method involves typing EVE commands on the EVE command line.

With keypad mode, you can easily manipulate text using simple keystrokes. Using the keys on the numeric keypad (VT100) or the auxiliary keypad (VT200), you can work with characters as well as with larger portions of text. Cursor position determines how text will be affected by the EVE commands, and you can move the cursor through the file in a variety of ways. In keypad mode, EVE keypad commands make it possible to delete, find, insert, substitute, and move text in a file with a single keystroke.

Line commands allow you to manipulate a range of one or more lines of text using any of the EVE line commands. The command line is activated with the DO keypad command. You type simple commands after the COMMAND: prompt on the command line, which is located at the bottom of your screen.

In addition, EVE provides the following features to make your editing easier:

- An on-line Help facility, which you can use at any time during an editing session without interrupting or affecting the work in progress
- A fail-safe mechanism, called a Journal facility, for retrieving lost files if your system crashes while you are editing
- Several methods of searching for text rapidly
- A variety of cursor movement functions
- Multiple windows in which two files can be viewed and edited on the screen during the current editing session

This chapter concentrates on editing in keypad mode. Occasionally, line commands essential to the editing process are discussed.

Before venturing any further, use the DCL CREATE command to set up a file, as explained in Experiment 4.1. You will use this file during the rest of the chapter.

Experiment 4.1   **Creating the Initial File**

1. Use the DCL CREATE command to create the file LETTER.TXT.

    ```
    $ create letter.txt
    ```

2. Type the following text exactly as shown, including the misspelled *Deer*.

    ```
    Deer Mr. Smith:
    Just a brief note to thank you for taking the time
    to talk with me today about the computer programming
    position you are looking to fill. I enjoyed our
    conversation and found your comments very helpful.
    Sincerely,
    ```

3. Exit by pressing <CTRL/z>.

    ```
    <CTRL/z>
    [Exit]
    $
    ```

4.2   **Getting Started with EVE**

To activate EVE, use the DCL EDIT command with the /TPU qualifier. Its syntax is

edit/tpu *filename*

Because the command to activate EVE may vary somewhat from computer to computer, you may need to check with your system manager to find out how to activate EVE on your system.

Once you have entered the EDIT command with the /TPU qualifier and the file name, you have activated EVE. EVE goes directly into keypad mode, and the first 21 lines of the file appear on the screen. A status line appears at the bottom of the screen and displays information about the current editing buffer. Also, it notifies you of the default editing mode (insert) and editing direction (forward) (see Figure 4.2).

When EVE is activated, it places a copy of the file in a buffer, a workspace where you can manipulate the text. This buffer is given the same name as the file you are editing. Activate EVE by following Experiment 4.2.

```
Deer Mr. Smith:
Just a brief note to thank you for taking the time
to talk with me today about the computer programming
position you are looking to fill.  I enjoyed our
conversation and found your comments very helpful.
Sincerely,
[End of file]
[Interrupt]
$
```

Figure 4.1 Interrupting an EVE Session

Experiment 4.2   ***Activating EVE***

1. First activate EVE by entering the **EDIT** command with the file name
    LETTER.TXT.

    `$ edit/tpu letter.txt`

    EVE will be in keypad mode and will display all six lines of the file and
    the **[End of file]** symbol, which signifies the end of the file.

2. Use the <DOWN ARROW> key to move the cursor past the **[End of file]**
    symbol.

3. Interrupt the EVE session by pressing <CTRL/y>. This returns you to the
    DCL prompt, as shown in Figure 4.1.

4. Activate EVE again by entering the **EDIT** command with the file name
    LETTER.TXT.

    Once EVE finishes painting the screen with text, the cursor appears in the
    upper left-hand corner; and the **[End of file]** symbol flags the end of the
    file, as shown in Figure 4.2.

```
Deer Mr. Smith:
Just a brief note to thank you for taking the time
to talk with me today about the computer programming
position you are looking to fill.  I enjoyed our
conversation and found your comments very helpful.
Sincerely,
[End of file]




Buffer: LETTER.TXT                    | Insert | Forward
```

Figure 4.2 The [End of file] Symbol

4.3   An Overview of the EVE Keypads

Many EVE editing commands are assigned to the numeric keypad on the
VT100 keyboard. On the VT200 keyboard, the auxiliary keypad (the eight-
key editing keypad with four arrow keys, which is between the main keyboard and the numeric keypad) and the function keys <F10> through <F14>
are assigned many EVE editing commands. The VT200's numeric keypad is
used by EVE only for numerical entries. Figure 4.3 shows the EVE editing
commands on the keypads.

4.4   The EVE Command Line

The command line is another way to communicate with EVE. You access the
command line with the DO command, which is issued by pressing the <DO>
key on the auxiliary keypad on the VT200 or the <PF4> key on the VT100
numeric keypad. After you press the <DO> key, EVE places the cursor on the
line below the status line and prompts you for the command, an English-like
word or phrase, by displaying COMMAND:. Once you type the command, you
must press <RETURN> to activate the function associated with that command.

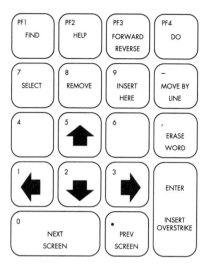

VT100 Terminal

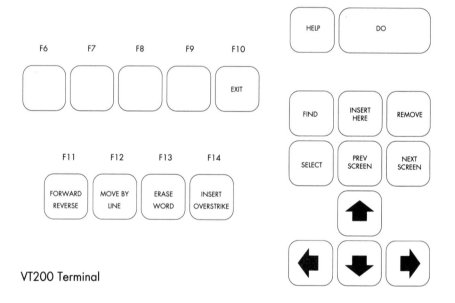

VT200 Terminal

Figure 4.3 The EVE Keypads

Some EVE commands require more information than just the command name. If you do not enter all the required information, EVE will prompt you for the needed information in the command line.

You can type line commands in either uppercase or lowercase letters, and you can abbreviate the commands. For example, BOTTOM, bottom, and BOT are all valid ways to type the BOTTOM line command. Command abbreviations must be unique. If not, EVE prompts you with the possible choices.

A line command can be repeated without typing it over each time. If you press the <DO> key twice in a row, EVE will repeat the last command entered. You can continue this process until you enter a different command.

Entering and Editing Text

When you work with EVE, you use the commands assigned to the keypad to modify and manipulate text. Some of the commands are used to move the cursor to particular places in the text. You can also use the arrow keys to move the cursor.

4.5.1 **Moving Around the File Using Cursor Movement Keys**

When you first start an EVE editing session, the cursor is positioned at the beginning of the file. You can move the cursor in any direction through the file using the arrow keys. The <LEFT ARROW> and <RIGHT ARROW> keys move the cursor one character to the left and right, respectively. The <UP ARROW> and <DOWN ARROW> keys move the cursor up and down one line.

There is also a quick way to move to the next line of text, the MOVE BY LINE command (the <F12> function key on the VT200 and <MINUS> on the VT100 numeric keypad). You can use the START OF LINE line command to move to the beginning of the current line and the END OF LINE line command to move to the end of the current line. In addition, you can use the MOVE BY WORD line command to move one word at a time.

Experiment with these cursor movement keys and commands by following the steps in Experiment 4.3.

Exploring Some Cursor Movement Functions

1. Try using the arrow keys to move around the file.

2. Move to the top of the buffer and then press the <UP ARROW> key.

3. Try using the MOVE BY LINE command (<F12> or <MINUS>) to move to the next line.

4. To move by the word, move to the beginning of a word and activate the command line by pressing <DO>. Type the **MOVE BY WORD** command and press <RETURN>. Also try out the line commands **START OF LINE** and **END OF LINE**.

5. When you are finished experimenting, move to the top of the buffer with the **TOP** line command.

There are several other ways to move around a file, which are introduced in later sections of this chapter.

4.5.2   Inserting Text

If need be, text can be added to a file by positioning the cursor where the text should be added and typing that text. The cursor and any text following it will be moved to the right as you type each character. You can insert a single character or many lines of text. The characters are always inserted to the left of the cursor.

Use <RETURN> when you want to start a new line. To break a line of text, position the cursor on the character that will be the first character of the new line and press <RETURN>.

The text file that you created in Experiment 4.1 is missing the second and third paragraphs. To practice using the EVE editor to make insertions, insert these paragraphs by following the steps in Experiment 4.4.

Inserting Text

1. Move the cursor to the letter *S* in *Sincerely* and type the following paragraphs. You can enter blank lines between the paragraphs by pressing <RETURN>. This enters an end-of-line character and moves the text that is to the right of the cursor plus the character the cursor is on to the next line.

```
As I told you during the interview, I would like
the chance to show how well I can handle the job.
I would be delighted to discuss the matter further
with you at your convenience.

I look forward to hearing from you. Thank you again
for your time and encouragement.
```

2. Notice the word *Sincerely* does not appear on a line by itself. Move it down two lines by pressing <RETURN> twice. The completed letter should appear as shown in Figure 4.4.

4.5.3 Deleting Text

Deleting text in EVE is a simple operation handled by a single keystroke or command. You can delete text by the character, the word, or the line. To delete characters, use the <x] key on the VT200 or <DELETE> on the VT100, which deletes the character to the left of the cursor, or the **ERASE CHARACTER** line command, which deletes the character at the cursor position.

Deleting a word is just as easy. Position the cursor on the word and use the ERASE WORD command (<F13> function key on the VT200 or <COMMA> on the VT100 numeric keypad). To delete a line of text, position the cursor at the beginning of the line and use the **ERASE LINE** line command.

Explore the use of these keys and commands by following Experiment 4.5.

Experiment 4.5 **Deleting Text**

1. The first text you need to delete is the misspelling in the word *Deer*. Move the cursor to the end of this word. Press the <x] key or <DELETE> twice to delete the last two characters. Then type **ar** to correct the spelling.

2. Move to the beginning of the second line of the first paragraph. Activate the command line by pressing <DO>. Use the **ERASE CHARACTER** line command to delete the *t* in *to*.

3. Move to the beginning of the third line and use the ERASE WORD command (<F13> or <COMMA>) to delete the first word, *position*.

4. Move to the beginning of the fourth line of text and use the **ERASE LINE** line command to delete the line. Notice that the lines below the deleted line move up.

```
┌─────────────────────────────────────────────────┐
│  Dear Mr. Smith:                                 │
│                                                  │
│  Just a brief note to thank you for taking the time │
│  to talk with me today about the computer programming │
│  position you are looking to fill.  I enjoyed our │
│  conversation and found your comments very helpful. │
│                                                  │
│  As I told you during the interview, I would like │
│  the chance to show how well I can handle the job. │
│  I would be delighted to discuss the matter further │
│  with you at your convenience.                   │
│                                                  │
│  I look forward to hearing from you.  Thank you again │
│  for your time and encouragement.                │
│                                                  │
│                                                  │
│  Sincerely,                                      │
│  [End of file]                                   │
│                                                  │
│                                                  │
│  Buffer: LETTER.TXT              | Insert | Forward │
└─────────────────────────────────────────────────┘
```

Figure 4.4 The Completed Letter

The deleted text is stored by EVE in a workspace called the Delete buffer. This buffer contains the most recently deleted character, word, or line. You can use the contents of the buffer to restore the most recent text that you have deleted.

4.5.4   Undeleting Text

To restore deleted text that is stored in the Delete buffer, use the RESTORE line command. Use this line command in Experiment 4.6 to restore the text you deleted previously.

Experiment 4.6   **Undeleting Text**

1. The last text deleted was the line previous to the current editing line. Use the RESTORE line command to restore the line.

2. You also deleted the character *t* from the word *to*, and the word *position*. Because EVE can only restore the most recently deleted text, you will need to retype these deletions.

3. If you want to work more with the delete and undelete functions, add several lines to the bottom of the file and work with the keys and commands using that text. When you are finished, delete the extra text from the file.

4.6 Leaving an EVE Editing Session

When you have finished editing a file of text, you need to leave the EVE editing session and save the completed file. You can use either the <CTRL/z> key sequence (VT200 and VT100) or the EXIT command (<F10> on a VT200) to save the results of an editing session. In either case, when you exit the editing session, EVE copies the contents of the Main buffer to a file in your user directory. The file has the same name but a higher version number, as illustrated in Figure 4.5.

During the course of an editing session, you may realize that you are editing the wrong file or that you have accidentally deleted information you need. To avoid saving the contents of the current buffer, you can leave an EVE editing session by using the QUIT line command rather than the EXIT command. The QUIT line command ends an editing session without saving the buffer's contents.

Experiment 4.7 demonstrates various methods of leaving an EVE editing session.

Experiment 4.7 Leaving an EVE Editing Session

1. First try leaving the EVE editing session and saving the changes using the <CTRL/z> key sequence.

2. You are at the DCL prompt, $. The changes to the file are now saved in a new version of LETTER.TXT. Verify this by using the DIRECTORY command to get a listing of files.

```
$ directory letter.txt
Directory DUA1:[YOURGROUP.YOU]
LETTER.TXT;2     LETTER.TXT;1
Total of 2 files.
$
```

3. Return to EVE as if you were going to edit LETTER.TXT.

```
$ edit/tpu letter.txt
```

4. This time, leave EVE using the QUIT line command.

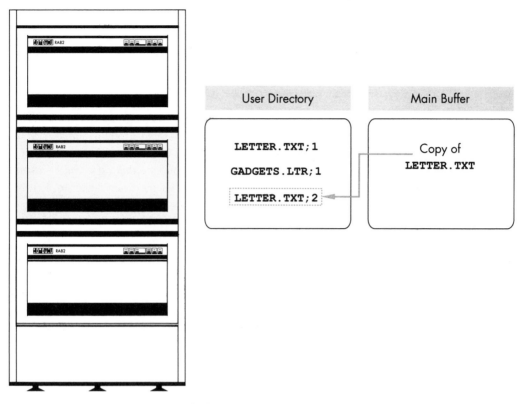

Figure 4.5 Saved File with Higher Version Number

5. With QUIT, the contents of the buffer are not saved in a file. Use the
    DIRECTORY command to check that a new version of LETTER.TXT has not
    been saved.

```
$ directory letter.txt
Directory DUA1:[YOURGROUP.YOU]
LETTER.TXT;2     LETTER.TXT;1
Total of 2 files.
$
```

4.7   Creating a File with EVE

Earlier in the chapter, you created the LETTER.TXT file using the DCL CREATE
command. You can also create a new file from EVE by specifying a new file
name when you enter the EDIT/TPU command. Experiment 4.8 demonstrates
how to create a new file, which contains a C program that prints Fahrenheit
temperatures and the centigrade, or Celsius, equivalents.

Creating a New File from EVE

1. Activate EVE using the file name TEMP.C.

   ```
   $ edit/tpu temp.c
   ```

   Once EVE finishes painting the screen with text, the cursor appears in the upper left-hand corner, and the symbol [End of file] flags the end of the file.

2. Enter the following text exactly as it appears. Remember to press <RETURN> to start a new line. Notice that as you enter more than 21 lines of text, the text scrolls off the top of the screen.

   ```
   /* This program will print a table of
      Fahrenheit temperatures and the
      corresponding temperatures in
      centigrade, or Celsius */


   main ()
   {
       int lowest, highest, increment;
       float fahrenheit, celsius;


       lowest = 0;         /* lowest temperature */
       highest = 300;      /* highest temperature */
       increment = 10;     /* temperature increment */

       fahrenheit = lowest;
       while (fahrenheit <= highest) {
          celsius = (5.0/9.0) * (fahrenheit - 32.0);
          printf("%4.0f %6.1f\n", fahrenheit, celsius);
          fahrenheit = fahrenheit + increment;
       }
   }
   ```

3. Return to the beginning of the file by using the arrow keys.

4.8 Getting Help with EVE Commands

EVE's on-line Help facility allows you to obtain help on a specific EVE key or command during your editing session.

While in keypad mode, you can use the HELP command (<HELP> on the VT200 or <PF2> on the VT100) to get help about keypad commands. A help screen appears. You can then press any key to obtain help about that key.

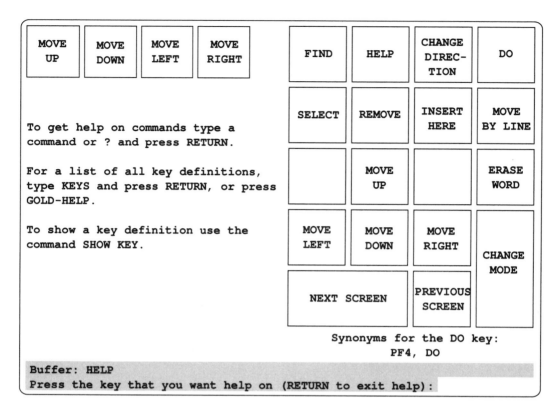

| MOVE UP | MOVE DOWN | MOVE LEFT | MOVE RIGHT | | FIND | HELP | CHANGE DIREC-TION | DO |

To get help on commands type a command or ? and press RETURN.

For a list of all key definitions, type KEYS and press RETURN, or press GOLD-HELP.

To show a key definition use the command SHOW KEY.

| SELECT | REMOVE | INSERT HERE | MOVE BY LINE |

| | MOVE UP | | ERASE WORD |

| MOVE LEFT | MOVE DOWN | MOVE RIGHT | CHANGE MODE |

| NEXT SCREEN | PREVIOUS SCREEN | |

Synonyms for the DO key:
PF4, DO

Buffer: HELP
Press the key that you want help on (RETURN to exit help):

VT100 Help Screen

Figure 4.6 Keypad Mode Help

To get help from the command line, type HELP at the Command: prompt and press <RETURN>. A help screen appears. You can then type HELP and the name of a command to obtain help about that command. For example, you could type HELP BOTTOM to see information about the BOTTOM command. To view a complete list of commands, type just HELP and press <RETURN>.

Experiment 4.9 explores the Help facility.

Experiment 4.9   **Getting Help**

1. You should be in EVE keypad mode to begin. If you have been following the experiments, the file TEMP.c will be on the screen. Issue the HELP command (<HELP> on the VT200 or <PF2> on the VT100). The screen should resemble Figure 4.6.

2. Read the instructions on the screen. Press any of the keypad keys to see information about that key's command.

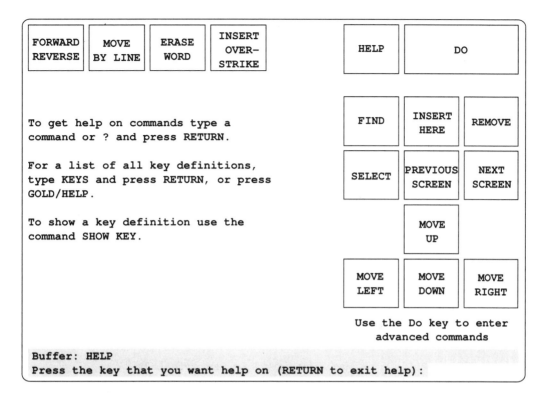

| FORWARD REVERSE | MOVE BY LINE | ERASE WORD | INSERT OVER-STRIKE | | HELP | DO |

To get help on commands type a command or ? and press RETURN.

For a list of all key definitions, type KEYS and press RETURN, or press GOLD/HELP.

To show a key definition use the command SHOW KEY.

FIND	INSERT HERE	REMOVE
SELECT	PREVIOUS SCREEN	NEXT SCREEN
	MOVE UP	
MOVE LEFT	MOVE DOWN	MOVE RIGHT

Use the Do key to enter advanced commands

Buffer: HELP
Press the key that you want help on (RETURN to exit help):

VT200 Help Screen

Figure 4.6 Keypad Mode Help (continued)

3. Once you have finished reading the help text, return to the editing session by pressing <RETURN>.

4. Use the <DO> key to activate the command line. The **Command:** prompt should appear on the screen.

5. Type **HELP** and press <RETURN>. The screen should resemble Figure 4.7.

6. Read the instructions on the screen. You can now obtain information about a particular command or topic. Enter text to explore a topic, for example, **DELETE**.

7. Once you have finished reading the help text, return to the keypad mode editing session by pressing <RETURN>.

```
Commands (List of Topics)

    For help on EVE topics, type the name of a topic and press RETURN.
    • For a keypad diagram, press HELP.
    • For help on VAXTPU builtins, type TPU and press RETURN.
    • To exit from help and resume editing, press RETURN.


EDITING TEXT

Change Mode              Erase Word            Restore Character
Copy                     Insert Here           Restore Line
Cut                      Insert Mode           Restore Selection
Delete                   Overstrike Mode       Restore Sentence
Erase Character          Paste                 Restore Word
Erase Line               Quote                 Select
Erase Previous Word      Remove                Select All
Erase Start of Line      Restore               Store Text


SEARCHES

Buffer: HELP           Press Down arrow to see more help
Type the topic you want help on (press RETURN if done):
```

Figure 4.7 Line Mode Help

4.9 More EVE Commands and Functions

There are many useful keypad functions that are provided by EVE for editing
a file or text. They include changing the editing direction, searching for text
strings, cutting and pasting portions of text, and so on. The following sections introduce many of these functions.

4.9.1 Changing the Editing Direction

When you begin an EVE editing session, the cursor movement through the
text in a file is forward, or toward the end of the buffer. This is the default
editing direction. For example, when you use the MOVE BY LINE command, the cursor moves to the end of lines; or when you use the FIND command to search for a text string, the search advances from the cursor toward
the end of the file.

By using the FORWARD/REVERSE command (<F11> on the VT200 or
<PF3> on the VT100), you can change the editing direction. After you issue

this command, movement through the file will be back toward the beginning of the file. To return to forward movement, you must press the same key again. The status line reflects the current editing direction each time this key is pressed.

Being able to control the editing direction is advantageous when working with many EVE functions, as demonstrated in Experiment 4.10.

Experiment 4.10   **Changing the Editing Direction**

1. Change the editing direction to reverse with the FORWARD/REVERSE command (<F11> or <PF3>). The status line should display **Reverse**.

2. Activate the command line by pressing <DO>. Then type the **MOVE BY WORD** command and press <RETURN>.

3. To move by the line, use the MOVE BY LINE command (<F12> on the VT200 or <MINUS> on the VT100). Notice that in reverse the MOVE BY LINE command moves the cursor to the beginning of lines. (If you are in the middle of a line, the cursor moves to the beginning of that line; if you are at the beginning of a line, the cursor moves to the beginning of the previous line.)

4. Use the FORWARD/REVERSE command to change the editing direction. Then use the MOVE BY LINE command again. In the forward direction, this command moves the cursor to the end of lines. (If you are in the middle of a line, the cursor moves to the end of that line; if you are at the end of a line, the cursor moves to the end of the next line.)

5. When you are finished experimenting, return the editing direction to forward.

4.9.2   *Other Ways of Moving the Cursor*

You have been moving the cursor around the screen up to this point by moving a character, word, or line at a time. In addition to these methods, EVE provides ways to move the cursor in larger increments. For example, the **TOP** and **BOTTOM** line commands move the cursor to the beginning or the end of the file quickly. These commands are particularly useful when you are working with large files.

You can also move the cursor through the file a screenful of text at a time using the PREV SCREEN (previous screen) command (<PREV SCREEN> on the VT200 or <PERIOD> on the VT100 numeric keypad) or the NEXT

SCREEN command (<NEXT SCREEN> on the VT200 or <0> on the VT100 numeric keypad). This brings a different section of text into view with a single keystroke.

Follow Experiment 4.11 to try out these commands.

More Cursor Movement Commands

1. First, activate the command line by pressing <DO>. Move to the end of the file with the **BOTTOM** line command.

2. To move to the top of the file, activate the command line again and enter the **TOP** line command.

3. Move to the bottom of the file using the **BOTTOM** line command.

4. Issue the PREV SCREEN command (<PREV SCREEN> or <PERIOD>) to move from the **[End of file]** marker up toward the beginning of the file.

5. Use the NEXT SCREEN command (<NEXT SCREEN> or <0>) to move from the current position toward the end of the file.

4.9.3 *A Simple Method of Locating Text*

Moving the cursor a character or a word at a time in a small file can be time-consuming but acceptable. However, using this method on large files can be tedious. EVE provides a simpler method of locating text with the FIND command (<FIND> on the VT200 or <PF1> on the VT100). FIND searches through the current file for a previously specified word, character, or short phrase. It quickly locates an item, minimizing the time required to scan the file.

When the FIND command is activated, it searches for the specified item in the current editing direction. EVE prompts you for the text string to search for, or the search string. You type the search string and press <RETURN>, and EVE searches for the string. EVE moves the cursor to the first occurrence of the search string that it encounters.

EVE accepts either lowercase or uppercase letters. If the word is typed in all lowercase letters, EVE finds the word whether it is in lowercase, uppercase, or a combination of the two. If the word is typed in all uppercase letters, EVE finds the word only if it is in all uppercase letters. If the word is typed in a combination of lowercase and uppercase, EVE finds only those occurrences that have the same combination of lowercase and uppercase letters.

If you want to find the next occurrence of the search string, you can press the <FIND> key twice and EVE will search for the previously entered search string.

This method of locating text can save a considerable amount of time when searching for a set of characters within a lengthy document. Keep in mind that when searching for text it is important to make the search string unique. You should try to include in the search string as many landmarks surrounding the text as possible so that EVE can locate the text on the first attempt.

If EVE is not able to locate a search string, it gives a message to that effect. This happens when a search string is mistyped, a string does not exist, or the direction of the search is moving away from the string in the text. In the last case, if the search string is found in the opposite direction, EVE will display a message indicating this and prompt you to continue the search.

You can try using the FIND command by following Experiment 4.12.

Experiment 4.12 **Using FIND to Locate Text**

1. Move the cursor to the beginning of the **TEMP.c** file.

2. Issue the FIND command (<FIND> or <PF1>). EVE prompts you for the search string, as shown in Figure 4.8.

3. Type the character { and press <RETURN>. EVE searches toward the end of the file for the first occurrence of {.

4. Search for the next occurrence by pressing the <FIND> key twice. EVE moves to the next occurrence of {.

5. Press the <FIND> key twice again. EVE did not find another occurrence of the search string in the current editing direction, and so it displays a message, as shown in Figure 4.9.

6. Type **y** or **yes** and press <RETURN>. EVE moves the cursor to the first occurrence of the search string in the reverse direction, or toward the beginning of the buffer.

4.10 Working with a Selected Range of Text

Up to this point, you have experimented with several methods of moving the cursor around the screen and manipulating small sections of text. EVE provides several additional features that enhance its editing abilities further. One

```
/* This program will print a table of
   Fahrenheit temperatures and the
   corresponding temperatures in
   centigrade, or Celsius */

main ()
{
   int lowest, highest, increment;
   float fahrenheit, celsius;

   lowest = 0;        /* lowest temperature */
   highest = 300;     /* highest temperature */
   increment = 10;    /* temperature increment */

   fahrenheit = lowest
   while (fahrenheit <= highest){
      celsius = (5.0/9.0) * (fahrenheit - 32.0);
      printf ("%4.0f %6.1f\n", fahrenheit, celsius);
      fahrenheit = fahrenheit + increment;
   }
}
```

Buffer: TEMP.C | Insert | Forward
Forward Find:

Figure 4.8 The Search Prompt

particularly useful feature allows you to select a larger portion of text that can be manipulated as a unit.

4.10.1   Selecting a Range of Text

The SELECT command (<SELECT> on the VT200 or <7> on the VT100 numeric keypad) allows you to select a section, or range, of text. The section of text can be made up of one or more words or one or more lines of text. On the screen a highlight identifies the selected text.

To select a range of text, move the cursor to the beginning of the text to be manipulated, press <SELECT> or <7>, then use any of the cursor movement keys or line commands to highlight the text. For example, you can use the arrow keys to extend the highlight up or down a line or left or right, or you can use the MOVE BY WORD line command. You can highlight text in either the forward or reverse direction simply by using FORWARD/REVERSE to change the editing direction.

```
/* This program will print a table of
   Fahrenheit temperatures and the
   corresponding temperatures in
   centigrade, or Celsius */

main ()
{
   int lowest, highest, increment;
   float fahrenheit, celsius;

   lowest = 0;         /* lowest temperature */
   highest = 300;      /* highest temperature */
   increment = 10;     /* temperature increment */

   fahrenheit = lowest
   while (fahrenheit <= highest){
      celsius = (5.0/9.0) * (fahrenheit - 32.0);
      printf ("%4.0f %6.1f\n", fahrenheit, celsius);
      fahrenheit = fahrenheit + increment;
   }
}
```

Buffer: TEMP.C | Insert | Forward
Found in reverse direction. Go there?

Figure 4.9 The FIND Message

Portions of text can be excluded from a selected range by moving the cursor back until the unwanted text is no longer highlighted. You can cancel any selection by pressing the <SELECT> key a second time.

You can practice selecting ranges of text by following Experiment 4.13.

Experiment 4.13 **Selecting a Range of Text**

1. In the earlier experiments in this section, you worked with the **LETTER.TXT** file. Retrieve that file by exiting EVE and then reactivating EVE with **LETTER.TXT** as the file name. When you exit EVE, you must enter a file name for the **TEMP.C** file because you created it in EVE and so it only exists in memory.

2. Select the first four lines of text with the **SELECT** command (<SELECT> or <7>) and highlight the lines. As you move the cursor down, EVE extends the highlight, as shown in Figure 4.10.

```
Dear Mr. Smith:

Just a brief note to thank you for taking the time
to talk with me today about the computer programming
position you are looking to fill.  I enjoyed our
conversation and found your comments very helpful.

As I told you during the interview, I would like
the chance to show how well I can handle the job.
I would be delighted to discuss the matter further
with you at your convenience.

I look forward to hearing from you.  Thank you again
for your time and encouragement.


Sincerely,
[End of file]


Buffer: LETTER.TXT                         | Insert | Forward
Selection Started, Press Remove when finished
```

Figure 4.10 Selecting Text

3. All the highlighted text is selected. You could now use other keys and com-
    mands to manipulate the selected range. Instead, press <SELECT> to cancel
    this selection.

4.10.2   *Removing and Inserting a Range of Text*

Previously, you deleted text by the character, word, or line. In addition to
these delete capabilities, EVE provides a REMOVE command (<REMOVE>
on the VT200 or <8> on the VT100 numeric keypad) that lets you delete the
text in a selected range. This method allows you to remove larger portions of
text with a single keystroke.

REMOVE erases any selected highlighted text or blank spaces. Removed
text is stored in the Insert buffer. The text remains in the Insert buffer until it
is replaced by other text or until the editing session is completed. If you select and remove another portion of text while the earlier one is in the Insert
buffer, the earlier text will be deleted from the buffer.

It is important to keep in mind when selecting a portion of text for removal that you should move the cursor one space beyond the last character you want to remove. The character or space the cursor is on is not included in the removed text.

Once the text has been removed, the contents of the Insert buffer can be placed anywhere in the current editing buffer. This is accomplished by positioning the cursor at the location where the text is to be placed and using the INSERT HERE command (<INSERT HERE> on the VT200 or <9> on the VT100 numeric keypad). All text to the right of the cursor will be moved to the right to accommodate the addition of the new text.

You can see how REMOVE and INSERT HERE work by following Experiment 4.14.

Experiment 4.14 **Removing and Inserting Text**

1. Move the cursor to the beginning of the file.

2. Use the SELECT command (<SELECT> or <7>) to move the cursor to the beginning of the blank line following the first paragraph.

3. Use the REMOVE command (<REMOVE> or <8>) to remove the selected text from the file. The selected text is now in the Insert buffer, as shown in Figure 4.11.

4. To restore the removed portion of text, you can insert it back into its previous location. If you wanted to insert it elsewhere, you would move the cursor to the new location. Leave the cursor in its current position and use the INSERT HERE command (<INSERT HERE> or <9>) to insert the contents of the Insert buffer into the file.

4.11 *Discovering Some of EVE's Special Features*

EVE has additional features that make it unique compared to other full-screen editors like EDT. These features are discussed in the following sections.

4.11.1 *Finding and Replacing Text*

EVE provides a way to find and replace text. You can use the REPLACE line command to specify which text should be replaced and what should replace it. This method is useful when you have numerous occurrences of text that

Insert Buffer

```
Dear Mr. Smith:

Just a brief note to thank you for taking the time
to talk with me today about the computer programming
position you are looking to fill.  I enjoyed our
conversation and found your comments very helpful.
```

Buffer: LETTER.TXT

```
As I told you during the interview, I would like
the chance to show how well I can handle the job.
I would be delighted to discuss the matter further
with you at your convenience.

I look forward to hearing from you.   Thank you again
for your time and encouragement.



Sincerely,
[End of file]
```

```
Buffer: LETTER.TXT                    | Insert | Forward
Remove completed.
```

Figure 4.11 The Insert Buffer

need to be replaced, because once you find and replace the first occurrence, you can continue replacing other occurrences easily.

When you enter the REPLACE line command, EVE prompts you for the string to be replaced, or the old string. When you enter the old string, EVE then prompts for the string that should replace the old string, the new string.

Once you have entered the new string, EVE highlights the first occurrence of the text to be replaced and prompts you for an action with REPLACE? TYPE YES, NO, ALL, LAST, OR QUIT:. You may respond by typing Y or YES to replace the occurrence, N or NO not to replace the occurrence, A or ALL to replace all occurrences without further prompting, **L** or **LAST** to replace the current occurrence and stop, or **Q** or **QUIT** to stop the replace process completely.

The **REPLACE** line command is case-sensitive. If the old string is all lowercase, EVE finds all uppercase and lowercase occurrences. If the old string is uppercase or mixed uppercase and lowercase, EVE finds only occurrences that match exactly. If the new string is lowercase, the replacement will match the case of the occurrence being replaced. If the new string is uppercase or mixed uppercase and lowercase, the replacement will be exact regardless of the case of the occurrence being replaced.

Follow Experiment 4.15 to see how the **REPLACE** line command works.

Finding and Replacing Text

1. Move the cursor to the beginning of the file, and press the <DO> key to move to the command line prompt.

2. Use the **REPLACE** line command to replace the word *you* with *YOU*. Type the string of text to be replaced, **you**, at the old string prompt and press <RETURN>. Type the new string, **YOU**, at the new string prompt and press <RETURN>.

3. EVE highlights the first occurrence of the old string and prompts you for an action. Type **ALL** and press <RETURN> to change all occurrences of *you* to *YOU*.

4. A message appears that the old string is found in the reverse direction. Remember that you entered **you** (all lowercase) as the old string and that EVE will match it with uppercase or lowercase letters. Because you started the search at the top of the file, the string found in the reverse direction has already been changed. Press <RETURN> to accept this default response, **N** for **NO**.

4.11.2   *Typing over Existing Text*

By default, when EVE is first activated, the editing session is in insert mode. As you type, the characters to the right of the cursor are moved to the right to make room for the newly typed characters. However, simple editing such as deleting and typing characters could become tedious. EVE provides the INSERT/OVERSTRIKE command (<F14> on the VT200 and <ENTER> on the VT100) as an efficient method for performing these simple edits. Use this key to change to overstrike mode so that you can type over an existing word, easily correcting typographical errors, reversing lowercase and uppercase letters, or replacing a word with another one of equal length.

To change from insert to overstrike mode, or vice versa, press the <INSERT/OVERSTRIKE> key. The status line on the bottom of the screen will reflect this change.

Try Experiment 4.16 to see how INSERT/OVERSTRIKE works.

Typing over Existing Text

1. Move to the first occurrence of **you**.

2. Change to overstrike mode with the INSERT/OVERSTRIKE command (<F14> or <ENTER>).

3. Type **you** in place of **you**.

4. Press the <INSERT/OVERSTRIKE> key to return the editing mode to insert mode.

4.11.3   *Reformatting a Paragraph*

The `FILL PARAGRAPH` line command fills, or reformats, the current paragraph so that all the lines of text run from the left to the right margin (columns 1 and 80, by default). This command is particularly useful when paragraphs you have edited extensively no longer fit properly between the margins.

EVE recognizes blank lines and Runoff (Digital's standard text-formatting program) command lines as paragraph boundaries. To reformat a paragraph, place the cursor anywhere in the paragraph and enter the `FILL PARAGRAPH` line command. The paragraph is reformatted and the cursor moves to the end of the paragraph.

Try Experiment 4.17 to see how the `FILL PARAGRAPH` command works.

Reformatting a Paragraph

1. Move the cursor to middle of the first paragraph and press <RETURN> to break the line.

2. Leaving the cursor in its current position, activate the command line and enter the `FILL PARAGRAPH` command.

4.11.4　Editing a Different File

There may be times when you want to view or edit a different file during an editing session. You can use the GET FILE line command to fetch the contents of the specified file, store it in an editing buffer, and display the file on the screen. The status line indicates the name of the new file being edited. This command becomes most useful when working with more than one file, or two editing windows, which is discussed in the next section.

You can see how the GET FILE command works by following Experiment 4.18.

　Editing a Different File

1. Activate the EVE command line by pressing <DO>, and type the GET FILE command followed by the file name TEMP.C. Then press <RETURN>. TEMP.C appears on the screen, replacing LETTER.TXT.

2. Activate the EVE command line again, but this time type GET FILE and the file name LETTER.TXT.

4.11.5　Creating Two Editing Windows

One of EVE's many powerful features is the ability to allow two files to be edited at the same time. This section explains how to split the screen to view two different sections of a long document or two different documents at the same time.

When EVE is first activated, the contents of the file to be edited are placed in a buffer having the same name. The file is then displayed on the screen in an area called a window. By using the TWO WINDOWS line command, you can split the screen into two sections, or windows.

When you do so, these two windows will contain the same file, which you can verify by looking at the status lines. Because the same file is displayed in both windows, whatever changes you make to the text in one window occur at the same time in the other. This is true even if you are viewing different portions of the file at the same time. If you want to view two different files on the screen, you can use the GET FILE command to retrieve a different file into one of the windows.

To move the cursor from one window to the other, use the OTHER WINDOW line command. You can use the ONE WINDOW line command to return the screen to its original state. The window the cursor is in becomes the current window.

Try splitting the screen into two windows by following the steps in Experiment 4.19.

Experiment 4.19 **Creating Two Windows**

1. Activate the command line by pressing the <DO> key. Create a second window by entering the TWO WINDOWS command. The cursor is positioned in the second, or lower, window.

2. Use the GET FILE command to retrieve the TEMP.c file. Activate the command line, type GET FILE followed by the file name TEMP.c, and press <RETURN>.

3. Now the LETTER.TXT file appears in the top window and the TEMP.c file appears in the lower window. Activate the command line again, but this time type ONE WINDOW. Then press <RETURN>. Notice which of the two files is now displayed on the screen.

4. Exit from EVE when you are finished. A message appears asking if the changes to LETTER.TXT should be saved; right now they only exist in the buffer in memory. Type Y or YES and press <RETURN>.

4.12   Recovering from Interruptions

There are four common circumstances that can interrupt or end your editing session without your consent:

1. Noise in a communication channel, which may cause extraneous characters to appear on the screen during an editing session

2. Accidentally pressing <CTRL/y>, which interrupts command processing

3. A system crash without warning

4. Exceeding your disk quota

The methods that allow you to recover from such circumstances are discussed in the sections that follow.

4.12.1 Deleting Extraneous Characters

During an editing session, you may receive broadcast messages or messages indicating that you have received electronic mail. In other instances, garbage characters may appear on the screen while you are using a dial-up modem to access the computer system.

To purge uninvited characters or messages, clear and redraw the screen by pressing <CTRL/w>. Using <CTRL/w> is especially important when foreign characters appear on the screen, as it will ensure that the cursor is in the correct position.

4.12.2 Resuming an Interrupted Editing Session

You can interrupt an editing session by mistakenly pressing <CTRL/y>. Luckily there is a simple solution. By entering the CONTINUE command at the DCL $ prompt, you can return to the EVE editing session. Follow Experiment 4.20 to see how this works.

Experiment 4.20 **Interrupting an Editing Session with CTRL/Y**

1. Activate EVE to edit the LETTER.TXT file.

2. Interrupt the editing session by pressing <CTRL/y>.

3. Locate the DCL $ prompt and the cursor. Type CONTINUE, and press <RETURN>.

4.12.3 Recovering a Lost Session

On some computers a system crash means that the contents of the file you were editing are lost. But with EVE you can recover text lost because of a system failure.

Like EDT, EVE has a Journal facility that records all your keystrokes during an editing session in a special file called a journal file. If your editing session ends abruptly because of a system crash, EVE saves the journal file. Even though the text of your editing work has been lost, the keystrokes you used are saved. Using the journal file, EVE can restore almost all your editing work. (Sometimes the last few commands you typed or the last few keys you pressed may not have been recorded in the journal file at the time of the interruption.)

The journal file is normally stored in the current directory with the same file name as the file you were working on, but with the file type **TJL**.

When you next activate EVE, use the **/RECOVER** qualifier and specify the name of the file you want to recover. When EVE begins the recovery process, do not touch the keyboard until the file is restored. EVE reproduces the editing session, reading the commands from the journal file and executing them on the screen. EVE re-edits your file in exactly the same fashion and sequence as you did prior to the interruption.

Once EVE has finished processing all the command information and keystrokes stored in the journal file, it will continue to use the same journal file during your editing session. If you are able to end your editing session successfully, using the EXIT command or the **QUIT** line command, EVE discards the journal file from your directory. However, if you find journal files in your directory that you do not plan to use, simply delete them.

To simulate a system crash, try Experiment 4.21.

Experiment 4.21 **Simulating a Crash and Recovering**

1. Add several lines to the **LETTER.TXT** file, perhaps repeating the last few lines of text.

2. Simulate a system crash by pressing <CTRL/y> and then logging off the system.

3. Log back into the system.

4. Activate EVE to edit **LETTER.TXT** but include the **/RECOVER** qualifier before the file name.

   ```
   $ edit/tpu/recover letter.txt
   ```

   Sit back and watch as EVE re-edits the file.

There are two important things to remember when you recover an interrupted EVE session. First, you must use the same type of terminal you used during the original editing session. In fact, the terminal should be identical in all characteristics. Second, never modify the file you were editing before you attempt its recovery.

4.12.4   *Exceeding Your Disk Quota*

There are essentially two ways you can exceed your disk quota while using EVE. Your disk quota might be full prior to activating EVE, or there may be enough disk storage in your user account prior to activating EVE but not enough to store the contents of the editing buffer upon leaving. These two events occur more often than you might think, especially in environments in which disk storage is limited and many computer programs are compiled.

When you exceed your disk quota prior to activating EVE, a message similar to the following appears:

```
Error opening DUA1:[USER]TOTAL.TXT as output
ACP file extend failed
Disk quota exceeded
```

To solve this problem, purge or delete files to recover space on the disk; or you may need to request additional disk space.

When you exceed your disk quota while saving a file, a message similar to the following appears:

```
Output file could not be created
Filename: DUA1:[USER]LIST.TXT
ACP file create failed
Disk quota exceeded
Press Return to continue
```

To solve this problem, press <RETURN> and then <CTRL/y> to return to the DCL $ prompt. This will not save the contents of the file you are working on, but it does save the journal file for later use.

Once out of EVE, you can purge or delete obsolete files. In some instances, you may have to request additional disk space.

To start editing your file again, type the same command line used to begin the original editing session but include the **/RECOVER** qualifier so that EVE can reconstruct your editing session. For example, to recover a file called **EXAMPLE.PAS**, you would type

```
$ edit/tpu/recover example.pas
```

Summary

EVE, the Extensible VAX editor, is an interactive text editor on the VMS operating system. You can use EVE to edit different types of files such as letters, memos, or complex programs. With EVE, you can create new files, insert text into them, and edit and manipulate that text. You can also edit and manipulate text in existing files. Changes being made to a file can be viewed on the screen as you make them.

To activate EVE, your terminal must be either a VT200 or a VT100 terminal. Each of these keyboards has an editing keypad and some additional keys that EVE uses to perform editing functions. EVE also uses the <CTRL> key with some main keyboard keys to perform other editing functions. In addition, EVE uses some of the function keys on the VT200 keyboard.

EVE assigns various commands to the numeric keypad on the VT100 terminal. The VT200 keyboard includes an eight-key auxiliary editing keypad and four arrow keys. The VT200's numeric keypad is used by EVE only for numerical entries.

As an interactive editor, EVE provides two ways to enter editing commands: keypad mode and line mode. You can move from one mode to the other during the same editing session. In addition, there are two ways to enter text: insert mode and overstrike mode. Both of these modes can be used interchangeably.

You gain access to EVE by typing the **EDIT/TPU** command at the DCL **$** prompt. If a requested file does not exist, EVE displays the **[End of file]** marker and a message that the file does not exist. If the file exists in your user directory, EVE puts a copy of the file into the main editing buffer and displays a portion of it on the screen.

EVE's on-line Help facility allows you to get help during your editing session without disturbing your work. In keypad mode, you press <HELP> or <F2> to get information about keypad functions. For help on line commands, you type **HELP** on the command line.

EVE's Journal facility acts as a safety net for your editing work. It can save you hours of work should your editing session stop unexpectedly because of a system interruption. While you are editing or inserting text, EVE keeps track of every keystroke you enter at your terminal. EVE records this information in a buffer until the buffer is full, and then transfers the information to a journal file. This journal file is deleted as soon as you use the EXIT command or the `QUIT` line command.

This chapter has only introduced some of the editing capabilities of EVE. However, it describes and demonstrates the most commonly used editing features. You can explore features that are not discussed in this chapter, such as defining keys and extended TPU, on your own. They expand EVE's editing capabilities further.

Tables 4.1–4.4 summarize the functions, commands, special characters, and important terms used in this chapter.

Table 4.1   Commands on the EVE Editing Keypads

Command	VT200 Key	VT100 Key	Result
DO	<DO>	<PF4>	Activates the EVE command line
ERASE WORD	<F13>	<COMMA>	Deletes the current word
EXIT	<CTRL/z> or <F10>	<CTRL/z>	Exits EVE and saves your current editing work in a new file with same name and a higher version number
FIND	<FIND>	<PF1>	Locates a search string
FORWARD/ REVERSE	<F11>	<PF3>	Switches the editing direction
HELP	<HELP>	<PF2>	Provides information on keypad mode editing keys
INSERT HERE	<INSERT HERE>	<9>	Inserts the contents of the Insert buffer to the left of the cursor

Table 4.1   Commands on the EVE Editing Keypads (continued)

Command	VT200 Key	VT100 Key	Result
INSERT/OVER-STRIKE	\<F14\>	\<ENTER\>	Switches the editing mode to insert or overstrike
MOVE BY LINE	\<F12\>	\<MINUS\>	Moves the cursor to the end of lines in the forward editing direction; to the beginning of lines in reverse
NEXT SCREEN	\<NEXT SCREEN\>	\<0\>	Moves the cursor vertically through a file, a screenful at a time, toward the end of the file
PREV SCREEN	\<PREV SCREEN\>	\<PERIOD\>	Moves the cursor vertically through a file, a screenful at a time, toward the beginning of the file
REFRESH	\<CTRL/w\>	\<CTRL/w\>	Clears and redraws the screen
REMOVE	\<REMOVE\>	\<8\>	Deletes the selected range of text and places it in the Insert buffer
RETURN	\<RETURN\>	\<RETURN\>	Inserts a line terminator in the text and moves the cursor to the beginning of a new line
SELECT	\<SELECT\>	\<7\>	Marks one end of a selected range

Table 4.2 DCL and EVE Line Commands

Command	Result
BOTTOM	Moves the cursor to the end of a file
CREATE	Establishes a new file
EDIT/TPU	Activates the EVE editor
/RECOVER	Instructs EVE to use the journal file to restore a file editing after a system interruption
END OF LINE	Moves the cursor to the end of the current line
ERASE CHARACTER	Erases the character the cursor is on
ERASE LINE	Erases the remainder of the line from the current cursor position to the end of the line
FILL PARAGRAPH	Reformats a paragraph within current margins.
GET FILE	Gets the contents of a specified file, stores it in an editing buffer, and displays it on the screen.
HELP	Provides on-line help for the EVE command line interface
MOVE BY WORD	Moves the cursor to the beginning of the current or next word, depending on the editing direction
ONE WINDOW	Deletes a second editing window
OTHER WINDOW	Switches cursor from one editing window to the other
QUIT	Exits EVE without saving your current editing work in a new file
REPLACE	Replaces the next occurrence of the current search string with a new string
RESTORE	Restores the text last erased
START OF LINE	Moves the cursor to the beginning of the current line
TOP	Moves the cursor to the beginning of the current buffer
TWO WINDOWS	Creates a second editing window

Table 4.3   Special Characters

Character	Meaning
`Command:`	Command line prompt
`[End of file]`	Designates the end of the file

Table 4.4   Important Terms

Term	Definition
Buffer	Temporary workspace in EVE specifically for manipulating text
Character	Letter or symbol
Command	Instruction specifying an action for EVE to perform
Cursor	Used by EVE to indicate the current editing position
Editor	Application software package used to create and modify text files
EVE	VMS full-screen editor
Insert buffer	Storage area used in conjunction with the REMOVE command
Journal file	File containing commands from the current editing session
Numeric keypad	Group of keys located on the far right-hand side of the keyboard
Screen editor	Text editor that allows you to view the contents of a file on the screen
Scrolling	Movement of lines of text up or down the screen
Searching	Locating specified text within a text file
Selected range	Portion of text that has been flagged to be manipulated by an EVE command
String	Group of characters
Text file	File containing ASCII characters

Exercises

1. Name the two EVE editing modes.

2. While in EVE, interrupt your editing session using <CTRL/y>. Once out of EVE, type the following DCL commands: **DIRECTORY, SHOW PROCESS, PHONE**. Now try to reinstate your editing session using the **CONTINUE** command. Did it work? How can you resume the session?

3. In question 2, you entered DCL commands before reinstating your interrupted EVE session. This time execute a command file, such as **LOGIN.COM**, and then type the **CONTINUE** command. What happened?

4. Try pressing the <REMOVE> key without selecting a range of text first. What happened?

5. Name the various methods of locating text within a buffer.

6. What is the default direction and default editing mode when EVE is first activated?

7. Name the terminals on which you can activate EVE. Why?

8. What is the programming language in which EVE is written?

9. How does EVE indicate the current editing mode and direction?

10. Explore how to redefine the function of a specific key using the **DEFINE KEY** line command.

11. You can execute DCL commands from EVE's command line. Explain the steps to accomplish this process. Experiment with using various DCL commands such as **DIRECTORY** and **SHOW PROCESS**, and see what happens.

12. Explain the process in which EVE searches for text or a search string. How does EVE respond if the search string is not found in the current editing direction?

13. Name all the methods for exiting an EVE editing session.

Review Quiz

Indicate whether the following statements are true or false:

1. The contents of the Main buffer can only be saved to the file specified at the time you activate EVE.

2. The **CHANGE** command is used in EVE to move from line mode editing to keypad mode editing.

3. The default editing direction when you first enter EVE is forward.

4. Searches using the <FIND> key can only occur in the reverse direction.

5. <CTRL/a> allows you to clear and redraw the screen.

6. EVE can be activated only on the VT200 and VT100 type of terminals.

7. The **REPLACE** line command exchanges a selected range of text, established using the <FIND> key, with the contents of the Insert buffer.

8. The <INCREMENT FORWARD> key moves the cursor in increments of 16 lines at a time.

9. The default editing mode when EVE is first activated is overstrike.

10. When one uses the <FIND> key, the characters to be searched for must be typed exactly as they appear in the current editing buffer.

4.16   *Further Reading*

Order from Digital Equipment Corporation, POB CS2008, Nashua, NH 03061:

VAX Text Processing Utility Manual. Order no. AA-LA14A-TE.

VMS General User's Manual. Order no. AA-LA98A-TE.

VMS Mini-Reference. Order no. AA-LA96A-TE.

Chapter 5

The Phone and Mail Utilities

At the instant I first became aware of the cosmos we all infest I was sitting in my mother's lap and blinking at a great burst of lights, some of them red and others green, but most of them only the bright yellow of flaring gas.

—H. L. Mencken, *Happy Days*, 1940

VMS provides two utilities that help you communicate with other system users: the Phone utility and the Mail utility. This chapter explores these two utilities. In this chapter, you will

- Learn to place a call using the Phone utility
- Learn to answer a phone call from someone else
- Explore different methods of sending mail messages
- Understand the use of mail folders
- Create a file from a mail message

5.1   *Using the Phone Utility*

The Phone utility is an interactive utility that makes it possible for you to talk to other users on your system via your terminal screen. You can place a call, answer an incoming call, get a list of users that you can call, and even place conference calls.

To enter the Phone utility, type

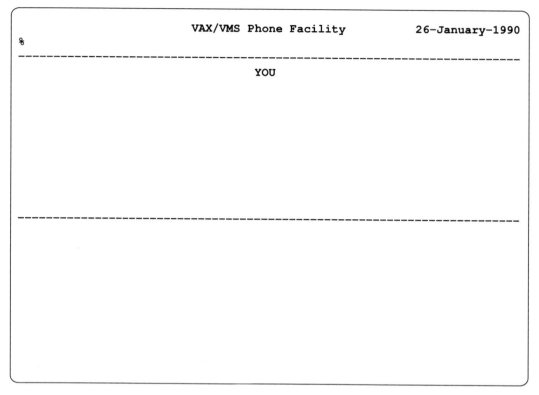

```
                    VAX/VMS Phone Facility              26-January-1990
  %
----------------------------------------------------------------------
                              YOU




----------------------------------------------------------------------




```

Figure 5.1 The Phone Utility Screen

$ phone

The Phone utility screen appears, as shown in Figure 5.1. The % is the Phone prompt. You can type Phone commands after this prompt, such as **DIRECTORY** to see a list of available users or **HELP** to get information about the various Phone features.

The two sections of the split screen are used to carry on a conversation. The upper section, or window, will display your comments, and the lower window will display the other person's comments.

You generally do not move to the Phone utility screen unless you are placing or answering a call.

5.1.1 Placing a Call

To place a call to another person, type

$ phone *username*

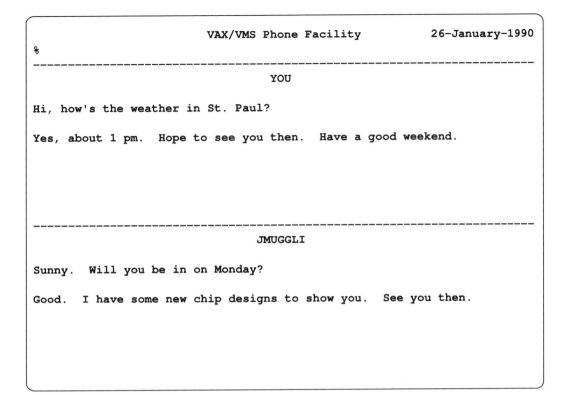

VAX/VMS Phone Facility   26-January-1990
%
_____
                            YOU

Hi, how's the weather in St. Paul?

Yes, about 1 pm. Hope to see you then. Have a good weekend.

_____
                          JMUGGLI

Sunny. Will you be in on Monday?

Good. I have some new chip designs to show you. See you then.

Figure 5.2 A Sample Phone Conversation

The screen changes to the Phone utility screen, and a message appears indicating that the utility is ringing the other person. When the person answers, another message appears, the user name of the person you are calling appears in the lower window, and you can begin your conversation.

As you type your comments, they appear in the upper window. The other person's responses appear in the lower window. For example, the conversation might be something like that shown in Figure 5.2.

If you need to issue a Phone command during a conversation, you can move back to the Phone prompt by typing %. When the conversation is over, press <CTRL/z> to hang up and move back to the Phone prompt. Exit the Phone utility by typing

% exit

5.1.2   *Answering a Call*

If someone calls you, you will receive a message to that effect. You can answer the call by moving to the Phone utility and then, at the Phone prompt, entering the **ANSWER** command. The **ANSWER** command completes the connection when someone is calling you.

You can experiment with the Phone utility by calling yourself. By doing this, you avoid bothering others on the system while you learn to use Phone. Follow the steps in Experiment 5.1.

Experiment 5.1   **Phoning Yourself**

1. Phone yourself by entering the **PHONE** command and your user name.

    `$ phone` *your-username*

2. When the phone rings, the call is answered automatically because you are calling yourself. (If the call were from another user, you would enter the **PHONE** command at the $ prompt and then the **ANSWER** command at the % prompt.)

3. Your user name appears in both the upper and lower windows because you are calling yourself. Enter some text as a conversation. Both windows will reflect your comments. To finish the conversation and to hang up, press <CTRL/z>.

4. Use the **EXIT** command to exit the Phone utility.

    `% exit`

Once you understand how the Phone utility works, try calling someone else. Use the **SHOW USERS** command at the DCL $ prompt to get a list of people currently logged on and then select a person to phone. Or you can move to the Phone utility and use the **DIRECTORY** command to see a list of users available for phoning. The directory listing indicates whether a user is accepting broadcast messages and so can be phoned.

5.1.3   *Phone Courtesies*

Keep in mind that this phone dialogue is carried on in silence. The other person can only guess when you are finished saying something. Thus, it helps to have some sort of symbols that simulate CB talk. For example, try using (o) for over and (oo) for over and out at the end of your comments.

There may be times when you do not want to be interrupted by phone messages. You can use the **SET BROADCAST** command to disable incoming phone calls. For example, you might type

```
$ set broadcast = nophone
```

To enable incoming phone messages, you would type

```
$ set broadcast = phone
```

5.2

Using the Mail Utility

Using the Mail utility, you can exchange messages with other system users. You can send a file using the **MAIL** command at the $, or you can move to the Mail utility, where you can create and send messages, read messages, and perform other mail management tasks.

If mail messages have been sent to you since the last time you logged in, you will see a message like the following when you log in:

You have 2 new mail messages.

You will also receive a message if someone sends you mail while you are logged in.

5.2.1

Sending and Reading Mail

To mail a file to another person, use the **MAIL** command, which has the following syntax:

mail [*filespec*] [*recipient-name*]

The file specification is that of the file you want to mail. The recipient name is the user name of the person to whom you are sending the file. For example, to mail a copy of the **LOGIN.COM** file to jmuggli, you would type

```
$ mail login.com jmuggli
```

Alternatively, you could compose and send a message to someone while in the Mail utility. To move to the Mail utility, type

```
$ mail
MAIL>
```

The **MAIL>** prompt indicates you are in the Mail utility.

To send a mail message from within the Mail utility, enter the **SEND** command. The Mail utility then prompts you for the recipient's user name, a subject line, and the text of the message. Enter this text, pressing <CTRL/z> when you are finished in order to send the message. To send a message to jmuggli, you would type

```
$ mail
MAIL> send
To:        jmuggli
Subj:      schedule
Enter your message below. Press CTRL/Z when complete, or
CTRL/C to quit:
Jim,
The new schedule will be out next week.
Joe
<CTRL/Z>
[EXIT]
MAIL>
```

To send a mail message to more than one user, simply enter a list of user names at the **To:** prompt, separating the names with commas.

To read your mail, move to the Mail utility. A message tells you how many new mail messages you have. Press the <RETURN> key to see the first new message. If you have more than one message, press <RETURN> after reading each message to see the next message.

You can begin exploring the Mail utility's capabilities by sending mail to yourself, following the steps in Experiment 5.2.

Experiment 5.2 **Sending Mail to Yourself**

1. Begin by creating a short file using the **CREATE** command.

    ```
    $ create mail.txt
    This file can be sent as a mail message
    <CTRL/Z>
    [Exit]
    $
    ```

2. Now use the **MAIL** command in a single command line to send a copy of the existing file to yourself. (In the following command line, enter your user name in place of **YOU**.)

```
$ mail mail.txt YOU
New mail from YOU
$
```

3. Now move to the Mail utility, where you can create and send messages as well as read your mail.

```
$ mail
You have 1 new message.
MAIL>
```

4. You can read the new message by pressing <RETURN>.

```
MAIL> <RETURN>
#1                 27-JAN-1990 13:54:57
From:      YOU
To:        YOU
Subj:
This file can be sent as a mail message
MAIL>
```

5. Now create and send a message from within the Mail utility. Use the SEND command, which prompts you for the name of the user or users to whom you want to send the message, the subject, and then the message. When you are finished entering the message, press <CTRL/Z>.

```
MAIL> send
To:        YOU
Subj:      exper. with send
Enter your message below. Press CTRL/Z when complete,
or CTRL/C to quit:
. . . message from me
<CTRL/Z>
[Exit]
New mail from YOU
MAIL>
```

6. You have sent yourself a second message. Now exit the Mail utility.

```
MAIL> exit
$
```

5.2.2 Using Folders

The Mail utility stores messages in "folders." By default, it stores unread messages in a folder called NEWMAIL and read messages in a folder called MAIL. There is also a WASTEBASKET folder that Mail uses to temporarily store messages you have deleted. When you exit the Mail utility, the **WASTEBASKET** folder is discarded.

You can create as many additional folders as you like, and you can move messages between folders.

Use the **MOVE** command to move a message to a different folder. For example, if you have just read a new message and you want it stored in a folder called **SCHEDULES**, you would type

```
MAIL> move schedules
```

You create a folder by moving a message to it and responding to the prompts so that the new folder is created. For example, if the folder called **SCHEDULES** did not exist, the Mail utility would respond as follows:

```
MAIL> move schedules
Folder SCHEDULES does not exist
Do you want to create it (Y/N, default is N)? Y
%MAIL-I-NEWFOLDER, folder SCHEDULES created
MAIL>
```

By default, the Mail utility begins in the **NEWMAIL** folder or, if no new messages exist, the **MAIL** folder. To access a different folder, use the **SELECT** command and specify the folder's name. For example, to access the **SCHEDULES** folder, you would type

```
MAIL> select schedules
%MAIL-I-SELECTED, 1 message selected
```

5.2.3   *Listing Messages*

When you are in the Mail utility, you can perform other mail management tasks. For example, you can ask for a directory listing of your messages, using the **DIRECTORY** command. This command lists the messages, who they are from, and each one's date, subject, and message number. You can use the message number to refer to that message during mail management tasks.

Unless you specify a folder name or have selected a different folder, the **DIRECTORY** command lists the messages in the **NEWMAIL** folder or, if that is empty, in the **MAIL** folder. Here is a sample directory listing:

```
MAIL> directory
#    From      Date           Subject
1    YOU       27-JAN-1990    exper. with send
2    SMITH     28-JAN-1990    test
3    OSOKO     30-JAN-1990
MAIL>
```

Try Experiment 5.3 to see how to use the DIRECTORY command to read mail messages.

Experiment 5.3

Using the DIRECTORY Command

1. First move to the Mail utility.

    ```
    $ mail
    You have 1 new message.
    MAIL>
    ```

2. Because you have not read the last message you received, you have one message in the NEWMAIL folder. Ask for a directory listing of your mail messages in this folder.

    ```
    MAIL> directory
    #    From      Date           Subject
    1    YOU       27-JAN-1990    exper. with send
    MAIL>
    ```

3. Press <RETURN> to read this message.

    ```
    #1                      27-JAN-1990
    From:            YOU
    To:              YOU
    Subj:            exper. with send
    . . . message from me
    MAIL>
    ```

4. Now that the message has been read, it is copied to the MAIL folder. Get a listing of messages in the MAIL folder.

    ```
    MAIL> directory mail
    #    From      Date           Subject
    1    YOU       27-JAN-1990
    2    YOU       27-JAN-1990    exper. with send
    MAIL>
    ```

5. To read a message, select the message by specifying the message's number. Try reading message 2.

```
MAIL> 2
#2                  27-JAN-1990 14:07:32
From:               YOU
To:                 YOU
Subj:               exper. with send
. . . message from me
MAIL>
```

6. Now exit the Mail utility.

```
MAIL> exit
$
```

5.2.4   *Two Useful SEND Qualifiers*

The Mail utility's **SEND** command has two qualifiers that are often useful. The **/SELF** qualifier lets you send a copy of a message you send to someone else back to yourself. The syntax for this form of the **SEND** command is

send/self

You can also specify the subject of the message with the **/SUBJECT** qualifier. If you specify a subject in the command, the Mail utility does not prompt you for that information, and the information appears in the mail message directory. The syntax for this form of the **SEND** command is

send/subject = "*subject text*"

Notice that you must enter the subject text enclosed in quotation marks if it is longer than a single word.

Try using these two qualifiers in Experiment 5.4.

Experiment 5.4   **Sending a Message to Another User and Yourself**

1. Move to the Mail utility.

```
$ mail
MAIL>
```

2. Now use the **SEND** command with both the **/SELF** and **/SUBJECT** qualifiers to create and send a new message.

```
MAIL> send/self/subject = "Secret life"
To:     another user
Enter your message below. Press CTRL/Z when complete,
or CTRL/C  to quit:
Marcel Vogel found plants reading persons' thoughts.
```

```
Peter Thompkins, Christopher Bird. The Secret Life
of Plants. Avon, 1974, p. 43.
<CTRL/Z>
```
[Exit]
New mail from YOU
MAIL>

3. The message has been sent to another user and to yourself. Use the
   DIRECTORY command to check this. Because there is a new message, the
   DIRECTORY command lists the contents of the **NEWMAIL** folder. Notice that
   this last message has a subject listed.

```
MAIL> directory
#   From    Date         Subject
1   YOU     27-JAN-1990  Secret life
MAIL>
```

4. Press <RETURN> to read the new message.

```
#1            27-JAN-1990    14:22:56
From:     YOU
To:       another user
CC:       YOU
Subj:     Secret life
Marcel Vogel found plants reading persons' thoughts.
Peter Thompkins, Christopher Bird. The Secret Life
of Plants. Avon, 1974. p. 43.
MAIL>
```

5. Now exit from the Mail utility.

```
MAIL> exit
$
```

5.2.5   Extracting Mail Messages

A mail message created and sent through the Mail utility is not a VMS file.
However, you may find that you want a message's information to be in a file.
The Mail utility has an **EXTRACT** command that makes it possible to write a
mail message to a file. The Mail **EXTRACT** command has the following syntax:

extract *filespec*

The file specification is the name of the file you want to create.

To extract a mail message, first read the message and then extract it to a new
file. To see how the **EXTRACT** command works, try Experiment 5.5.

Extracting a Mail Message

1. First, activate Mail and check your mail directory. Because there are no new messages, the **DIRECTORY** command lists the messages in the **MAIL** folder.

```
$ mail
MAIL> directory
#    From    Date            Subject
1    YOU     27-JAN-1990
2    YOU     27-JAN-1990     exper. with send
3    YOU     27-JAN-1990     Secret life
MAIL>
```

2. Read the "secret life" message.

```
MAIL> 3
#3          27-JAN-1990 14:22:56
From:       YOU
To:         another user
CC:         YOU
Subj:       Secret life
Marcel Vogel found plants reading persons' thoughts.
Peter Thompkins, Christopher Bird. The Secret Life
of Plants. Avon, 1974, p. 43.
MAIL>
```

3. Now use the **EXTRACT** command to copy the message to a new file.

```
MAIL> extract plantlife.dat
%MAIL-I-CREATED, DUA1:[YOURGROUP.YOU]PLANTLIFE.DAT;1
created
```

4. Exit from Mail and verify that you now have a new file named **PLANTLIFE.DAT** in your current directory.

```
MAIL> exit
$ directory plantlife.dat
Directory DUA1:[YOURGROUP.YOU]
PLANTLIFE.DAT;1
Total of 1 file.
$
```

When the message is extracted to the file, it includes the To, From, and Subject headings from Mail. If you use the **TYPE** command to inspect the new file, these headings will appear. You can prevent the headings from being copied when you extract a message by using the /NOHEADER qualifier for the Mail EXTRACT command. For example, after reading the message, you could type

```
MAIL> extract/noheader secretlife.dat
```

The copy of the message in this new file would not have the Mail headers.

5.3   *Summary*

The VMS Phone and Mail utilities make it possible for system users to communicate with each other. With these utilities, you have a choice of either interactive exchanges via the Phone utility or sending messages to other users via the Mail utility.

Both utilities provide a HELP command. When you begin using either utility, you can get help on a topic by typing

HELP [*topic*]

For example, while you are in Mail, you can obtain information on all the Mail commands by typing

```
MAIL> help *
```

To display a list of available topics, type

```
MAIL> help
```

Experiment with the HELP command to see what commands are available for each utility.

The Phone utility only works if the user you wish to talk to is logged in when you make the call by entering

$ PHONE *username*

When you enter this command line, the phoned user will see the "Ringing You . . ." message flash on the screen. You will want to use this utility with care to avoid distracting another user unnecessarily.

You can print a list of users you may call on your system by entering the DIRECTORY command while you are in Phone. The Mail utility also has a DIRECTORY command that you can use to see a listing of your mail messages.

In both cases, you need to be *inside* the utility to use the commands provided by the utility. You can tell if you are inside either utility by observing the special prompt that is displayed.

The Phone utility prompt is %, and the Mail utility prompt is **MAIL>**.

Exercises

1. Give the command lines to do the following things:

   a. Mail a file named **EXPRESS.DAT** to a user named **SUSAN**.

   b. Mail version 14 of **EXPRESS.DAT** to **SUSAN**.

2. Using the **HELP** command provided by the Phone utility, list and give a brief explanation of each of the Phone commands available on your local system.

3. Using the **HELP** command provided by Mail, list and give a brief explanation of each of the Mail commands available on your local system.

4. Give the command line to mail a file named **T.DAT;5** to yourself.

5. Which Phone command allows you to respond to another user phoning you while you are using Phone?

6. Give the command used by both Phone and Mail to terminate a utility session.

7. What happens when you type the following while you are in the Mail utility?

   MAIL> mail

8. Give two ways to terminate a Phone session.

9. What technique is used to block incoming phone messages? Give the command line to do this.

10. If you have blocked incoming phone messages, how do you remove the block? Give the command line to do this.

11. Assume you have 12 mail messages. Give the Mail command lines to do the following:

   a. List your mail messages.

   b. Delete messages 5 and 9.

   c. Copy message 6 to a file named **MSG.6**.

Indicate whether the following statements are true or false:

1. The **SET** command can be used to block incoming phone messages.

2. You can use the **WRITE** command to copy a mail message to a file while you are in Mail.

3. Extracting a mail message means writing the message to a designated file.

4. The Mail **SEND** command has a **/SUBJECT** qualifier that must be used when you send a mail message.

5. You can use the Mail **SEND** command to mail a file to yourself.

6. If you type the following, then the Mail utility next prompts you for the message to send:

   MAIL> send

7. The Mail utility allows you to copy messages you send back to yourself.

8. The Phone utility allows you to reject calls from designated users.

9. The Phone **FACSIMILE** command makes it possible to send the contents of a file as part of a Phone conversation.

10. You must type the following to respond to an incoming Phone message:

    $ respond

5.6   Further Reading

McBride, R. A., K. W. Wong, J. F. Peters, and E. A. Unger. *Rule-Based Active Message Systems*. Proceedings of the Association for Computing Machinery Workshop on Applied Computing, March 30–31, 1989.

VMS Utilities and Commands. Digital Equipment Corporation, 1989. *Address:* Educational Services BUO/E55-193, 12 Crosby Drive, Bedford, MA 01730-9964.

Order from Digital Equipment Corporation, POB CS2008, Nashua, NH 03061:

VMS Mail Utility Manual. Order no. AA-LA07A-TE.

Chapter 6

More Work with Files

The brain is, in fact, an associating machine. To recall a name, date, or fact, what the brain needs is a cue, a clue.
— Robert L. Montgomery, *Memory Made Easy*, 1979

Yea, from the table of my memory
I'll wipe away all trivial fond records.
— Shakespeare, *Hamlet*, I, v

Chapter 2, A Beginner's Guide to VMS File Management, introduced you to some basics of file handling with VMS. This chapter extends your understanding of working with files. In this chapter, you will

- Learn how to search files
- Explore uses of the Sort and Merge utilities
- Explore another way to create files
- Begin using logical names
- Learn how to print files
- Learn how to set up local help libraries

Searching Files

The **SEARCH** command scans one or more files for a specified string or strings and lists all occurrences of the lines containing the string or strings. This command is useful in constructing special-purpose glossaries, for example. Even though a text may have a mixture of ideas, you can cull from it all lines pertaining to a selected set of keywords.

The **SEARCH** command has the following syntax:

search *filespec* [, . . .] *search-string* [, . . .]

The file specification is the name of at least one file that should be searched. If more than one file should be searched, list the names, separating them with commas. You may include wildcard characters in the file specification.

The search string is the string of characters to be searched for. If it includes any spaces, lowercase letters, or nonalphanumeric characters, the search string must be enclosed in double quotation marks (").

For example, to search the **VAXDEF.TXT** file (created in Experiment 2.1 in Section 2.1.1) for occurrences of the string **one file**, you would type

```
$ search vaxdef.txt "one file"
A wildcard char. can specify more than one file.
$
```

To list all lines in **VAXDEF.TXT** with the string **information**, you would type

```
$ search vaxdef.txt INFORMATION
A file is a named piece of information.
$
```

You can practice using the **SEARCH** command by following the steps in Experiment 6.1.

Experiment 6.1 **Searching Files**

1. Use the **CREATE** command to create the following sample file.

```
$ create authors.dat
Cather, Willa Five Stories
Cather, Willa A Lost Lady
Cather, Willa My Mortal Enemy
Cather, Willa Obscure Destinies
Cather, Willa One of Ours
```

```
Cather, Willa The Professor's House
Camus, Albert The Stranger
Bolt, Robert A Man for All Seasons
<CTRL/Z>
```
[Exit]
$

2. Now search the file for the string **one**.

```
$ search authors.dat "One"
```
Cather, Willa *One* of Ours
$

3. The **SEARCH** command also has a **/LOG** qualifier, which displays the file name, number of records, and number of matches for each file searched. For example, to search all your files of type **TXT** for the string **file**, you would type

```
$ search/log *.txt "file"
```
%SEARCH-S-NOMATCH, DUA1:[YOURGROUP.YOU]A.TXT;1 -1 record
%SEARCH-S-NOMATCH, DUA1:[YOURGROUP.YOU]AI.TXT;1 -13 records

   .
   .
   .

****
DUA1:[YOURGROUP.YOU]MAIL.TXT;1
This *file* can be sent as a mail message
%SEARCH-S-MATCHED, DUA1:[YOURGROUP.YOU]MAIL.TXT;1 -1
record, 1 match**

   .
   .

****
DUA1:[YOURGROUP.YOU]VAXDEF.TXT;1
A wildcard char. can specify more than one *file*.
A *file* is a named piece of information.
%SEARCH-S-MATCHED, DUA1:[YOURGROUP.YOU]VAXDEF.TXT;1 -4
records, 2 matches**
$

6.2   *Another Method of Creating Files*

Up to this point, you have used the **CREATE**, **EDIT**, **COPY**, and Mail **EXTRACT** commands to establish new files. VMS also offers a variety of other ways to create new files. For example, many DCL commands have an **/OUTPUT** qualifier that makes it possible to create a new file. By default, VMS sends a command's response or output to the terminal or, in a batch job, to a batch

Table 6.1   Commands with the /OUTPUT Qualifier

Command	Example	Result
`DIRECTORY`	`directory/output = d.dat`	Writes the output from a `DIRECTORY` command to a new file, in this case, `D.DAT`
`RUN`	`run/output = r.dat pgm`	Writes the output from the execution of `pgm`, an executable program, to a file, in this case, `R.DAT`
`SEARCH`	`search/output = se.dat pgm begin`	Writes the output from a `SEARCH` command; in this case, the search scans the `pgm` file for occurrences of *begin*, and the output file is `SE.DAT`
`SHOW`	`show/output = sh.dat users`	Writes the output from a `SHOW` command that lists current users to a file, in this case, `SH.DAT`
`TYPE`	`type/output = t.dat`	Writes the output from a `TYPE` command to a file, in this case, `T.DAT`

job log file. (This default output stream or file is specified by `SYS$OUTPUT`, a system logical name.) The `/OUTPUT` qualifier directs the output from a command to a specified file instead. Table 6.1 lists a selection of DCL commands that have this qualifier.

6.2.1   *Redirecting the DIRECTORY Command Output*

You can use the `/OUTPUT` qualifier with the `DIRECTORY` command to redirect the listing of files from the terminal to a specific file. You might do this to save a copy of the listing from an old directory when you anticipate making many changes to it and want to have a record of the old directory structure.

The `DIRECTORY` command with the `/OUTPUT` qualifier has the following syntax:

directory/output [= *filespec*]

Although the file specification is optional for the /OUTPUT qualifier, if you do not enter it, the output is sent to the default output device (generally, the terminal) rather than to a file. Try redirecting the output of the DIRECTORY command by following Experiment 6.2.

Experiment 6.2   **Redirecting the Output from a DIRECTORY Command**

1. Send the output from a DIRECTORY operation to a file named DIR.OUT.

   ```
   $ directory/output = dir.out
   $
   ```

2. The directory history is now in a new file called DIR.OUT. Verify this by entering a DIRECTORY command for DIR.OUT files.

   ```
   $ directory dir.out
   Directory DUA1:[YOURGROUP.YOU]
   DIR.OUT;1
   Total of 1 file.
   $
   ```

3. You can see the contents of the DIR.OUT file by entering a TYPE command.

   ```
   $ type dir.out
   Directory DUA1:[YOURGROUP.YOU]
   A.TXT;1    AI.TXT;1    AUTHORS.DAT;1    BUBBLE.PAS;1
      .
      .
      .

   Total of 35 files.
   $
   ```

When you create a file of the directory results, everything that would normally appear on the screen is placed in the file. You can suppress the directory heading, which contains the device and directory names, by using the /NOHEADING qualifier. For example, you could type

```
$ directory/noheading/output = dirnh.out
```

The /NOHEADING qualifier tells the DIRECTORY command to use single-column format in its output. As a result, the pathname of each file appears with each file name. To see this, type

```
$ type dirnh.out
DUA1:[YOURGROUP.YOU]A.TXT;1
DUA1:[YOURGROUP.YOU]AI.TXT;1
   .
   .
   .
```

```
DUA1:[YOURGROUP.YOU]VAXMAN.DAT;1
DUA1:[YOURGROUP.YOU]VMS.DIR;1
Total of 35 files.
$
```

If you want to direct the output to a different directory, be sure to include the pathname for that directory or subdirectory when you enter the file specification. Remember, pathnames are enclosed in brackets. For example, to direct the output to a file in a subdirectory called DIRLISTS, you would type

```
$ directory/output = [.dirlists]dir.out
```

6.2.2 Redirecting the SEARCH Command Output

You can redirect the output from the SEARCH command to a specified file using the /OUTPUT qualifier. By redirecting the output from the SEARCH command, you can establish special-purpose files that provide a permanent record of the output. The syntax for this form of this command is

search/output [= *filespec*] *filespec* [, . . .] *string* [, . . .]

For example, to create a file that contains the lines in VAXDEF.TXT with the string information, you would type

```
$ search/output = info.dat vaxdef.txt INFORMATION
$
```

6.3 Sorting File Contents

Sorting the contents of a file is a useful procedure that can help you organize information in a specific way. A sorted list is a list of items arranged in ascending or descending order. Each item is considered a record. A record can consist of one or more fields. For example, the list in Table 6.2 shows the most common English words, taken from Gaines [1939]. The list has two fields, Word and Frequency, and each word and its frequency number constitute one record.

A sort key is the field of the records that is used to order the list. For example, in the Gaines word list, the Frequency field has been used as the sort key. These most common English words appear in descending order relative to frequency counts.

The DCL Sort utility makes it possible to sort file records in terms of one or more sort keys.

Table 6.2 *Most Common English Words*

Word	Frequency
the	15,568
of	9,767
and	7,638
to	5,739
a	5,074
in	4,312
that	3,017
is	2,509

6.3.1 Sorting Files with the Sort Utility

You use the DCL Sort utility to sort the records of a file or files by one or more sort keys. The **SORT** command, which invokes the Sort utility, has the following syntax:

sort *input-filespec* [, . . .] *output-filespec*

The input file specification is the name of at least one file to be sorted. Up to ten files can be sorted to create one output file. If more than one file should be sorted, list the file names, separating them with commas. The output file specification is the file that will be created and that will contain the sorted records.

In its simplest form, without any qualifiers, the **SORT** command sorts the file using the entire record as the sort key and produces an output file with the records in ascending order. Follow the steps in Experiment 6.3 to explore how a simple sort works.

Experiment 6.3 **Using the SORT Command Without Qualifiers**

1. First create a file, **GAINES.DAT**, to be sorted.

```
$ create gaines.dat
the     15568
of       9767
and      7638
to       5739
a        5074
in       4312
```

```
that       3017
is         2509
<CTRL/Z>
[Exit]
$
```

2. Now enter a SORT command without qualifiers. This sorts the records of the file by the entire record. The input file is GAINES.DAT and the output file can be WORDS.DAT.

```
$ sort gaines.dat words.dat
$
```

3. Use the TYPE command to see the contents of WORDS.DAT.

```
$ type words.dat
a            5074
and          7638
in           4312
is           2509
of           9767
that         3017
the         15568
to           5739
$
```

If you want the output from a sort to be written directly to the screen, specify SYS$OUTPUT as the output file. Then the SORT command displays the results of the sort rather than creating a file containing the results. For example, to see the results of a sort of GAINES.DAT directly on the screen, you would type

```
$ sort gaines.dat sys$output
a            5074
and          7638
in           4312
is           2509
of           9767
that         3017
the         15568
to           5739
$
```

6.3.2 Using the SORT Command with the /STATISTICS Qualifier

At times it is helpful to use the /STATISTICS qualifier with the SORT command. This qualifier gives you a way of checking what the Sort utility has done because it lists information about the sort procedure—the number of records read and sorted, the elapsed time, and much more. For example, to produce statistics for a sort of the GAINES.DAT file, you would type

```
$ sort/statistics gaines.dat words.dat
              VAX Sort/Merge Statistics
Records read:            8      Input record length:     10
Records sorted:          8      Internal length:         12
Records output:          8      Output record length:    10
Working set extent:   2000      Sort tree size:         102
Virtual memory:        259      Number of initial runs:   0
Direct I/O:              7      Maximum merge order:      0
Buffered I/O:            4      Number of merge passes:   0
Page faults:            38      Work file allocation:     0
Elapsed time: 00:00:00.59      Elapsed CPU:   00:00:00.20
```

6.3.3   *Sorting with Sort Keys*

By default, the Sort utility uses the entire record as the sort key and sorts the records in ascending order. If you want to sort by a specific field in the records, you must specify that field by using the /KEY qualifier. The syntax for the /KEY qualifier is

sort/key = (pos:*column-number*, **siz**:*key-size*, [**type**], [**order**]) *input-filespec output-filespec*

The position and size arguments of the /KEY qualifier are mandatory, and the type and order arguments are optional. The position argument specifies the position of the leading column of the field that will be used as the sort key.

The size argument specifies the size, or the exact number of columns, of this key field. Acceptable values for this argument depend on the data type of the entries in the key field, or sort key, as follows:

- 1 to 32,767 characters for char (character) data
- 1, 2, 4, 8, or 16 bytes for binary data
- 1 to 31 digits for decimal data
- No value for floating-point data (f_floating, d_floating, g_floating, or h_floating)

The optional type argument specifies the data type of the sort key. Type char is the default type used by the Sort utility if no type is specified.

The optional order argument specifies the order of the sort operation and can be either ascending or descending. By default, the sort will be in ascending order.

For example, to sort the lines in the **GAINES.DAT** file in descending order using the first field as the sort key, you would type

```
$ sort/key = (pos:1,siz:4,descending) gaines.dat sys$output
to         5739
the        15568
that       3017
of         9767
is         2509
in         4312
and        7638
a          5074
$
```

Before you can specify a field of a record to be used as a sort key, you must first determine the position and size of a key in a file record. (The illustrations in this section will be in terms of stream files, or files of characters, and single sort keys.)

An easy way to pinpoint the position and size of a sort key is to use an editor such as EDT or EVE to add a line to the file that will be sorted. This line could contain alternating groups of five *x*s and five *y*s, or numbers, to serve as a counting mechanism, so that you can count over to the sort key field to determine the column in which the field starts and the size of the field.

For example, to determine the position and size of the Frequency field in **GAINES.DAT**, you could add a line, as follows:

```
a          5074
and        7638
xxxxxyyyyyxxxxxyyyyy
in         4312
is         2509
of         9767
that       3017
the        15568
to         5739
```

Alternatively, the line might contain numbers, as follows:

```
a          5074
and        7638
12345678901234567890
in         4312
is         2509
of         9767
that       3017
the       15568
to         5739
```

In either case, you can then determine that the Frequency field starts at position 10 and has a size of 5.

You can explore using a different sort key by following the steps in Experiment 6.4. This experiment creates a file of records with multiple fields by using the /DATE, /SIZE, and /OUTPUT qualifiers with the DIRECTORY command.

Experiment 6.4 **Sorting with Sort Keys**

1. Use the DIRECTORY command with the /DATE, /SIZE, and /OUTPUT qualifiers to create the file GOODPLACE.DAT. The directory listing can include only files of type DAT.

   ```
   $ directory/date/size/output = goodplace.dat *.dat
   $
   ```

2. Examine the contents of GOODPLACE.DAT by entering a TYPE command.

   ```
   $ type goodplace.dat
   Directory DUA1:[YOURGROUP.YOU]
   AUTHORS.DAT;1              1        7-JAN-1990 10:20
      .
      .
      .
   WORDS.DAT;1               1        7-JAN-1990 10:50
   Total of 9 files, 8 blocks.
   $
   ```

   The /DATE qualifier in the DIRECTORY command included the creation date of the file in the listing, and the /SIZE qualifier included the number of blocks used by the file.

3. Use EDT or EVE to edit GOODPLACE.DAT so that you can pinpoint the position and size of the field you will use as the sort key. Move to the second line and press <RETURN> to insert a blank line. Then enter alternating groups of five xs and five ys as follows:

```
Directory DUA1:[YOURGROUP.YOU]
AUTHORS.DAT;1              1        7-JAN-1990 10:20
xxxxxyyyyyxxxxxyyyyyxxxxxyyyyy
CSBKS.DAT;1              10         7-JAN-1990 11:38
   .
   .
   .
WORDS.DAT;1              1          7-JAN-1990 10:50
Total of 9 files, 8 blocks.
```

4. Count the groups of *x*s and *y*s to determine the first column used by the key field. In this example, the Blocks field starts in column 24 (this is the position), and this key uses two columns (this is the size). Your results might be slightly different. Exit the editor without saving a new version of the file.

5. Next, you need to determine the key data type. The /OUTPUT qualifier on the DIRECTORY command creates a stream file, or a file of characters; so each sort key chosen for such a file will have a type of char. Also, for easy reading, you will want the sort to be in descending order so that the largest files appear at the top.

6. Sort the GOODPLACE.DAT file and write the output from the sort to a NEW-LIST.DAT file. Use the values for the position and size arguments that you determined in step 4.

```
$ sort/key = (pos:24,siz:2,char,descending)
goodplace.dat newlist.dat
$
```

7. Now display the contents of the NEWLIST.DAT file by using the TYPE command. (Your results might be slightly different.)

```
$ type newlist.dat
Total of 9 files, 8 blocks.
Directory DUA1:[YOURGROUP.YOU]
CSBKS.DAT;1              10         7-JAN-1990 11:38
LIST.DAT;1               9         7-JAN-1990 07:57
GAINES.DAT;1             1         7-JAN-1990 09:46
   .
   .
   .
$
```

You may have found the **NEWLIST.DAT** file produced by the **SORT** command in Experiment 6.4 surprising. It puts the Directory header line and Total files line at the top of the sorted file. Keep in mind that, by default, the **SORT** command uses the ASCII table to determine the order of a character. (The block number symbols are evaluated as characters, not as integers.) The lowercase letters *ck* (in the word *blocks*) occupy columns 24 and 25 in the Total files line, as do the uppercase letters *UP* in the word *YOURGROUP*. Because you specified that the sort keys were to be put in descending order, and uppercase letters and lowercase letters come after any of the numerals in the ASCII table (see Table B1, Appendix B), the **SORT** command puts the Total files line and the Directory header line at the top of the sorted file. The keys with the highest ASCII character values move to the top of the sorted file.

6.4 Merging Sorted Files

If you have sorted several files and then decide you want the results of these sorts in one file, you can use the **MERGE** command to merge together the sorted files into a single sorted file. The syntax for the **MERGE** command is the same as the syntax for the **SORT** command (with the exception of several qualifiers):

merge *input-filespec, input-filespec* [, . . .] *output-filespec*

The input file specifications are the names of the files to be merged. The files must be sorted by the same key, or they cannot be merged. Up to ten files may be merged to create one output file. Separate the input file specifications with commas.

The output file specification is the file that will be created and that will contain the merged list of sorted records.

In its default form, the **MERGE** command is simple to use, as you can see by following Experiment 6.5. In this experiment, you set up a second list of the most common English words, sort this new file and the **GAINES.DAT** file, and then merge these two files together.

Experiment 6.5 **Merging Sorted Files**

1. Begin by creating a second file to sort, **GAINES2.DAT**.

```
$ create gaines2.dat
it        2255
for       1869
```

```
with        1849
you         1336
<CTRL/Z>
[Exit]
$
```

2. Sort the **GAINES.DAT** file and the **GAINES2.DAT** file just created. The output files for these sorts can be **FIRST.DAT** and **SECOND.DAT**.

```
$ sort gaines.dat first.dat
$ sort gaines2.dat second.dat
```

3. Both files were sorted by the same key (in this case, the entire record), so the sorted files can be merged. Merge the two files created by the sort. Instead of sending the results to an output file, you can have them displayed on the screen by entering **SYS$OUTPUT**.

```
$ merge second.dat, first.dat sys$output
a           5074
and         7638
for         1869
in          4312
is          2509
it          2255
of          9767
that        3017
the        15568
to          5739
with        1849
you         1336
$
```

6.5   Logical Names

A logical name is a name that you can use in place of a file specification, part of a file specification, or another logical name. You can use logical names to assign a short, easy-to-remember name to a file whose file specification is long and complex. For instance, a file may be nested within subdirectories or be on a device other than your default. Typing a logical name is quicker and easier than typing full specifications. Because logical names can represent devices, such as disks or tape, they are useful for ensuring device independence.

6.5.1   *Defining Logical Names*

Use the **DEFINE** command to create logical names. This command has the following syntax:

define *logical-name equivalence-string* [, . . .]

The equivalence string is the file specification or the part of a file specification that you are equating to the logical name. It is a sequence of from 1 to 255 characters and can be any string such as [.**vms**] or **DUA1**: or [**YOURGROUP**.**YOU**].

For example, to create the logical name **AGENDA** for the file specification **DUA1**:[**YOURGROUP**.**YOU**.**MTGS**] **AG3**.**DAT**, you would type

```
$ define agenda dua1:[yourgroup.you.mtgs]ag3.dat
```

You could then use the logical name **AGENDA** anywhere you need to enter the file specification. For example,

```
$ copy agenda report.dat
```

To define a logical name for a device, for example, DUA1:, you would type

```
$ define disk dua1:
```

When defining a logical name for a device, be sure to end the equivalence string with a colon to indicate that it is a device.

If you define only a part of a file specification with a logical name, the logical name must be the leftmost component of the file specification. Then, when you use the logical name, you must separate it from the rest of the specification with a colon. For example, you could define a subdirectory by typing

```
$ define mtgs dua1:[yourgroup.you.mtgs]
```

To create a file in that subdirectory, you would type

```
$ create mtgs:newfile.dat
```

Finally, you can check the equivalence of a logical name by using the **SHOW LOGICAL** command. For example, to check the meaning of the logical name **AGENDA**, you would type

```
$ show logical agenda
"AGENDA" = "DUA1:[YOURGROUP.YOU.MTGS]AG3.DAT" (LNM$PROCESS_TABLE)
$
```

To explore logical names, follow the steps in Experiment 6.6.

Defining and Using Logical Names

1. Begin by creating a subdirectory of your current directory. If you already have a **vms** subdirectory, go on to step 2.

   ```
   $ create/directory [.vms]
   $
   ```

2. Define **vms** as a logical name for the **vms** subdirectory.

   ```
   $ define vms [.vms]
   $
   ```

3. Use the **show logical** command to display the value of the logical name **vms**.

   ```
   $ show logical vms
   "VMS" = "[.VMS]" (LNM$PROCESS_TABLE)
   $
   ```

4. Try using the logical name to copy files to the **vms** subdirectory. Then get a directory listing of the files just copied.

   ```
   $ copy *.txt vms
   $ directory vms:*.txt
   Directory DUA1:[YOURGROUP.YOU.VMS]
   A.TXT;1    AI.TXT;1    FLEAS.TXT;4    FLEAS1.TXT;1
     .
     .
     .
   Total of 11 files.
   $
   ```

6.5.2   *System Logical Names*

VMS defines a number of logical names whenever the system comes up. It uses these logical names when it processes the DCL commands that you issue. These logical names identify devices and files, and all have the SYS$ prefix.

Some of these system logical names are specifically associated with your process, while others are systemwide. Table 6.3 lists some of the most common system logical names associated with a process.

Table 6.3 Common System Logical Names

Logical Name	Equivalence Name
SYS$COMMAND	Name of the file or input stream from which DCL reads commands (usually, the name of your terminal)
SYS$DISK	Name of the default disk
SYS$ERROR	Name of the device that displays all error messages (usually, the name of your terminal)
SYS$INPUT	Name of the file or input stream from which data and commands are read (usually, the name of your terminal)
SYS$OUTPUT	This is the default file or output stream to which DCL sends its output (usually, the name of your terminal)
SYS$login	

When you log in, the files named by the process logical names identify the default files that DCL uses for its input and output streams. When you execute a file of commands like your LOGIN.COM file, DCL uses SYS$COMMAND to keep track of the original input stream. It then redefines SYS$INPUT to identify a file of commands it is executing as the file from which to read its input.

6.5.3 Logical Name Tables

VMS stores logical names in logical name tables. There are different types of logical name tables; each type contains the logical names available for specific groups of users. For example, the system logical name table lists the logical names available to all users of the system, and the group logical name table lists the logical names available to all users in your user identification code (UIC) group. The job logical name table contains the logical names available to your process and any of its subprocesses, and the process logical name table contains the logical names available only to your process.

When you define your own logical names, they are stored in the process logical name table. To see the list of logical names you defined as well as the process logical names defined by the system, you can use the SHOW LOGICAL command with the /PROCESS qualifier. Follow Experiment 6.7 to see how this works.

Viewing Your Process Logical Name Table

Use the SHOW LOGICAL command to see your process logical name table.

```
$ show logical/process
(LNM$PROCESS_TABLE)
"SYS$COMMAND" = "_TXG5:"
"SYS$ERROR" = "_TXG5:"
"SYS$INPUT" = "_TXG5:"
"SYS$OUTPUT" = "_TXG5:"
    .
    .
    .
```

You will probably see other logical names in your process logical name table besides those shown in this sample output. LNM stands for Logical NaMe. The logical name LNM$PROCESS is equivalent to LNM$PROCESS_TABLE. The equivalence string "_TXG5:" identifies a local terminal.

6.6 Printing Files

When you want to print a file, use the PRINT command. This command sends the file to the specified (or default) print queue. The print queue is the list of jobs waiting to be printed on a device. Only one job is printed at a time, and jobs are printed in turn, with the actual order of printing dependent on the priority, size, or submission time of each job.

The syntax for the PRINT command is

print *filespec* [, . . .]

The file specification can be replaced with a logical name. It can also be for more than one file, with each file specification separated from the others by a comma. For example, to print two files, GAINES.DAT and GAINES2.DAT, in one print job, you would type

```
$ print gaines.dat,gaines2.dat
Job gaines (queue SYS$PRINT, entry 231) started on
SYS$PRINT
```

This command sends the print job to the default print queue, SYS$PRINT. The message that appears shows the job's name, which is taken from the first file specified; the queue name; the job number; and whether the job has started or is pending. Once a job is submitted to a queue, use the job number to refer to it.

For example, if you want to delete an entry that you have entered in the queue, use the **DELETE** command with the **/ENTRY** qualifier and specify the entry number, as follows:

```
$ delete/entry = 231
```

To see a list of your jobs in the print queue, use the **SHOW ENTRY** command. This command displays each job's status in the queue. For example,

```
$ show entry
```

Jobname	Username	Entry	Blocks	Status
GAINES	YOU	231	10	Printing

`On printer queue SYS$PRINT`

The **PRINT** command has many useful qualifiers. If you want the system to notify you when your print job is done, you can use the **/NOTIFY** qualifier. To send the print job to a print queue other than the default print queue, use the **/QUEUE** qualifier and specify the queue name. (**SHOW QUEUE** displays a list of all queues initialized for the system and their job lists.)

You can use the **/COPIES** qualifier to specify the number of copies that should be printed. The default number of copies is 1. For example, to print three copies of **GAINES.DAT**, you would type

```
$ print/copies = 3 gaines.dat
```

If you are printing more than one file in a print job, the position of the **/COPIES** qualifier is important. If you place **/COPIES** immediately after the **PRINT** command, all the listed files will be printed that number of times. If you place the **/COPIES** qualifier after one of the file specifications, only that file will be printed that number of times.

6.7   *Creating Library Files*

The VMS Librarian utility allows you to create specially formatted files called library files. A library file can store groups of files as modules. Library files make it possible to maintain a single file of related modules rather than having a group of individual files. For example, you could have different files, each of which describes a procedure; or you could have a library file whose modules each describe a procedure. Manipulating the single library file is easier than working with many different files.

You can use library files in various ways. You might create a library of program source code or of technical references. One particularly good application is to create your own help library. This discussion of library files focuses on creating a help library.

To create a library file, use the **LIBRARY** command with a qualifier that indicates the type of library and the **/CREATE** qualifier. Possible library types are

/TEXT

/HELP

/SHARE

/OBJECT

/MACRO

The specified type controls the default file type specification for the library file and the input files that make up the modules. For example, the syntax to create a help library file is

library/help/create *library-filespec* [*input-filespec* [, . . .]]

The **/HELP** qualifier specifies that a help library is being created and that the library file specification will be type **HLB** and the input file specification will be type **HLP**. The *input-filespec* is optional; you can create the library file and then later add input files containing a module or modules, or you can create the library file and at the same time enter input files in it.

6.7.1   *Creating a Help Library File*

Before creating the help library, you can create an input file that contains the modules for the library. Input files are created with a program or a text editor. Each input file can contain one or more modules.

The input files for help libraries must have a particular format. Each module in the input file is made up of the lines of text that relate to a single topic, or key. The topic can have up to eight levels of subtopics. The topic, or module name, is key 1; the subtopics are keys 2 through 9. As in an outline, each key level is subordinate to the next higher key level. The lines containing the topic and subtopics begin with the key number indicating their level.

Here is the sample format for a help input file:

1 *topic/module name*	(this identifies a help topic)
first-level text	(any number of lines)
2 *subtopic name*	(each subtopic name begins with a 2)
second-level text	(any number of lines)
3 *sub-subtopic name*	(optional topic related to subtopic)
third-level text	(any number of lines)

(Other subtopics on levels below 3 go here. The presence of subtopics is optional.)

2 *next subtopic name*
second-level text
3 *sub-subtopic name*
third-level text
1 *next topic/module name*   (identifies next help topic)
first-level text
2 *subtopic name*
second-level text

(Other modules will have similar structures.)

By default, each module name can be up to 15 characters long in a help library. If you want to increase the acceptable length, you can use the **KEYSIZE** option with the **/CREATE** qualifier when you create the help library file. For example, to create a help library file with module names that can be 30 characters, you would type

```
$ library/help/create = (keysize:30) library-filespec input-filespec
```

Similarly, there is an initial number of modules the library can contain; this default size is 128 modules. Another option for the **/CREATE** qualifier, however, **MODULES**, allows you to change the default. Thus, if your input file has more than 128 modules (more than 128 level-1 topics), you can increase the number allowed. For example,

```
$ library/help/create = (modules:350) library-filespec input-filespec
```

Once you have set up the input file or files, use the **LIBRARY** command with the **/HELP** and **/CREATE** qualifiers, specifying the name of the library file you are creating and the name of the input file or files that contain the modules for the library file. You can explore this procedure by following the steps in Experiment 6.8.

1. Use the DCL **CREATE** command or a text editor (EDT or EVE) to create a file named **IO.HLP** that contains the following lines. Remember that each key 1 topic and its subtopics will become a separate module.

```
1 module_format
Starts with level-1 text with possible subtopics.
2 level-2
Always starts with a 2 followed by a level-2 name. The
level-2 heading is followed by level-2 text. There may be
more than one level-2 topic.
3 level-3
Always starts with a 3 followed by a level-3 name. There may
be more than one level-3 topic. (Level-3 topics give
ideas related to the nearest level-2 topic.)
3 other-notes
Keep module names short.
2 limitations
defaults: module names have 15 characters, libraries have
an upper limit of 128 modules.
2 structure
A help library has a tree structure.
1 gethelp
Type help/library = DUA1:[YOURGROUP.YOU]io.hlb
1 startlib
Type library/help/create libraryfile inputfile
```

2. Now use the **LIBRARY** command and the **/HELP** and **/CREATE** qualifiers to create the help library file. You can use **IO** as its name; because of the **/HELP** qualifier, the file type will be **HLB**. Change the default keysize to 32 so that the module names can be up to 32 characters long. Also, add a **/LOG** qualifier. This qualifier simply causes VMS to verify each operation.

```
$ library/help/create = (keysize:32)/log io io
%LIBRAR-S-INSERTED, module module_format inserted in
DUA1:[YOURGROUP.YOU]IO.HLB;1
%LIBRAR-S-INSERTED, module gethelp inserted in
DUA1:[YOURGROUP.YOU]IO.HLB;1
%LIBRAR-S-INSERTED, module startlib inserted in
DUA1:[YOURGROUP.YOU]IO.HLB;1
$
```

6.7.2   *Accessing a Local Help Library*

You can list the contents of a help library by using the /LIST qualifier and specifying the file name. Besides a list of module names, this qualifier displays the creation and last revision dates, the number of modules, the maximum key length, and so on. For example,

```
$ library/help/list io
Directory of HELP library DUA1:[YOURGROUP.YOU]IO.HLB;1 on
9-JAN-1990 10:34:15
Creation date: 20-DEC-1989    Creator: VAX-11 Librarian VO4
Revision date: 9-Jan-1990     Library format 3.0
Number of modules: 3          Max. key length: 32
Other entries: 0              Preallocated index blocks: 15
Recoverable deleted blocks: 0 Total index blocks used: 1
Max. no. history records: 20  Library history records: 14

gethelp
module_format
startlib
$
```

The Librarian utility has an /EXTRACT qualifier that makes it possible to display a selected module in a library. When used alone, /EXTRACT writes the module to a file in the current directory. When used with the /OUTPUT qualifier set to SYS$OUTPUT, /EXTRACT displays the module on the screen. For example, to display the GETHELP module, you would type

```
$ library/help/extract = gethelp/output = sys$output io
1 gethelp
Type help/library = DUA1:[YOURGROUP.YOU]io.hlb
$
```

Generally, however, you want to access the entire help library. Your system probably has a systemwide help library that you can access by typing

```
$ help
```

To get information from your local help library, you use the HELP command with the /LIBRARY qualifier and the file specification. For example, to tell DCL you want to get help from the IO.HLB library, you would type

```
$ help/library = dua1:[yourgroup.you]io.hlb
Sorry, no documentation on HELP
Additional documentation available:
gethelp    module_format    startlib
Topic?
```

After you get the `Topic?` prompt, you can enter any of the topics listed (including the names of other local libraries your system might have) to get help on that topic. To exit from a help library, simply press <RETURN>.

The first line of the previous example points to another feature of help libraries. If you include in your help library a module named `HELP`, this module will be displayed first. You can use this `HELP` module to give instructions on how to use your local help library.

6.7.3   *Adding Modules to the Help Library*

Once you have created a help library file, you can add more modules to it at any time. Use the `/INSERT` qualifier to add modules from one or more new input help files. Use of this qualifier has the following syntax:

library/help/insert *library-filespec input file-spec* [, . . .]

The library file specification is the help library file to which you are adding. The input file specification(s) are of type `HLP`, and if more than one file is listed, the file specifications are separated by commas.

Following the steps in Experiment 6.9, you can add modules to the `IO.HLB` library file.

Experiment 6.9   **Adding Modules to a Help Library**

1. Begin by creating three new input files. Because each file is short, use the DCL **CREATE** command to do so.

```
$ create t1.hlp
1 ideas
See LIBRARIAN Utility Reference Manual.
<CTRL/Z>
[Exit]
$ cr t2.hlp
1 insert
See LIBRARIAN-27.
<CTRL/Z>
[Exit]
$ create help.hlp
1 help
```

```
This library gives details on various ways to create a
local help library. Enter ideas to see information on
the librarian utility.
<CTRL/z>
```
[Exit]
$

2. Now insert these new modules into **IO.HLB** by using the **/INSERT** qualifier and listing the input files. Use the **/LOG** qualifier as well so that you can see the operations being performed.

```
$ library/help/insert/log io t1, t2, help
%LIBRAR-S-INSERTED, module ideas inserted in
DUA1:[YOURGROUP.YOU]IO.HLB;1
%LIBRAR-S-INSERTED, module insert inserted in
DUA1:[YOURGROUP.YOU]IO.HLB;1
%LIBRAR-S-INSERTED, module help inserted in
DUA1:[YOURGROUP.YOU]IO.HLB;1
$
```

3. Use the **HELP** command with the **/LIBRARY** qualifier to access the help library. Notice that the contents of the newly added help module appear before the **Topic?** prompt.

```
$ help/library = dua1:[yourgroup.you]io.hlb
HELP
This library gives details on various ways to create a
local help library. Enter ideas to see information on
the librarian utility.

Additional information available:

gethelp   help   ideas   insert   module_format
startlib
Topic?
```

6.7.4   *Replacing Library Modules*

You can replace an old module with a revised version by employing the **/REPLACE** qualifier. Before you use the **/REPLACE** qualifier, either edit the original version of an input help file or create an entirely new one with the same module name as the module you will be replacing. The **/REPLACE** qualifier deletes any existing modules in the library that have the same name as modules in the input files and inserts the modules of the input files into the library.

Practice replacing a module by following the steps in Experiment 6.10.

Replacing a Library Module

1. Use the **CREATE** command to create **CHANGE.HLP**.

   ```
   $ create change.hlp
   1 change
   See LIBRARIAN-38.
   <CTRL/Z>
   [Exit]
   $
   ```

2. Insert this module into **IO.HLB**.

   ```
   $ library/help/log/insert io change
   %LIBRAR-S-INSERTED, module change inserted in
   DUA1:[YOURGROUP.YOU]IO.HLB;1
   $
   ```

3. Use either EDT or EVE to edit **CHANGE.HLP** so that the file contains the following text.

   ```
   1 change
   See LIBRARIAN-38 and VAX/VMS User's Guide, 2-50
   ```

4. Use the **/REPLACE** qualifier to replace the old **CHANGE** module with the edited module. Use the **/LOG** qualifier to verify the operation.

   ```
   $ library/help/replace/log io change
   %LIBRAR-S-REPLACED, module change replaced in
   DUA1:[YOURGROUP.YOU]IO.HLB;1
   $
   ```

5. Finally, use the **/EXTRACT** qualifier to see the **CHANGE** module.

   ```
   $ library/help/extract = change/output = sys$output io
   1 change
   See LIBRARIAN-38 and VAX/VMS User's GUIDE, 2-50
   $
   ```

6.7.5 *Deleting Library Modules*

At times, you will want to delete a module altogether from a help library. The **/DELETE** qualifier makes it possible to do this. This form of the **LIBRARY** command has the following syntax:

library/help/delete = (*module-name* [, . . .]**)** *library-filespec*

For example, to delete the **IDEAS** module from **IO.HLB**, you would type

```
$ library/help/delete = ideas/log io
%LIBRAR-S-DELETED, module IDEAS deleted from
```

```
DUA1:[YOURGROUP.YOU]IO.HLB;1
$
```

If you want to delete more than one module, enclose the list in parentheses and separate the module names with commas. For example, to delete the **HELP** and **GETHELP** modules, type

```
$ library/help/log/delete = (help,gethelp) io
%LIBRAR-S-DELETED, module HELP deleted from
DUA1:[YOURGROUP.YOU]IO.HLB;1
%LIBRAR-S-DELETED, module GETHELP deleted from
DUA1:[YOURGROUP.YOU]IO.HLB;1
$
```

When you delete modules, the space they occupied remains in the library. To recover the space generated by deleting modules, use the **/COMPRESS** qualifier with the **LIBRARY** command. When you use **/COMPRESS**, the **LIBRARY** command creates a new library. By default, this new library is in your current directory and has the same file name and type as the original library. The syntax for this form of the **LIBRARY** command is

library/compress [= (*option*)[, . . .])]

6.8   *Summary*

There are many ways to work with files using DCL. You can search for occurrences of specific strings and you can sort the contents of files by any specified field. By merging sorted files, you can create a new file of all the information. You can redirect the output from a DCL command using the **/OUTPUT** qualifier to create a file containing that output so that you have a permanent record. By printing a file, you obtain hard copies of the file's contents.

Logical names provide you with a shortcut when referring to file specifications, thus facilitating your work with files. VMS also automatically defines a number of logical names, which it uses when it processes DCL commands. VMS stores logical names in logical name tables, which you can examine.

DCL also provides a Librarian utility, which has a variety of uses. One helpful application of this utility is creation and management of help libraries. The Librarian utility makes it possible to organize and retrieve information you might otherwise forget.

Tables 6.4–6.6 give an overview of the commands, special characters, and important terms used in this chapter.

Table 6.4 DCL Commands

Command	Result
DEFINE	Defines a logical name
DELETE	
/ENTRY	Deletes the specified entry from the print queue
/LOG	Displays what the **DELETE** command has done
DIRECTORY	
/NO HEADING	Removes the directory heading from the directory listing
/OUTPUT	Redirects the directory listing to an output file
HELP/LIBRARY	Accesses a help library
LIBRARY	Runs the Librarian utility
/COMPRESS	Restores free space after a deletion
/CREATE	Creates a library
/DELETE	Deletes a library module
/EXTRACT	Extracts a selected module from a library
/HELP	Specifies a help library
/INSERT	Inserts a module into a library
/LIST	Lists the contents of a library
/LOG	Displays what the **LIBRARY** command has done
/REPLACE	Replaces a library module
MERGE	Merges up to ten sorted files
PRINT	Prints the specified file(s)
/COPIES	Prints the specified number of copies
SEARCH	Searches a file or files for a specified string or strings
/LOG	Displays a record of the search procedure
/OUTPUT	Redirects the results of the search to an output file
SHOW ENTRY	Lists your jobs in the print queue
SHOW LOGICAL/PROCESS	Displays the process logical name table
SORT	Sorts the records of a file or files
/KEY	Sorts by the specified key
/STATISTICS	Lists information about the sort procedure

Table 6.5   Special Characters

Character	Meaning
LNM	Logical name
LNM$PROCESS_TABLE	Name of the process logical name table
SYS$COMMAND	Default process-permanent file used to identify initial file from which DCL takes its input
SYS$ERROR	Default process-permanent file to which DCL writes its error messages
SYS$INPUT	Default process-permanent file from which DCL reads its input
SYS$OUTPUT	Default process-permanent file to which DCL writes its output
-	The command line continuation operator
_$	Printed by DCL after the - continuation operator is entered to continue entering a command on the next line
( )-library delete	Encloses specification deletion of a library module
( )-merge key	Encloses specifications for a merge key
( )-sort key	Encloses specifications for a sort key

6.9   *Exercises*

Before you do the exercises in this section, create the following file:

```
$ create ada.dat
mesg-based systems: a task can send a mesg to or receive
    a mesg from another task.
tasks: components of an Ada program that can execute in
    parallel.
task spec: task id is <entry decls> <rep clauses> end id;
rendezvous: communication between two tasks.
<CTRL/Z>
[Exit]
$
```

1. Use the **SEARCH** command to display the following:

    a. Lines in **ADA.DAT** containing the word *entry*.

    b. Lines in **ADA.DAT** containing a colon (:).

Table 6.6   Important Terms

Term	Definition
Help library	Library of specially formatted modules; each module begins with a line of the form **1** *module-name*
Library	File used to store library modules that have been established by the Librarian utility
Logical name	Name associated with an equivalence string that is all or part of one or more file specifications and possibly other logical names; established with the **DEFINE** command
Process logical name table	Table that holds definitions of logical names; named **LNM$PROCESS_TABLE**
Sort key	The field of a record used by **SORT** and **MERGE** to order file records

2. Give the command line to write the output from 1(a) and 1(b) to a file named **ENTRY.DAT**.

3. Give the **SEARCH** command line that will display all lines in **ADA.DAT** following the first occurrence of the word *task*. (*Hint*: Use the **/REMAINING** qualifier with **SEARCH**.)

4. Give the command line to sort the **ENTRY.DAT** file that was created in exercise 2.

5. What would be the effect of executing the **SORT** command in terms of **ADA.DAT**? Try it to see what happens. Explain the output you get.

6. What is the default output file used by the **SEARCH** command?

7. List and explain each of the logical names in your process logical name table.

8. Give the **SEARCH** command line that would search all your files of type **DAT** for the string **VAX** and write the lines found to a file named **VAXLINES.DAT** in your current directory.

9. Use the **SORT** command with a file (constructed like the **GAINES.DAT** file) of the command words most used in this chapter.

   a. Create this file, calling it **FILEWORDS.DAT**.

   b. Sort the **FILEWORDS.DAT** file in ascending order using the default sort key (each entire record). Use **SYS$OUTPUT** as the output file.

c. Sort the **FILEWORDS.DAT** file in descending order using the default sort key. Use **SYS$OUTPUT** as the output file.

d. Sort the **FILEWORDS.DAT** file in descending order with the Frequency (or second) field as the sort key. Use **FIRST.DAT** as the output file name.

e. Sort the **GAINES.DAT** file in descending order with the Frequency field as the sort key. Use **SECOND.DAT** as the output file name.

10. Show how to merge together the **FIRST.DAT** and **SECOND.DAT** files from 9(d) and 9(e).

11. Show how to set up a local help library that gives help on each of the VMS topics covered in this chapter. Call the library file **VMS.HLB**. In doing this, you should include the following:

a. Give an example of a module named **FILES-11** with at least two levels of subtopics. Construct this module in a file named **FILES11.HLP**. Give the command line to add this module to your **VMS.HLB** library.

b. Give an example of a module named **CREATE** (constructed in a file named **CR.HLP**) with three second-level topics and at least two third-level topics for each second-level topic. Give the command line to re-place a module named **CREATE** in your **VMS.HLB** file with the new module in your **CR.HLP** file.

6.10 *Review Quiz*

Indicate whether the following statements are true or false:

1. By default, the output from the **SORT** command is written to **SYS$OUTPUT**.

2. **SYS$OUTPUT** is the logical name for a process-permanent file.

3. Every help library module begins with a 1.

4. By default, the **HELP** command opens the most recently created local help library.

5. Unlike the **TYPE** command, the **DIRECTORY** command does not have an **/OUTPUT** qualifier.

6. The Librarian utility creates files of type **HLP**.

Gaines, H. F. *Cryptanalysis: A Study of Ciphers and Their Solutions.* New York: Dover Publications, 1939. See page 226 for most common English words.

Marotta, R. E. *The Digital Dictionary: A Guide to Digital Equipment Corporation's Technical Terminology.* 2d ed. Bedford, Mass.: Digital Press, 1986.

Order from Digital Equipment Corporation, POB CS2008, Nashua, NH 03061:

Guide to VMS File Applications. Order no. AA-LA78A-TE.

Guide to VMS System Security. Order no. AA-LA40A-TE.

VMS DCL Dictionary. Order no. AA-LA12A-TE.

VMS General User's Manual. Order no. AA-LA98A-TE.

VMS Librarian Utility Manual. Order no. AA-61A-TE.

VMS Sort/Merge Utility Manual. Order no. AA-LA09A-TE.

Chapter 7

Command Procedures

The guiding principle for making the choice [whether to add a new action or write a new program] should be that each program does one thing.
—Richard Pike and B. W. Kernighan
Program Design in the UNIX Environment, 1984

Command procedures and the various features you can use in them provide you with a way of simplifying and streamlining your use of VMS. In this chapter, you will

- Explore the main features of command procedures
- Form command procedures with familiar groups of command lines
- Experiment with new ways to use logical names
- Begin using global and local symbols to simplify the entry of command lines
- Customize your working environment with enhanced versions of your `LOGIN.COM` file
- Explore file-handling commands used in command procedures
- Experiment with uses of parameters for command procedures
- Explore uses of literals and quoted strings
- Employ commenting techniques to specify key features of command procedures

A command procedure is a file containing DCL commands and perhaps some data used by the commands. These procedures can help you to simplify and clarify your use of VMS because you can use them to execute many commands with one statement. Command procedures can be short yet powerful, or they can be more complex, performing programlike functions. Using command procedures for repetitive or complex tasks will save you time.

7.1.1   ### Rules and Guidelines for Writing Command Procedures

You can use an editor such as EVE or EDT to write command procedures, or if it is a short procedure, you can use the DCL **CREATE** command. The file type of a command procedure is **COM**. Within the command procedure file, the lines containing commands must begin with a dollar sign ($), lines containing comments must begin with a dollar sign and an exclamation point (!), and lines containing data used by the commands (responses to DCL prompts) do not begin with a dollar sign. A command procedure can terminate with an **EXIT** command.

The basic structure for a command procedure is as follows:

```
$ ! introductory comments
$ !
$ ! comment about next command
$ !
$ command
data used as response to command prompt
$ !
$ ! comment
$ !
$ command
$ command
$ exit
```

Spaces, tabs, and blank lines should be used liberally to improve readability. Comments themselves are an essential part of command procedures. They identify and explain the actions of the procedure and are useful when you need to debug or modify a procedure. There are a variety of techniques from software engineering that can be used to decide what kind of comments to insert into a procedure. A selection of these commenting techniques are given in this chapter.

To execute a command procedure, type the procedure file specification preceded by an at-sign (@). For example, to execute a command procedure named CDUP.COM, you would type

```
$ @cdup
```

Sample Command Procedures

Command procedures are often quite short, simple, and designed for a single purpose. For example, you could create the following command procedure to change to the next directory one level up from your current directory and execute the SHOW DEFAULT command.

```
$ ! cdup.com
$ !
$ ! action: change directories one level up from the current
$ ! directory and execute show default command.
$ !
$ set default [-]      ! move up one directory level
$ show default
$ exit
```

Your LOGIN.COM file is also a command procedure file. Because it is executed each time you log into your system, you can use it to customize the login procedure. For example, your LOGIN.COM file might look like this:

```
$ ! commands executed each time you log in
$ write sys$output "     Hello, Jim!"
$ show users
$ show quota
$ exit
```

With this LOGIN.COM file, when you log in, the message *Hello, Jim!* will appear, followed by a list of users and your disk quota.

As with other command procedure files, you can execute your LOGIN.COM file by entering @ and the file name. For example,

```
$ @login
```

When you are customizing LOGIN.COM, it is helpful to execute the file each time you change it.

Creating a Simple Command Procedure

One guideline for when to write a command procedure is that whenever you find it necessary to type two or more command lines together repeatedly, they can be placed in a command procedure. Suppose you often change from your login directory up to the next directory and then change back to your login directory. Following the steps in Experiment 7.1, you can write command procedures to automate these changes of directories.

Experiment 7.1 **Creating a Command Procedure to Automate Directory Changing**

1. Use the **SHOW DEFAULT** command immediately after you log in to determine the name of your login directory.

```
$ show default
DUA1:[YOURGROUP.YOU]
```

2. Use EVE, EDT, or the DCL **CREATE** command to write the following command procedure. Call the command procedure file **CDUP.COM** and use the **SET DEFAULT [-]** command to move up one directory level.

```
$ ! cdup.com
$ !
$ ! action: change directories one level up from the current
$ ! directory and execute show default command.
$ !
$ set default [-]
$ show default
$ exit
```

3. Use EVE, EDT, or the DCL **CREATE** command to write the following command procedure, **GOHOME.COM**, which changes back to the login directory. Be sure to enter your disk and login directory in place of **DUA1:[YOURGROUP.YOU]**.

```
$ ! gohome.com
$ !
$ ! action: change back to login directory and display name
$ !
$ set default DUA1:[YOURGROUP.YOU]
$ show default
$ exit
```

4. Starting in your login directory, move up one directory level by executing CDUP.COM.

```
$ @cdup
DUA1:[YOURGROUP]
```

5. Now change back to your login directory by executing GOHOME.COM. Because GOHOME.COM resides in your login directory, which is no longer the current directory, you must give the file specification for GOHOME.COM when you execute it. Otherwise, VMS will not be able to find and execute the command procedure.

```
$ @dual:[yourgroup.you]gohome
DUA1:[YOURGROUP.YOU]
```

7.2   Using Logical Names in Command Procedures

Using logical names instead of complete file specifications with command procedures can save you time and keystrokes. For example, in Experiment 7.1, you had to specify the complete file specification for the GOHOME.COM procedure because the file did not reside in the current directory. If you define a logical name for that file specification, you can invoke that command procedure from any directory by entering @ and the logical name. For instance, you could define the logical name GOHOME for the file GOHOME.COM by typing

```
$ define gohome dual:[yourgroup.you]gohome
```

Then, to execute the GOHOME.COM procedure, you use the logical name, which by your definition includes the entire file specification. You would type

```
$ @gohome
```

The choice of a logical name that is the same as the file name for the command procedure is optional. You can choose any logical name for a command procedure.

Try using logical names for both the CDUP.COM and GOHOME.COM files. Follow the steps in Experiment 7.2.

Experiment 7.2   **Using Logical Names with Command Procedures**

1. Your login directory should be the current directory. Define logical names for CDUP.COM and GOHOME.COM, giving their full file specifications.

```
$ define cdup dual:[yourgroup.you]cdup.com
$ define gohome dual:[yourgroup.you]gohome.com
```

2. Move up one directory level using the logical name to execute CDUP.COM.

```
$ @cdup
DUA1:[YOURGROUP]
```

3. Change back to your login directory using the logical name to execute GOHOME.COM.

```
$ @gohome
DUA1:[YOURGROUP.YOU]
```

The use of logical names simplifies the use of command procedures. However, the lifespan of a logical name is limited to the time when you are logged into your system. When you log in the next time, you will have to redefine the logical names you want to use. Solve this problem by adding the definition of a logical name to your LOGIN.COM file. This automates the creation of the logical names you need. It is good practice to develop a logical names section of your LOGIN.COM file. Follow Experiment 7.3 to see how to do this.

Experiment 7.3   **Defining Logical Names in LOGIN.COM**

1. Use EDT or EVE to edit your LOGIN.COM file so that it looks like the following. Remember to enter your disk and login directory in place of DUA1:[YOURGROUP.YOU].

```
$ ! login.com
$ !
$ ! action: commands executed each time you log in
$ !
$ ! logical names section:
$ !
$ define cdup DUA1:[YOURGROUP.YOU]cdup.com
$ define gohome DUA1:[YOURGROUP.YOU]gohome.com
$ !
$ ! welcoming actions:
$ !
$ write sys$output "    Hello, Jim!"
$ show users
$ show quota
$ exit
```

2. Because you have changed your LOGIN.COM file, execute it to test the changes.

```
$ @login
```

3. Now use the logical names to move up a directory level and then back to the login directory.

```
$ @cdup
DUA1:[YOURGROUP]
$ @gohome
DUA1:[YOURGROUP.YOU]
```

Introduction to Symbols

A symbol is a name used to represent a character string, integer value, or logical value.

DCL checks the first word, or token, of a command line for a symbol and explicitly substitutes its value. You can equate a symbol to a command string and then use the symbol as a synonym for the command. You can use symbols to represent data in commands and command procedures or as shortcuts for commands themselves.

A symbol name can be from 1 to 255 characters long. It must begin with a letter, an underscore (_), or a dollar sign ($). In a symbol name, lowercase and uppercase letters are treated as uppercase letters, so it does not matter what case you use when defining or using them. You should be careful, however, not to create a symbol using a name that is already a DCL command.

There are two kinds of symbols, local and global. Local symbols are created using a single equal sign, and global symbols using two equal signs. A local symbol is available to the command level that defined it and to lower command levels. A global symbol is available to all command levels.

DCL level is command level 0 and is the highest command level. It is the level at which you log in. When you execute a command procedure interactively, the procedure's commands are executing at command level 1. Execution of a command procedure from within another command procedure moves to the next lower command level. Table 7.1 provides examples of creating a local and a global symbol.

Local symbols typically appear inside command procedures for a variety of reasons shown later in this chapter. Global symbols also are often used to represent command lines. Both local and global symbols remain defined until you exit the command level at which they were defined.

Table 7.1 Local and Global Symbols

Symbol Type	Meaning	Operator	Example
Global	Accessible at all command levels	==	`dirs == "directory/ since"`
Local	Accessible only at the command level at which it is defined and lower levels	=	`history = "recall/all"`

Symbol values that are character strings should be enclosed in quotation marks. Values that are numeric need not be enclosed in quotation marks.

7.3.1   *Working with Symbols*

In addition to creating symbols, you can use the SHOW SYMBOL command to see symbols' values. To see the value of a specific symbol, specify the symbol name. For example, to see the value of the symbol HISTORY, type

```
$ show symbol history
HISTORY = "recall/all"
```

To see the values of all local symbols, you can use the /ALL qualifier. For example,

```
$ show symbol/all
HISTORY = "recall/all"
ADDRESS = "type DUA1:[YOURGROUP.YOU]address.dat"
```

To see all global symbols, use the /GLOBAL qualifier and the /ALL qualifier. For example,

```
$ show symbol/global/all
DIRS == "directory/since"
USERS == "show users"
$RESTART == "False"
$SEVERITY == "1"
$STATUS == "%X0000001"
```

$RESTART, $SEVERITY, and $STATUS are reserved global symbols that DCL maintains.

If you want to delete a symbol, use the DELETE command with the /SYMBOL qualifier and specify the symbol name. (If the symbol is a global symbol, you must also use the /GLOBAL qualifier.) For example, to delete the local symbol ADDRESS, you would type

```
$ delete/symbol address
```

If ADDRESS were a global symbol, you would delete it by typing

```
$ delete/global/symbol address
```

You can try creating a symbol by following Experiment 7.4, which creates a symbol to represent a command line. The DIRECTORY/SINCE/DATE command line produces a directory of all files created on the current day (/SINCE) and includes each file's creation date in the listing (/DATE).

Experiment 7.4   **Working with Symbols**

1. Create a global symbol for the DIRECTORY/SINCE/DATE command line.

   ```
   $ dirnow == "directory/since/date"
   $
   ```

2. Use the SHOW SYMBOL command to see the value of DIRNOW. Because it is a global symbol, you should use the /GLOBAL qualifier; otherwise DCL would look for a local symbol.

   ```
   $ show symbol/global dirnow
   DIRNOW == "directory/since/date"
   ```

3. Use the symbol to get a directory listing of the files created today.

   ```
   $ dirnow
   Directory DUA1:[YOURGROUP.YOU]
   CDUP.COM;1       20-JAN-1990     10:00
   GOHOME.COM;1     20-JAN-1990     10:20
   LOGIN.COM;1      20-JAN-1990     11:14
   Total of 3 files.
   $
   ```

7.3.2   *Abbreviating Symbols*

You can include an asterisk (*) abbreviation marker when you define a symbol so that you can abbreviate the symbol name when you use it. Any characters to the right of the asterisk appearing in the symbol may be omitted when you enter the symbol. For example, you can create the following useful global symbol:

```
$ h*istory == "recall/all"
```

Then you can execute the command by entering any of the following for the symbol name:

```
h
hi
his
hist
histo
histor
history
```

7.3.3   Using Symbols with Command Procedures

Symbols can play a role in simplifying the entry of command lines. For example, you can create a global symbol whose value is the command line @cdup, which executes the CDUP.COM procedure, by typing

```
$ cd == "@cdup"
```

Try creating symbols for the execution of both CDUP.COM and GOHOME.COM by following the steps of Experiment 7.5. Remember that you have already defined logical names for these files and so can use them in the command lines.

Experiment 7.5   **Using Symbols to Execute Command Procedures**

1. Create global symbols for the command lines that execute CDUP.COM and GOHOME.COM. Use the logical names defined for each file.

```
$ cd == "@cdup"
$ go == "@gohome"
```

2. Now execute the procedures by simply entering the appropriate global symbol. First execute CDUP.COM to move up one directory and then execute GOHOME.COM to return to your login directory.

```
$ cd
DUA1:[YOURGROUP]
$ go
DUA1:[YOURGROUP.YOU]
```

Like logical names, global symbols remain defined until you log out. You can add the creation of symbols to your LOGIN.COM file, however, so that every time you log in, the symbols will be available. Follow Experiment 7.6 to add a symbol section to your LOGIN.COM file.

1. Use EDT or EVE to edit your LOGIN.COM file so that it looks like the following. Remember to enter your disk and login directory in place of
   DUA1:[YOURGROUP.YOU].

   ```
   $ ! login.com
   $ !
   $ ! action: commands executed each time you log in
   $ !
   $ ! logical names section:
   $ !
   $ define cdup DUA1:[YOURGROUP.YOU]cdup.com
   $ define gohome DUA1:[YOURGROUP.YOU]gohome.com
   $ !
   $ ! global symbols section:
   $ !
   $ cd == "@cdup"
   $ go == "@gohome"
   $ h*istory == "recall/all"
   $ !
   $ ! welcoming actions:
   $ !
   $ write sys$output "    Hello, Jim!"
   $ show users
   $ show quota
   $ exit
   ```

2. Because you have changed your LOGIN.COM file, execute it to test the
   changes.

   ```
   $ @login
   ```

3. Try using the symbol HISTORY to execute the RECALL/ALL command, which
   recalls the previous command lines you entered.

   ```
   $ h
   1 @login
   2 edit/edt login.com
     .
     .
     .
   20 @gohome
   $
   ```

Lexical functions are built-in VMS routines that return information about character strings and attributes of the current process. For example, the lexical function **F$TIME ( )** returns the current date and time.

The results of a lexical function are returned to the point at which the lexical function is used. This allows you to assign the results of the lexical function to a symbol, which you can then use in a command or command procedure. Assign a lexical function to a symbol as you would assign any symbol: enter the symbol, the equals operator (=), and the lexical function name. For example,

```
$ now = f$time()
```

Lexical functions have the following syntax:

f$*lexical-function-name* (*argument* [, . . .])

The name of a lexical function always begins with f$. After the lexical function name, specify arguments enclosed in parentheses and separated by commas. Some arguments are required and others are optional; the number and type of arguments varies from lexical function to lexical function. For instance, **F$LENGTH**, which returns the length of a character string, requires one argument:

f$length (*string*)

F$TIME ( ) has no required or optional arguments. If no arguments are required, you must enter an empty set of parentheses after the lexical function name.

Experiment 7.7 explores the use of **F$LENGTH**.

Experiment 7.7   **Using the F$LENGTH *Lexical Function***

1. First set up a string variable by typing the following:

    ```
    $ greeting = "Hello, world!"
    ```

2. Store the length of this string in the symbol **LEN**, which gets its value from the **F$LENGTH** function.

    ```
    $ len = f$length(greeting)
    ```

3. Now you can inspect the value of the symbol using the SHOW SYMBOL command.

```
$ show symbol len
LEN = 13  Hex = 0000000D  Octal = 00000000015
```

File-Handling Commands for Command Procedures

Within command procedures, it is often necessary to read and write data from and to files. To do this, use the OPEN, READ, WRITE, and CLOSE commands. Although these DCL commands are normally used only within command procedures, you can explore how they function by working with them at the DCL prompt, outside of a command procedure.

Opening a File

The OPEN command opens a file for reading or writing. You can use the OPEN command to open either an existing file or a new file. When this command opens a file, it assigns a logical name to the opened file and places the name in the process logical name table. The syntax for the OPEN command is

open *logical-name filespec*

If you do not specify a file type in the file specification, the system will use type DAT as the default type. For example, to open the file VAXBKS.DAT, using the logical name OURFILE, you would type

```
$ open ourfile vaxbks
```

To open a file that is not type DAT, you must include the type. For example, to open the file AI.TXT, you would type

```
$ open aifile ai.txt
```

Once opened, the file is referred to by its logical name.

When you finish working with an opened file, use the CLOSE command to close the file. The CLOSE command deassigns the logical name assigned to the opened file. The syntax for the CLOSE command is

close *logical-name*

7.5.2   *Reading an Open File*

To open a file for reading, use either just the OPEN command or the OPEN command with the /READ qualifier. Because /READ is the default qualifier for the OPEN command, OPEN and OPEN/READ yield the same results. For example, each of the following command lines opens VAXBKS.DAT and prepares it for reading:

```
$ open ourfile vaxbks
```

or

```
$ open/read ourfile vaxbks
```

In each case, the OPEN command sets up a pointer to the first line of the file.

If you are opening a file for reading with OPEN or OPEN/READ, you must specify an existing file.

The READ command is used to read from an opened file. The READ command assigns the contents of a file record to a symbol. A file record is a collection of related items, such as the characters in a line of text. The READ command has the following syntax:

read *logical-name symbol-name*

The logical name is the logical name given the file by the OPEN command. The symbol name is the symbol assigned to the first file record.

Once you have used READ to assign a file record to a symbol, you can use either the WRITE command or the SHOW SYMBOL command to display the value of the symbol. The syntaxes for these two commands are

write sys$output *symbol-name*
show symbol *symbol-name*

In both cases, VMS will display the file record that the READ command has equated to the symbol.

For example, if you open VAXBKS.DAT with the logical name OURFILE, you can use READ to assign the first record to the symbol THISLINE and use WRITE to see the symbol's value.

```
$ read ourfile thisline
$ write sys$output thisline
Kenah, L.J. Goldenberg, R.E. Bate, S.F. VAX/VMS
```

Alternatively, you can use **SHOW SYMBOL** to see the symbol's value.

```
$ show symbol thisline
THISLINE = "Kenah, L.J. Goldenberg, R.E. Bate, S.F.VAX/VMS"
```

After each **READ** operation, the file pointer set up by the **OPEN** command moves to the beginning of the next file record. Thus, you can issue the **READ** command again, assigning the second file record to the symbol, and then view the symbol's new value. In this way, you can read all the records in the file. If you try to read past the end of the file, you get an end-of-file error message.

To explore using the **OPEN**, **READ**, and **CLOSE** commands, follow the steps in Experiment 7.8.

Experiment 7.8   ***Opening and Reading a File***

1. Use EVE, EDT, or the DCL **CREATE** command to create a file containing the following text. Name the file **QUOTE1.TXT**.

   ```
   concurrency control is the activity of coordinating
   accesses to a database in a multiuser database
   management. Concurrency control permits users to
   access a database in a multiprogrammed fashion while
   preserving the illusion that each user is executing
   alone on a dedicated system (Bernstein, P.A., Goodman, N.,
   "Concurrency Control in Distributed Database Systems,"
   ACM Computing Surveys 13 (1981):185-221.)
   ```

2. Open **QUOTE1.TXT** for reading, specifying the logical name **MYFILE**.

   ```
   $ open myfile quote1.txt
   ```

3. Use the **READ** command to assign the file's first record to the symbol **THISLINE**.

   ```
   $ read myfile thisline
   ```

4. Use the **WRITE** command to display the value of the **THISLINE** symbol.

   ```
   $ write sys$output thisline
   concurrency control is the activity of coordinating
   $
   ```

5. Read the next two records of the file, assigning them to the **THISLINE** symbol and displaying the symbol's value.

   ```
   $ read myfile thisline
   $ write sys$output thisline
   ```

```
          accesses to a database in a multiuser database
          $ read myfile thisline
          $ write sys$output thisline
          management. Concurrency control permits users to
          $
```

6. You are finished reading from the open file, so close it.

```
          $ close myfile
```

The **CLOSE** command closes the file and deassigns the logical name.

7.5.3   *Opening a File for Writing*

In addition to opening a file for reading, you can open a file for writing. To do this, use the **OPEN** command with the **/WRITE** qualifier, which prepares a file for writing. This form of the **OPEN** command has the following syntax:

open/write *logical-name filespec*

If the file specification is for a new file, the **OPEN/WRITE** command creates and opens a new file. If the file specification is for an existing file, then the command creates and opens a new file with a version number greater than the highest version of the existing file. This new version of the file will not contain the contents of the old version of the file.

For example, to open and create a new file, **QUOTES.TXT**, you would type

```
          $ open/write newfile quotes.txt
```

To open and create a new version of an existing file, **QUOTE1.TXT**, you would type

```
          $ open/write newfile quote1.txt
```

If **QUOTE1.TXT;2** is the highest version of **QUOTE1.TXT**, the new file will be **QUOTE1.TXT;3**.

The **OPEN/WRITE** command positions the file pointer at the beginning of the opened file. You can then use the **WRITE** command to add records to the file. The syntax for the **WRITE** command is

write *logical-name expression* [, . . .]

The logical name is the logical name of the file given by the **OPEN** command. The expression can be a character string, a value returned by a lexical function, or the value of a symbol, or it can be an expression such as a + b. You may enter a list of expressions separated by commas. If the expression is a character string, you must enclose it in quotation marks. For example, to write a character string as the first line of an opened file, you could type

```
$ write newfile "Collected Quotes:"
```

To enter a blank line, enter " " as the expression. Explore opening a file for writing by following Experiment 7.9.

Opening and Writing to a New File

1. Open a new file named **QUOTES.TXT** for writing. Use the logical name **PEARLS**.

   ```
   $ open/write pearls quotes.txt
   ```

2. Add some lines of text to the **QUOTES.TXT** file.

   ```
   $ write pearls "Collected Quotes:"
   $ write pearls " "
   $ write pearls "The requirements for mastering the art"
   $ write pearls "of memory are visualizing, a desire to"
   $ write pearls "remember, and a love of people. —R. L."
   $ write pearls "Montgomery, Memory Made Easy, NY.:"
   $ write pearls "AMACOM(Amer. Management Assoc.), 1979."
   ```

3. Close the file.

   ```
   $ close pearls
   ```

4. Examine the contents of **QUOTES.TXT** by using the **TYPE** command.

   ```
   $ type quotes.txt
   Collected Quotes:

   The requirements for mastering the art
   of memory are visualizing, a desire to
   remember, and a love of people. —R. L.
   Montgomery, Memory Made Easy, NY.:
   AMACOM(Amer. Management Assoc.), 1979.
   ```

7.5.4   Opening and Appending to a File

If you want to add to an existing version of a file, you can use the **OPEN** command with the **/APPEND** qualifier. The **OPEN/APPEND** command opens an existing file for writing and positions the file pointer at the end of the file. Any records you add using the **WRITE** command are appended to the end of the file.

The **/APPEND** and **/WRITE** qualifiers for the **OPEN** command are mutually exclusive.

This form of the OPEN command has the following syntax:

open/append *logical-name filespec*

Try using the **/APPEND** qualifier to add to the QUOTES.TXT file. Follow the steps in Experiment 7.10.

Experiment 7.10 **Appending to an Existing File**

1. Open the QUOTES.TXT file using the **/APPEND** qualifier.

   ```
   $ open/append pearls quotes.txt
   ```

2. The file pointer is at the end of the file. Append three records to the file.

   ```
   $ write pearls " "
   $ write pearls "Time flies like an arrow."
   $ write pearls "—Anonymous"
   ```

3. Close the file and then examine its contents by using the TYPE command.

   ```
   $ close pearls
   $ type quotes.txt
   Collected Quotes:

   The requirements for mastering the art
   of memory are visualizing, a desire to
   remember, and a love of people. —R. L.
   Montgomery, Memory Made Easy, NY.:
   AMACOM(Amer. Management Assoc.), 1979.

   Time flies like an arrow.
   —Anonymous
   ```

7.5.5 Using File-Handling Commands in a Command Procedure

Now that you are familiar with the file-handling commands OPEN, READ, WRITE, and CLOSE, you can try using them in a command procedure. In Experiment 7.11, you create a command procedure, DTODAY.COM, which creates a file containing the current date and a list of the files created today.

Using File-Handling Commands in a Command Procedure

1. Use EVE, EDT, or the DCL CREATE command to write the following command procedure. Call the command procedure file DTODAY.COM. Remember to begin each line with $.

```
$ ! dtoday.com
$ !
$ ! assign f$time() to a symbol
$ !
$ now = f$time()
$ !
$ ! open a new file for writing
$ ! and write current time and a heading
$ !
$ open/write infile dir.dat
$ write infile now
$ write infile " "
$ write infile "Files created today:"
$ close infile
$ !
$ !open dir.dat and append the list
$ ! of new files created today
$ !
$ open/append infile dir.dat
$ directory/since/output = infile
$ close infile
$ exit
```

2. Execute DTODAY.COM. Then examine the file it created, DIR.DAT, using the TYPE command.

```
$ @dtoday
$ type dir.dat
20-JAN-1990 17:05:57.81

Files created today:

Directory DUA1:[YOURGROUP.YOU]
CDUP.COM;1    DIR.DAT;1    DTODAY.COM;1    GOHOME.COM;1
  .
  .
  .


Total of 8 files.
$
```

3. Each time you execute `DTODAY.COM` a new version of `DIR.DAT` is created with a new time stamp and a new list of files. Execute `DTODAY.COM` again.

```
$ @dtoday
```

Passing Data with Parameters

Command procedures often require that the user provide data to be processed by the procedure. If the data are always the same each time the procedure executes, you can include the data in the command procedure in a data line that follows the command requiring the data. A data line does not begin with $.

If the data are always different each time the procedure executes, you can use one of several mechanisms to specify them. One such mechanism lets you pass the data as one or more parameter values.

There are eight reserved local symbols, P1 through P8, which are called parameters and which are available for use with command procedures. When you invoke a command procedure, you can pass it up to eight parameters, which will automatically be equated to the symbols P1 through P8.

Specify parameters on the command line that invokes the command procedure, separating the parameters with one or more spaces or tabs. A parameter can be a character string, integer, or symbol. For example, you might have a command procedure that adds the parameter values and returns the sum. To execute the procedure, you would type

```
$ @add 13 10 37 8
```

You could add up to eight parameters in this example.

If the parameter is a character string that contains spaces, you must enclose the string in quotation marks. Otherwise, each word will be treated as a separate parameter. For example, to execute a command procedure that requires a name as a parameter, you could type

```
$ @name "Fred Bennett"
```

The entire string would be assigned to P1. If you entered

```
$ @name Fred Bennett
```

Fred would be assigned to P1, and Bennett would be assigned to P2.

VMS assigns the parameters to the parameter symbols sequentially. If you want to skip a parameter symbol, you must enter a null string, " ", for that parameter. For example,

```
$ @data "Fred Bennett" " " "East St"
              (P1)        (P2)    (P3)
```

Experiment 7.12 explores features of using parameters and shows you a method for displaying parameter values.

Experiment 7.12 **Displaying Parameter Values**

1. Use EDT, EVE, or the DCL CREATE command to create the following command procedure. Call the command procedure file SHOWME.COM.

```
$ ! showme.com
$ !
$ ! action: display values of local symbols P1-P8
$ !
$ show symbol/local/all
$ exit
```

2. Execute the SHOWME.COM procedure using two parameters.

```
$ @showme Wolfgang Mozart
P1 = "WOLFGANG"
P2 = "MOZART"
P3 = ""
P4 = ""
P5 = ""
P6 = ""
P7 = ""
P8 = ""
```

In this sample run of SHOWME.COM, local parameters P3 through P8 have null values, which are indicated by the empty pairs of quotation marks.

3. Execute SHOWME.COM again, but this time specify that the name be treated as a single parameter by enclosing it in quotation marks.

```
$ @showme "Wolfgang Mozart"
P1 = "Wolfgang Mozart"
P2 = ""
P3 = ""
P4 = ""
P5 = ""
```

```
P6 = ""
P7 = ""
P8 = ""
```

Now the local parameter P1 has been assigned the string "**Wolfgang Mozart**".

4. Now try running **SHOWME.COM** without any parameters.

```
$ @showme
P1 = ""
P2 = ""
P3 = ""
P4 = ""
P5 = ""
P6 = ""
P7 = ""
P8 = ""
```

This time each of the local symbols P1 through P8 has a null value.

If you attempt to enter more than eight parameters, VMS will give you the following error message:

```
$ @showme a b c d e f g h i
%DCL-W-DEFOVE too many command procedure parameters—limit
to eight.
$
```

You can pass the value of a symbol by enclosing the symbol in apostrophes ('). For example,

```
$ dowjones = "1936"
$ @showme 'dowjones'
P1 = "1936"
P2 = ""
P3 = ""
P4 = ""
P5 = ""
P6 = ""
P7 = ""
P8 = ""
```

The apostrophes request symbol substitution. In other words, '**dowjones**' requests that the value of 1936 be substituted when this parameter is passed to **SHOWME.COM.** You could verify this by leaving out the apostrophes:

```
$ dowjones = "1936"
$ @showme dowjones
P1 = "dowjones"
P2 = ""
P3 = ""
P4 = ""
P5 = ""
P6 = ""
P7 = ""
P8 = ""
```

To request symbol substitution for a symbol within a character string, put *two* apostrophes before it and one apostrophe after it. For example,

```
$ samplesymbol = " The Vikings can beat the Redskins!"
$ write sys$output "Superbowl_talk: ''samplesymbol'"
Superbowl_talk: The Vikings can beat the Redskins!
```

Passing Data with the INQUIRE Command

When you use parameters to pass data to a command procedure, you must know what parameters the procedure requires. The procedure does not prompt you for them.

The INQUIRE command can be used in a command procedure to prompt for an input value during the execution of a procedure. This command has the following syntax:

inquire *symbol-name* [*prompt-string*]

The symbol name is the symbol that will be equated to the data you enter. The prompt string is the prompt that displays on the screen telling you what data are required.

For example, to prompt for the count value, you would type

```
$ inquire count "count"
count: 2010
```

To see the value of the count symbol, you could then type

```
$ show symbol count
COUNT = "2010"
```

Notice that DCL automatically appends a colon and a space to the prompt string. You can prevent this by using the INQUIRE command with the /NOPUNCTUATION qualifier. For example,

```
$ inquire/nopunctuation count "count? "
count? 2011
```

Concatenating Strings

The + operator makes it possible to concatenate, or glue together, strings. You might concatenate strings when you assign a symbol value. Concatenation of two strings has the following syntax:

symbol **=** *firststring* **+** *secondstring*

For example,

```
$ here = "Wobegon, Minnesota"
$ write sys$output "Lake " + here
Lake Wobegon, Minnesota
```

One practical application of string concatenation can be seen in Experiment 7.13. The command procedure in this experiment simplifies specifying files for the **PURGE** and **DELETE** commands. It copies the specified files and deletes the original files. You can use it to move files to another directory.

Experiment 7.13 **Concatenating Strings in a Command Procedure**

1. Use EDT, EVE, or the DCL **CREATE** command to create the following command procedure. Call the command procedure file **MV.COM**.

```
$ ! mv.com
$ !
$ ! action: copy specified files and delete originals
$ !          (perform equivalent of UNIX mv command)
$ !
$ wildcard = p1 + ";*"
$ copy/log 'p1' 'p2'
$ delete/confirm 'wildcard'
$ exit
```

This procedure requires two parameters. The first parameter, P1, is the file specification for the file or files you want copied. The second parameter, P2, is the directory to which the files should be copied. The wildcard symbol is assigned to the value of the first parameter, the file specification, concatenated with the specification for all versions of the file. Thus, the **DELETE** command will delete all versions of the specified files.

2. Before trying out the command procedure, create a subdirectory called **QUOTES**.

```
$ create/directory [.quotes]
```

3. Use the GOHOME command procedure to move back to your login directory.

```
$ @gohome
```

4. Now use the MV.COM procedure to move QUOTE1.TXT and QUOTES.TXT to the new subdirectory.

```
$ @mv quote*.txt [.quotes]
%COPY-S-COPIED, DUA1:[YOURGROUP.YOU]QUOTE1.TXT;1 copied to
DUA1:[YOURGROUP.YOU.QUOTES]QUOTE1.TXT;1 (1 block)
%COPY-S-COPIED, DUA1:[YOURGROUP.YOU]QUOTES.TXT;1 copied to
DUA1:[YOURGROUP.YOU.QUOTES]QUOTES.TXT;1 (1 block)
%COPY-S-NEWFILES, 2 files created
DELETE DUA1:[YOURGROUP.YOU]QUOTE1.TXT;1? [N]
```

5. Because of the /CONFIRM qualifier used with the DELETE command, you must confirm whether the files should be deleted from their original location. Confirm the deletions.

```
DELETE DUA1:[YOURGROUP.YOU]QUOTE1.TXT;1? [N] Yes
DELETE DUA1:[YOURGROUP.YOU]QUOTES.TXT;1? [N] Yes
$
```

6. Get a directory listing of the files in the QUOTES directory.

```
$ directory [.quotes]
Directory DUA1:[YOURGROUP.YOU.QUOTES]
QUOTE1.TXT;1     QUOTES.TXT;1
Total of 2 files.
$
```

7.9 Conditional Execution of Command Procedures

The IF command makes possible conditional execution inside a command procedure. The IF command tests the value of a condition and causes a DCL command to be executed when the condition is true. This command has the following syntax:

if *condition* **then** *command*

The condition used in an IF command line can be one or more numeric constants, string literals, symbols, or lexical functions separated by logical, arithmetic, or string operators. DCL has a rich selection of logical operators that can be used to form expressions. These operators are given in Table 7.2.

There are many applications of the IF command. For example, Experiment 7.14 creates one command procedure that combines the operations of CDUP.COM and GOHOME.COM.

Table 7.2 Logical Operators

Operator	Result	Example
.EQS.	Tests if two character strings are equal	`if p1 .eqs. "y" then recall/all`
.GES.	Tests if the first string is greater than or equal to the second string	`if p1 .ges. " " then recall/all`
.GTS.	Tests if the first string is greater than the second	`if p1 .gts. " " then gohome`
.LES.	Tests if the first string is less than or equal to the second string	`if p1 .les. "aha" then directory`
.LTS.	Tests if the first string is less than the second string	`if p1 .lts. "yes" then recall 1`
.NES.	Tests if two strings are not equal	`if p1 .nes. "no" then directory`
.EQ.	Tests if two integer expressions are equal	`if n .eq. 1 then recall/all`
.GE.	Tests if the first integer expression is greater than or equal to the second integer expression	`if n .ge. 0 then exit`
.GT.	Tests if the first integer expression is greater than the second integer expression	`if n .gt. 50 then exit`
.LE.	Tests if the first integer expression is less than or equal to the second integerexpression	`if n .le. 9 then directory`
.LT.	Tests if the first integer expression is less than the second integer expression	`if n .lt. 1 then exit`
.NE.	Tests if two integer expressions are not equal	`if n .ne. 0 then recall/all`
.AND.	Combines two expressions with a logical AND	`if (p1 .eqs. "y") .and. (p2 .nes. "n") then directory`
.OR.	Combines two expressions with a logical OR	`if (p1 .ges. "n") .or. (p2 .nes. "y") then recall/all`
.NOT.	Logically negates an expression	`x = 1 if .not. x then recall/all`

Using the IF Command in a Command Procedure

1. Use EDT, EVE, or the DCL CREATE command to create the following command procedure. Call the command procedure file CD.COM.

```
$ ! cd.com
$ !
$ ! action: change to directory one level below or
$ !         one level up from the current directory
$ !
$ if p1 .eqs. "" then set default [-]
$ if p1 .nes. "" then set default [.'p1']
$ show default
$ exit
```

This procedure references one parameter, the specification for your login directory. If you do not specify a directory, P1 will be null and the procedure will move up one directory level. If you specify a directory one level down, P1 will not equal null, and the procedure will move down to that directory.

2. Before trying the command procedure, simplify the use of CD.COM by creating a global symbol in your LOGIN.COM file. Add the following line to the global symbols section of LOGIN.COM. If LOGIN.COM already has this symbol defined, edit the line as follows:

```
$ cd == "@cd"
```

3. Reexecute LOGIN.COM.

```
$ @login
```

4. Now use the procedure to move up one directory level.

```
$ cd
DUA1:[YOURGROUP]
```

5. Use the procedure to move down one directory level. Enter cd and a subdirectory name without the brackets or period.

```
$ cd you
DUA1:[YOURGROUP.YOU]
```

Branching with the GOTO Command

The GOTO command causes a branch to a labeled location, transferring execution of the command procedure to the commands in that location. You can use GOTO to go around a segment of commands based on a condition tested with the IF command. The syntax for the GOTO command is

goto *label*

A label is a name assigned to a command or group of commands in the procedure. The label appears before the command or command and always has a colon (:) suffix. The GOTO command transfers execution to those commands.

Arithmetic Operators

If you need to manipulate numbers within command procedures, you can use arithmetic operators to do so. For instance, you may need to add parameter values or divide the first parameter by the second. Table 7.3 lists the arithmetic operators.

Examine the following command procedure to see how the arithmetic operators are used in this example of computing averages. As you examine the example, notice also the use of the IF and GOTO commands.

```
$ ! av.com
$ !
$ ! action: compute arithmetic average
$ !
$ count = 1
$ sum = 0
$ while:
$     inquire term "term (enter positive integer, or 0 to stop)"
$     if term .eq. 0 then goto doorway
$     sum = sum + term
$     count = count + 1
$     goto while
$ doorway:
$     result = sum / count
$     write sys$output "count   sum   average"
$     write sys$output count, " ", sum, " ", result
$ exit
```

In this procedure, as long as you enter a nonzero value in response to the prompt **term (enter positive integer, or 0 to stop)**, a new value of SUM and COUNT will be computed and control will be transferred back to the WHILE

Table 7.3   Arithmetic Operators

Operator	Result	Example
*	Multiplies two numbers	`count = count * 2`
/	Divides two numbers	`tally = count / 4`
+	Adds two numbers	`sum = sum + 1`
-	Subtracts two numbers	`diff = sum - 1`

label. If you enter a zero, control transfers to the line of this procedure labeled DOORWAY. There are lots of variations to this procedure that you might want to try.

7.12   Debugging Techniques

If a command procedure does not execute as you expected, you need to discover where the error in the procedure occurred. DCL offers a variety of tools that can be used in debugging a faulty command procedure. Table 7.4 lists a selection of these tools.

The SET VERIFY command is easy to use and is helpful in tracing what happens during the execution of a command procedure. SET VERIFY displays each line of the procedure before it is executed so that you can see the line that generated the error. This command and its counterpart, SET NOVERIFY, are used in the following context:

```
$ set verify
$ !
$ ! sequence of commands you want to trace
$ !
$ set noverify
```

For example, you could modify AV.COM, the command procedure that computes averages, to trace the actions in the While loop of the procedure (the changes to the file appear in color):

```
$ ! av.com
$ ! version 1.1
$ !
```

Table 7.4 Debugging Tools

Command	Result
SET VERIFY	Traces the execution of commands in the procedure
SET NOVERIFY	Turns off verify mode
SHOW SYMBOL	Displays the values of local symbols P1 through P8 as well as any other symbols used in the procedure

```
$ ! action: compute arithmetic average
$ !
$ count = 1
$ sum = 0
$ set verify
$ while:
$    inquire term "term (enter positive integer, or 0 to stop)"
$    if term .eq. 0 then goto doorway
$    sum = sum + term
$    count = count + 1
$    goto while
$ doorway:
$    set noverify
$    result = sum / count
$    write sys$output "count   sum   average"
$    write sys$output count, " ", sum, " ", result
$ exit
```

You could also try using the **SHOW SYMBOL** command to display the symbol values of the symbols involved in the error.

7.13   *Responding to Execution Errors*

You can use the **ON** command to branch to an error-handling section of a command procedure when an error occurs. For example, the following procedure, **LEAVE.CO**, automates purging and deletion of unneeded files (in this case, of type **OBJ**) when you log out:

```
$ ! leave.com
$ !
$ ! action: purge current directory and delete files of
$ !         type obj
$ on error then goto doorway
$ purge
$ delete/confirm *.obj;*
```

```
$ goto clean_exit
$ doorway:
$    write sys$output "Sorry, there are no files of type obj"
$    logout
$ clean_exit:
$    write sys$output "Purged, deleted files of type obj"
$    write sys$output "completed at: "
$    show time
$    logout
$ exit
```

When no files of type OBJ exist, an error condition occurs. When the error occurs, the procedure displays a message and then logs out. Otherwise, the files are deleted, the procedure displays a message to that effect, and then the procedure logs out.

7.14   Commenting Techniques

In the design of command procedures, there are some fairly simple commenting techniques that you should routinely use to clarify the actions of the procedures. Table 7.5 lists the types of comments.

Preconditions and postconditions are assertions that specify the *required* input and output for the command procedure. For example, you could change AV.COM so that it contained comments explaining the required parameters and the resulting output (the changes to the file appear in color):

```
$ ! filename: av.com
$ ! version 1.2
$ !
$ ! precondition: 0 or more positive integers
$ ! postcondition: (1) number of entries averaged
$ !                (2) sum of entries
$ !                (3) average entry value
$ !
$ ! action: compute arithmetic average
$ !
$ count = 1
$ sum = 0
$ set verify
$ while:
$    inquire term "term (enter positive integer, or 0 to stop)"
$    if term .eq. 0 then goto doorway
$    sum = sum + term
```

Table 7.5 Types of Comments

Type	Example
File specification	`! forever.com`
	`! version 1.0`
Preconditions (required input)	`! pre: p1 = file type`
Postconditions (required output)	`! post: print average value`
Action	`! action: purge specified directory`

```
$    count = count + 1
$    goto while
$ doorway:
$    set noverify
$    result = sum / count
$    write sys$output "count   sum   average"
$    write sys$output count, " ", sum, " ", result
$ exit
```

7.15   Summary

Command procedures offer a means of simplifying the daily use of your system. This simplification starts with collecting commonly used groups of command lines that you find yourself repeatedly having to enter. Once you have a command procedure, it is simple to execute it:

`$ @command-procedure-specification`

Chief among the command procedures you will want to maintain and refine is your LOGIN.COM file. This command procedure makes it possible to customize your working environment. Thanks to your LOGIN.COM file, you have a means of tailoring your VMS environment to your individual needs.

It is also helpful to become comfortable with the creation and use of logical names and symbols. With logical names, you can simplify the entry of complex file specifications. With symbols, you can simplify the entry of commands. For example, suppose your name is Abbot in the Music department. The Music department is listed in the directory ALLDEPTS, which is a directory of all departments. Then you can create the following logical name for your login directory:

`$ define homeplate dual:[alldepts.music.abbot]`

Then for any command procedure you have in your login directory, you can employ the **HOMEPLATE** logical name to specify the access path for these procedures. For instance, if you are in your **VMS** subdirectory and want to list your **LOGIN.COM** file in your login directory, you would just type

```
$ type homeplate:login.com
```

You can also experiment with assigning commonly used command lines to global symbols. For example,

```
$ showlog == "type homeplate:login.com"
```

The use of logical names and global symbols can become the basis for various refinements of your **LOGIN.COM** file. As a result, you should find that your use of your local system becomes easier and more enjoyable.

Tables 7.6 and 7.7 present the commands and important terms used in this chapter.

7.16   Exercises

1. When is your **LOGIN.COM** automatically executed?

2. Construct simple, complete command procedures to accomplish the following tasks, and give sample runs for each procedure:

    a. Delete, with confirmation, all your files of type **DAT**, and list the remaining files in your current directory.

    b. Delete, with confirmation, all your files of type **TXT**, and list the remaining files in your current directory.

    c. Produce a combination of (a) and (b).

3. One procedure can execute another one. Write a command procedure called **STEP**, which calls a procedure called **STEP2**, which in turn calls a procedure called **STEP3**, which in turn calls a procedure called **STEP4**. Each time one of these procedures is executed, have it print the message "Hello, this is procedure *name*."

4. Give an example of a command line that starts with @showme (see Experiment 7.12) and that does the following:

    a. Has eight parameters, each of which is a pair of words.

    b. Has one parameter with eight pairs of words.

    c. Has one parameter with Mozart's full name.

5. Write a command procedure named **GOV.COM** that does the following:

Table 7.6 DCL Commands

Command	Result
CLOSE	Closes a file
EXIT	Terminates the execution of a command procedure
GOTO	Directs the flow of execution to a label that identifies a block of commands
IF	Tests the value of an expression and executes a given command if the result of the expression is true
INQUIRE	Issues a prompt, reads the user's response from the terminal, and assigns it to a symbol
ON	Specifies an action to be performed if an error occurs
OPEN	Opens a file for reading or writing
READ	Reads a single record from a specified input file and assigns the contents of the record to a specified symbol name
RECALL	Displays previously entered commands so that you can reprocess them
SET NOVERIFY	Inhibits the displaying of command and data lines in a procedure as the system reads the procedure (the default condition)
SET VERIFY	Causes the system to display each command or data line in a procedure as it reads the procedure
WRITE	Writes specified data to the output file indicated by the logical name

a. Uses the local parameter P1 to determine whether to branch to your **VMS** subdirectory or to any of the following subdirectories:

Subdirectory **VMS1** in **VMS**
Subdirectory **VMS2** in **VMS**
Subdirectory **VMS3** in **VMS**
Subdirectory **VMS4** in **VMS**

For example, if you type **@gov**, you will branch to **VMS**. If you type **@gov 2**, you will branch to **VMS2** in **VMS**, and so on.

b. Displays the name of the new subdirectory. Give the sample runs that result from typing each of the following:

Table 7.7   Important Terms

Term	Definition
Command level	Equated with the input stream for DCL; it is at level 0 when you log in, and each subsequent execution of a command procedure changes the command level
Command procedure	File of commands
Global	Command language symbol that is accessible at all command levels
Label	Name assigned to a statement or group of statements
Literal	Character string enclosed in quotes, or a number
Local	Command language symbol that is accessible only at the current command level and lower levels
Postcondition	Required output for a command procedure
Precondition	Required input for a command procedure
Symbol	Name representing a character string or an integer value

```
$ @gov
$ @gov 2
$ @gov 1
$ @gov 3
```

6. Enhance the GOV.COM procedure created in exercise 5 so that it uses P2 to decide whether or not to display a copy of the new subdirectory.

7. Create a logical symbol that makes it possible for you to execute the GOV.COM procedure from exercise 5 from any of your directories. Give some sample runs.

8. Create a global symbol that makes it possible for you to execute the GOV.COM procedure from exercise 5 by typing g, go, or gov to change to your VMS subdirectories. With this new symbol, for example, you should be able to change to your VMS1 subdirectory by typing any of the following:

```
$ g 1
$ go 1
$ gov 1
```

Give some sample runs.

9. Incorporate the global symbol from exercise 8 into your **LOGIN.COM** file and do the following:

   a. Give a listing of the new version of **LOGIN.COM**.

   b. Give sample runs to verify that the new version works correctly.

10. Write a command procedure named **ERASE.COM** that uses the P1 parameter to select all files of type **P1** to purge. Give sample runs with the following:

    a. Files of type **OBJ**

    b. Files of type **DAT**

11. Enhance **ERASE.COM** from exercise 10 so that it receives confirmation from you before files of type **P1** are purged. Give some sample runs.

12. Enhance **ERASE.COM** so that it purges all the files in your current directory if P1 is null.

13. Create a global symbol that makes it possible to execute **ERASE.COM** by typing any of the following:

    ```
    $  e      parameter
    $  er     parameter
    $  era    parameter
    $  eras   parameter
    $  erase  parameter
    ```

    Give some sample runs.

14. Incorporate the global symbol from exercise 13 into your **LOGIN.COM** file and do the following:

    a. Give a listing of the new version of **LOGIN.COM**.

    b. Execute **LOGIN.COM** and then verify that the new global symbol works by doing the following:

       (1) Create empty files **AI.SKY**;x, for $x = 1, \ldots , 10$.

       (2) Create empty files **BI.RED**;x, for $x = 1, \ldots , 5$.

       (3) Create empty files **CI.TNT**;x, for $x = 1, 2$.

       (4) Purge files of type **SKY**.

       (5) Purge files of type **RED**.

       (6) Purge files of type **TNT**.

15. Enhance **ERASE.COM** from exercise 13 so that it uses parameters P1, P2, and P3 in the following ways:

   a. If P1 is null, it purges all files in your current directory and eliminates all but the most recent version of each file.

   b. If P1 is not null, it purges all files of type **P1**.

   c. If P2 is not null, it purges all files of type **P2** as well as files of type **P1**.

   d. If P3 is not null, it purges all files of type **P3** as well as files of types **P1** and **P2**.

   Give sample runs of the new version of **ERASE.COM** by creating new versions of the files of type **SKY**, **RED**, and **TNT** from exercise 14.

16. (Debugging) Enhance the **ERASE.COM** file from exercise 13 with error-checking command lines so that it does the following:

   a. Prints a "you need 2 parameters" error message and exits if P2 is not null and P1 is null.

   b. Prints a "you need 3 parameters" error message and exits if P3 is not null and either P1 or P2 is null.

   Give some sample runs.

7.17   Review Quiz

Indicate whether the following statements are true or false:

1. Any file of type **COM** is a command procedure.

2. A command procedure containing only the following line cannot be executed:

   ```
   $ !
   ```

3. A command procedure **YES.COM** can be executed by typing either **@yes** or **@yes.com**.

4. A value is assigned to a global symbol with the = operator.

5. Assuming the symbol **G*OPHER** represents a command line, that command line can be entered by typing **g**.

6. Command procedures always have a minimum of nine local symbols.

7. If command procedure **YES.COM** is executed by typing **@yes**, then P1 of **YES.COM** is null when the execution of **YES.COM** begins.

The next three statements refer to execution of the command procedure `YES.COM` using the following command line:

```
$ @yes I think he said "Hello, Sam!" twice
```

8. Parameter P7 of `YES.COM` will be null.

9. Parameter P5 will be `Hello,`.

10. Every parameter in `YES.COM` will not be null.

7.18   Further Reading

Marotta, R. E., ed. *The Digital Dictionary: A Guide to Digital Equipment Corporation's Technical Terminology.* Bedford, Mass.: Digital Press, 1985.

Pike, Richard, and B. W. Kernighan. Program Design in the UNIX Environment. *AT&T Bell Laboratories Technical Journal* 63 (no. 8, pt 2, Oct. 1984): 1595–1605.

Order from Digital Equipment Corporation, POB CS2008, Nashua, NH 03061:

Guide to Using VMS Command Procedures. Order no. AA-LA11A-TE.

VMS DCL Dictionary. Order no. AA-LA12A-TE.

VMS General User's Manual. Order no. AA-LA98A-TE.

Appendix A

Reference Guide to
Selected DCL Commands

APPEND

Appends one or more specified input files to the end of a specified output file.

Syntax

append *input-filespec* [, . . .] *output-filespec*

Example

```
$ append tool_box.com login.com
```

ASSIGN

Creates a logical name and assigns an equivalence string, or a list of strings, to the specified logical name.

Syntax

assign *equivalence-name* [, . . .] *logical-name*[:]

Example

```
$ assign test_data.lst sys$output
```

Command Qualifiers

/GROUP	Places the logical name in the group logical name table. Other users with the same UIC group number can access the logical name.
/PROCESS	Places the logical name in the process logical name table. If a logical name table is not specified with this command, the logical name will be placed in the process logical name table by default.
/USER_MODE	Logical names assigned with user mode are placed in the process logical name table and are used during the execution of a single image.

BASIC (compiled)

Activates the VAX BASIC compiler.

Syntax

basic [*filespec* [, . . .]]

If one or more file specifications are supplied, BASIC will compile the source file(s). If each source file specification is separated by commas, BASIC will compile each module separately and produce multiple object files.

Example

```
$ basic sample1, sample2
```

If each source file specification is separated by a plus sign (+), BASIC will append the files and produce a single object module.

Example

```
$ basic sample1 + sample2
```

BASIC (interactive)

Activates the VAX BASIC interactive programming environment.

Syntax

basic

Example

```
$ BASIC
VAX BASIC 3.2
Ready
```

For further information, type the word **HELP** after activating the BASIC programming environment.

CLOSE

Closes a file that was opened for input or output with the OPEN command.

Syntax

close *logical-name*

Example

```
$ close test_file
```

CONTINUE

Resumes execution of a DCL command, a program, or a command procedure that was interrupted by pressing <CTRL/y> or <CTRL/c>. This command also serves as the target command for an IF or ON command in a command procedure.

Syntax

continue

Example 1

```
$ run test_program
<CTRL/y>
$ show users
```

```
                VAX/VMS Interactive Users
                24-OCT-1987 20:07:34.60
                Total number of interactive users = 5

Username          Process           Name PID      Terminal
BBTHOMPSON        BBTHOMPSON        00001D8A      TXE4:
CABAUMHOVER       CABAUMHOVER       00001DB2      TXF1:
JJLYNCH           JJLYNCH           00001B29      TXE5:
PAT               PAT               00001AB0      TXB2:
SJPERRY           SJPERRY           00001AA2      TXC3:
$ continue
```
```
[text_program execution continues]
```

Example 2

```
$ on error then continue
```

COPY

Makes a copy of the specified input file(s) and stores the contents in the specified output file.

Syntax

copy *input-filespec* [, . . .] *output-filespec*

Example 1

```
$ copy login_backup.com login.com
```

Example 2

```
$ copy test_data_3.dat,test_data_2.dat test_data_1.dat
```

CREATE

Creates a new sequential file that contains the typed input or commands entered at the DCL level. The command is terminated and the file closed after <CTRL/z> key press.

Syntax

create *filespec* [, . . .]

Example

```
$ create test.dat
13579
24680
12450
<CTRL/z>
$
```

Command Qualifier

/PROTECTION = (*code*)   Defines the protection to be assigned to the file.

CREATE/DIRECTORY

Creates a new directory or subdirectory for cataloging files.

Syntax

create/directory *directory-specification* [, . . .]

Example

```
$ create/directory [.basic]
```

Command Qualifier

/PROTECTION = (*code*)   Defines the protection to be applied to the directory.

DEASSIGN

Removes a logical name assignment from the specified logical name table.

Syntax

deassign [*logical-name*[:]]

Example

```
$ deassign sys$output
```

Command Qualifiers

/GROUP	Specifies that the logical name is in the group logical name table.
/PROCESS	Specifies that the logical name is in the process logical name table.
/USER_MODE	Specifies that the logical name is in the process name table.

DEFINE

Creates a logical name and assigns an equivalence string, or a list of strings, to the specified logical name.

Syntax

define *logical-name equivalence-string* [, . . .]

Example

```
$ define sys$output test.dat
```

Command Qualifiers

/GROUP	Places the logical name in the group logical name table. Other users with the same UIC group number can access the logical name.
/PROCESS	Places the logical name in the process logical name table. If a logical name table is not specified with this command, the logical name will be placed in the process logical name table by default.
/USER_MODE	Logical names assigned with user mode are placed in the process logical name table and are used during the execution of a single image.

DEFINE/KEY

Assigns a set of attributes and an equivalence string to a specified key on the terminal keyboard.

Syntax

define/key *key-name equivalence-string*

Example

```
$ define/key PF1 "show users" /terminate
```

Command Qualifiers

/[NO]ECHO   Controls whether the equivalence string is displayed on the terminal.

/TERMINATE   Inserts carriage-return/line-feed characters after the specified key press. Similar to pressing <RETURN> after typing a command.

DELETE

Deletes one or more files from a user directory.

Syntax

DELETE *filespec; version-number* [, . . .]

Example 1

```
$ delete test.dat;1
```

Example 2

```
$ delete letter.txt;*
```

DELETE/ENTRY

Deletes one or more plant or batch job entries from a specified queue.

Syntax

delete/entry = *entry-number queue-name*[:]

Example

```
$ delete/entry = 231 sys$print
```

DELETE/KEY

Removes the key definition for a specified terminal key established using the **DEFINE/KEY** command.

Syntax

delete/key [*key-name*]

Example

```
$ delete/key PF1
```

DIRECTORY

Displays a list of files stored in a specified user directory and its corresponding information. If no file specification is given, information for the current directory will be displayed.

Syntax

directory [*filespec* [, . . .]]

Example

```
$ directory [.basic]*.bas
```

Command Qualifiers

/[NO]DATE	Displays the backup, creation, expiration, and modification dates for each specified file.
/FULL	Displays all relevant information about a specified file.
/PROTECTION	Displays the file protection for the specified file.
/[NO]SIZE	Displays the file size in blocks used for the specified file.
/TOTAL	Suppresses the listing of all file information and only displays the trailing lines.

EXIT

Terminates the processing of the current command procedure.

Syntax

exit

Example

```
$ show users
$ exit
```

GOTO

Transfers control to a specified label statement within a DCL command procedure.

Syntax

goto *label*

Example

```
$ if pl .eqs. "stop" then GOTO done
$ show users
$ done:
```

HELP

Displays information on a specified topic (for example, DCL commands).

Syntax

help [*keyword*]

Example

```
$ help copy
```

IF

Tests the value of an expression and executes the command following the
THEN keyword if the test is true.

Syntax

if *test-expression* **then** *do-command*

Example

```
$ if p1 .neq. "stop" then goto fetch_nxt_num
```

INQUIRE

Allows for interactive input from the terminal.

Syntax

inquire *symbol-name* [*prompt-string*]

Example

```
$ inquire name "Enter your name"
```

Command Qualifier

/[NO] **PUNCTUATION**   Controls whether a colon (:) and a space will be dis-
                              played after the prompt message.

LINK

Activates the VAX linker to link one or more object modules into a program
image.

Syntax

link *filespec* [, . . .]

Example

```
$ link random
```

LOGOUT

Ends an interactive user session.

Syntax

logout

Example

```
$ logout
```

Command Qualifiers

/BRIEF	Displays the user name, date, and time.
/FULL	Displays a summary of accounting information.
/[NO]HANGUP	Controls whether the phone connected to your terminal will be hung up.

MAIL

Activates the VMS Mail utility.

Syntax

mail [*filespec*][*recipient-name*]

Example

```
$ mail
```

MERGE

Activates the VMS Sort utility to combine from two to ten similarly sorted files and creates a single output file.

Syntax

merge *input-filespec-1*, *input-filespec-2* [, . . .] *output-filespec*

Example

```
$ merge test_1.dat,test_2.dat final.dat
```

ON

Defines the default courses of action when a command or program within a command procedure encounters an error condition or is interrupted by a <CTRL/y>.

Syntax

on *condition* **then** *command*

Example

```
$ on error then goto exit
```

OPEN

Opens a file for reading or writing.

Syntax

open *logical-name*[:] *filespec*

Example

```
$ open test_data final_1.dat
```

PHONE

Activates the VMS Phone utility, which allows a user to communicate with other users during an interactive session.

Syntax

phone [*phone-command*]

Example

```
$ phone
```

PRINT

Sends one or more files to a particular print queue.

Syntax

print *filespec* [, . . .]

Example

```
$ print us_history.rpt
```

Command Qualifiers

/[NO]NOTIFY	Controls whether a message will be displayed on your terminal once the file has finished printing.
/QUEUE = *queue-name*[:]	Places the file to be printed into a specified print queue.

PURGE

Deletes all files located within a specified user directory except the highest-numbered version(s).

Syntax

purge [*filespec* [, . . .]]

Example

```
$ purge
```

Command Qualifier

/KEEP = *n*	Specifies the number of versions of the specified files to be retained in the directory.

RECALL

Displays up to the last 20 commands for reprocessing.

Syntax

recall [*command-qualifier*]

Example

$ `recall show`

Command Qualifier

/ALL   Displays all the commands currently stored in the
                                   Recall buffer.

RENAME

Allows you to change the file specification of one or more files to a specified
output file specification.

Syntax

rename *input-filespec* [, . . .] *output-filespec*

Example

$ `rename test.dat final.dat`

RUN

Activates a specified program image.

Syntax

run *filespec*

Example

$ `run square_roots`

SEARCH

Searches for a specified string or strings in one or more files and lists all
lines containing occurrences of the strings.

Syntax

search *filespec* [, . . .] *search-string* [, . . .]

Example

$ `search resume.txt VAX`

SET DEFAULT

Changes the default device or directory name for the current process.

Syntax

set default *device-name*[:][*filespec*]

Example

$ set default [.basic]

SET FILE

Modifies file characteristics.

Syntax

set file *filespec* [, . . .]

Example

$ set file test.dat

Command Qualifiers

/PROTECTION [= (*code*)]	Allows you to change or reset the protection for one or more files.
/VERSION_LIMIT [= *n*]	Specifies the maximum number of file versions a file can have.

SET PASSWORD

Allows for a password to be changed by the current user of an account.

Syntax

set password

Example

$ set password
Old password: (*typed characters will not be echo*ed)
New password: (*typed characters will not be echo*ed)
Verification: (*typed characters will not be echo*ed)

SET PROCESS

Changes the characteristics of the specified process. If no process is specified, changes the characteristics of the current process.

Syntax

set process [*process-name*]

Example

$ set process

Command Qualifier

/NAME = *string*   Changes the name of the current process.

SET PROMPT

Allows the current user to change the default DCL prompt.

Syntax

set prompt [= *string*]

Example

$ set prompt = "Home> "

SET PROTECTION

Changes the protection for a specified file or files.

Syntax

set protection [= (*code*)] *filespec* [, . . .]

Example

$ set protection = (W:RWED) final.dat

SET TERMINAL

Changes the system's interpretation of the terminal characteristics.

Syntax

set terminal [*device_name*[:]]

Example

$ set terminal/line_editing

Command Qualifiers

/INSERT   Characters will be inserted when editing command lines.

/[NO]LINE_EDITING   Enables the advanced line-editing features for editing command lines.

/OVERSTRIKE   Characters will be overwritten when editing command lines.

SHOW DEFAULT

Displays the current default device and directory names.

Syntax

show default

Example

$ show default

SHOW KEY

Displays the key definition for a specified key.

Syntax

show key [*key-name*]

Example

$ show key PF1

SHOW LOGICAL

Displays a logical name and its equivalence string or all logical names in one or more logical name tables.

Syntax

show logical [*logical-name*[:]]

Example

$ show logical sys$output

Command Qualifiers

/ALL	Displays all logical names in the specified logical name table.
/GROUP	Displays the logical name in the group logical name table.
/PROCESS	Displays the logical name in the process logical name table.

SHOW PROCESS

Displays information about a process and any subprocess in the current process tree.

Syntax

show process [*process-name*]

Example

$ show process

SHOW PROTECTION

Displays the current file protection that is applied to any new files created during the current interactive terminal session or batch job.

Syntax

show protection

Example

$ show protection

SHOW QUEUE

Displays information about a specified print or batch queue.

Syntax

show queue [*queue-name*]

Example

$ show queue sys$print

SHOW QUOTA

Displays the current disk quota that is authorized to the current user.

Syntax

show quota

Example

$ show quota

SHOW SYMBOL

Displays the current value of a local or global symbol.

Syntax

show symbol [*symbol-name*]

Example

$ show symbol my_basic

Command Qualifiers

/ALL	Displays all symbols in the specified symbol table.
/GLOBAL	Displays only the symbols in the global symbol table.
/LOCAL	Displays only the symbols in the local symbol table.

SHOW SYSTEM

Displays a list of processes in the system and information about the status of each one.

Syntax

show system

Example

$ show system

SHOW TERMINAL

Displays the current terminal characteristics of a specified terminal.

Syntax

show terminal [*device-name*[:]]

Example

$ show terminal

SHOW TIME

Displays the current date and time.

Syntax

show [day]time

Example

$ show time

SHOW USERS

Displays information pertaining to the current interactive users.

Syntax

show users [*username*]

Example

$ show users

SORT

Activates the VMS Sort utility to reorder the records in a file into a defined sequence and place them in a new file.

Syntax

sort *input-filespec* [, . . .] *output-filespec*

Example

$ sort temp.dat final.dat

SPAWN

Suspends the current process and creates a new process (subprocess).

Syntax

spawn [*command-string*]

Example

$ spawn phone

STOP/QUEUE/ENTRY

Stops the executing job on the specified batch queue.

Syntax

stop/queue/entry = *entry-number queue-name*[:]

Example

```
$ stop/queue/entry = 1234 sys$batch
```

SUBMIT

Submits one or more command procedures to a specified batch job queue.

Syntax

submit *filespec*

Example

```
$ submit square_roots
```

Appendix B

Tables

Table B.1 ASCII Characters

Char	Dec	Octal	Hex	Char	Dec	Octal	Hex	Char	Dec	Octal	Hex
Nul	0	0	0	+	43	53	2B	V	86	126	56
^A	1	1	1	,	44	54	2C	W	87	127	57
^B	2	2	2	-	45	55	2D	X	88	130	58
^C	3	3	3	.	46	56	2E	Y	89	131	59
^D	4	4	4	/	47	57	2F	Z	90	132	5A
^E	5	5	5	0	48	60	30	[	91	133	5B
^F	6	6	6	1	49	61	31	\	92	134	5C
bell	7	7	7	2	50	62	32	]	93	135	5D
bksp	8	10	8	3	51	63	33	^	94	136	5E
tab	9	11	9	4	52	64	34	_	95	137	5F
lnfeed	10	12	A	5	53	65	35	`	96	140	60
vtab	11	13	B	6	54	66	36	a	97	141	61
ff	12	14	C	7	55	67	37	b	98	142	62
cr	13	15	D	8	56	70	38	c	99	143	63
^N	14	16	E	9	57	71	39	d	100	144	64
^O	15	17	F	:	58	72	3A	e	101	145	65
^P	16	20	10	;	59	73	3B	f	102	146	66
^Q	17	21	11	<	60	74	3C	g	103	147	67
^R	18	22	12	=	61	75	3D	h	104	150	68

Char	Dec	Octal	Hex	Char	Dec	Octal	Hex	Char	Dec	Octal	Hex
^S	19	23	13	>	62	76	3E	i	105	151	69
^T	20	24	14	?	63	77	3F	j	106	152	6A
^U	21	25	15	@	64	100	40	k	107	153	6B
^V	22	26	16	A	65	101	41	l	108	154	6C
^W	23	27	17	B	66	102	42	m	109	155	6D
^X	24	30	18	C	67	103	43	n	110	156	6E
^Y	25	31	19	D	68	104	44	o	111	157	6F
^Z	26	32	1A	E	69	105	45	p	112	160	70
ESC	27	33	1B	F	70	106	46	q	113	161	71
FS	28	34	1C	G	71	107	47	r	114	162	72
GS	29	35	1D	H	72	110	48	s	115	163	73
RS	30	36	1E	I	73	111	49	t	116	164	74
US	31	37	1F	J	74	112	4A	u	117	165	75
space	32	40	20	K	75	113	4B	v	118	166	76
!	33	41	21	L	76	114	4C	w	119	167	77
"	34	42	22	M	77	115	4D	x	120	170	78
#	35	43	23	N	78	116	4E	y	121	171	79
$	36	44	24	O	79	117	4F	z	122	172	7A
%	37	45	25	P	80	120	50	{	123	173	7B
&	38	46	26	Q	81	121	51	|	124	174	7C
'	39	47	27	R	82	122	52	}	125	175	7D
(	40	50	28	S	83	123	53	~	126	176	7E
)	41	51	29	T	84	124	54	del	127	177	7F
*	42	52	2A	U	85	125	55				

Table B.2   Escape Sequences in DCL Command Procedures to Control Screen Displays

Escape Sequence	Function
<ESC> [0m (default)	Writes normal characters
<ESC> [1m	Writes bold characters
<ESC> [4m	Writes underlined characters
<ESC> [5m	Writes blinking characters
<ESC> [7m	Writes reverse video characters
<ESC> #3	Writes double height (top half)
<ESC> #4	Writes double height (bottom half)
<ESC> #5	Writes single width (default)
<ESC> #6	Writes double width
<ESC> 7	Saves cursor's column position and character attributes
<ESC> 8	Restores cursor's column position and character attributes

Table B.3   Escape Sequences in DCL Command Procedures to Erase Screen Displays

Escape Sequence	Erase Function
<ESC> [0K	From the cursor to the end of the line
<ESC> [1K	From the beginning of the line to the cursor
<ESC> [2K	The entire line
<ESC> [0J	From the cursor to the end of the screen
<ESC> [1J	From the bottom of the screen to the cursor
<ESC> [2J	The entire screen

Appendix C

EDT Line Mode Commands

You can use line mode editing in EDT on any interactive terminal. This mode focuses on the line as the unit of text. Whenever you see the line mode asterisk prompt (*), you can type a line mode command.

Line mode commands use qualifiers and specifiers in addition to command words. Qualifiers, which modify the way EDT processes the command, are always optional. You must precede a qualifier with a slash (for example, /QUERY).

Specifiers tell EDT on which part of the text to operate. Optional specifiers are enclosed in square brackets (for example, [=buffer]). The main specifier is range, which references the line or lines affected by the command.

Table C.1 contains a brief description of the most commonly used line mode commands, along with their corresponding qualifiers and specifiers. The underlined letters in the line mode syntax statements in Table C.1 indicate the minimum allowable abbreviations for command words.

Table C.1   Line Mode Commands

Command	Description
C̲HANGE	Shifts EDT to keypad mode.
C̲LEAR *buffer*	Deletes the entire contents of the specified EDT buffer (text storage area) from your EDT session.
<CTRL/Z>	Causes EDT to exit from keypad mode to line mode editing. An asterisk prompt (*) will appear at the lower left margin of the terminal screen. To reenter keypad mode, type **C** (for **CHANGE**) and press <RETURN>. The cursor will return to its former location in the text.
E̲X̲I̲T̲ [/SAVE][*filespec*]	Ends the EDT editing session, saving a copy of the main buffer text in an external file. If you supply a file specification, EDT creates a file with that name and copies the contents of the main buffer into that file. A new version of an existing file is created only if the file is modified. The /SAVE command line qualifier tells EDT to save the journal file upon exiting.
H̲E̲L̲P̲ [*topic* [*subtopic* . . .]]	Displays information on various EDT topics on your terminal. If you supply no topic, HELP gives information on how to use the EDT Help facility.
IN̲CLUDE *filespec* [= *buffer*]	Copies the specified file into the current EDT session. If you give no location specifiers, the copy is placed above the current line. *Buffer* represents the name of an EDT buffer where you want the external file stored. The equal sign (=) must appear before the buffer name.
Q̲U̲I̲T̲ [/SAVE]	Ends your EDT session without saving a copy of your editing work. The /SAVE qualifier saves only the journal file, not the edited file.
S̲E̲T̲ S̲C̲REEN *width*	Sets the maximum number of characters that EDT displays on a line of text.
S̲E̲T̲ W̲R̲AP *number*	Determines whether EDT wraps text being inserted in keypad mode. Also determines the maximum line length for filling text. To remove word wrap, use the SET NOWRAP line mode command. The default is SET NOWRAP.
S̲H̲OW B̲U̲FFER	Lists all buffers currently in use during your EDT session. Also lists the number lines in each buffer. An equal sign (=) indicates the current buffer. An asterisk (*) next to Main indicates that there are more lines in the main buffer, but EDT has not yet seen them.

EDT2: A Sample TPU-Based Editor

EDT2 is an interactive text editor that demonstrates the versatility and extensibility of the VAXTPU programming language. This editor emulates the keypad functions and some of the line mode commands of the EDT text editor. It also has many of the features of EVE, including windowing. Most of the line-editing functions currently available in EDT have been implemented in EDT2 using the <GOLD> key and a single keyboard key. The purpose of presenting EDT2 is to provide you with a familiar editing interface. It is hoped that you will use this editor as you have used EDT, but then go on to enhance the editor.

The EDT2 editor supports ANSI CRT terminals. These include the VT200 and VT100 family of terminals and the VK100. The editor will run under any VMS operating system supporting the VAXTPU programming language.

EDT2 not only offers the complete numeric keypad functionality of EDT but also many other features to make text editing easy and efficient. These features include the following:

- Two ways to enter editing commands: keypad mode and line mode.
- Insert and overstrike mode.
- Transpose characters.
- Word wrap mode.
- A new on-line Help facility.

- A Journal facility that protects your editing work in case of a system interruption.
- Multiple windows. You can view two files on the same screen.
- Section files. You can customize the characteristics of your editing session using the VAXTPU language.
- Key definition facility. You can store a VAXTPU command in a single key using the DEFINE command or store one or more keystrokes in a single key using the LEARN command to minimize repetitive typing.
- DCL command execution directly from EDT2. You can Spawn a single command, create a subprocess to use the Mail and Phone facility, or execute a DCL command using the DCL Window function.

Before activating EDT2, you should define a symbol in your `LOGIN.COM` file. For example, add the following line to `LOGIN.COM`.

```
$ edt2 :== edit/tpu/section-edtsecini2.tpu$section
```

This will minimize the number of characters you need to enter each time you use the EDT2 text editor. Execute `LOGIN.COM` so that the new symbol can be established. Then you can activate the new editor by simply typing the new symbol and the name of a file. For example,

```
$ edt2 login.com
```

You should attempt to modify EDT2 only after you have become comfortable with the VAXTPU programming language.

Because EDT2 is too large to include in this appendix, specific modules that might be of interest are found on the next few pages. Contact the publisher of this book if you would like a copy of the EDT2 editor and the corresponding on-line help file.

```
!
!
!EDT2 - Return Key
!
PROCEDURE edt$return
local left_margin;
left_margin: = get_info (current_buffer, "left_margin");
split_line;
if      mark (none = end_of (current_buffer)
then
        move_vertical (-1);
endif;
edt$indent_line_to (left_margin);
ENDPROCEDURE;
```

```
!
!
! EDT2 - Capitalize String
!
!
! Capitalize a string—like change_case (string, capital)
! would be. Ignore leading punctuation, so things like "Hi"
! and (foo) can be capitalized.
!
! Parameters
!
!     cap_string          string to be capitalized - input/output
PROCEDURE edt$capitalize_string (cap_string)
local initial_letter,       ! initial substring ending at
                            ! first letter
      initial_index,        ! Loop index used in search for
                            ! first letter
      cap_string_length,    ! Length of cap_string parameter
      rest_of_string;       ! Remainder of cap_string after
                            ! initial_letter

initial_index    := 1;
cap_string_length  := length (cap_string);

loop
        initial_letter := substr (cap_string, 1, initial_index);
        exitif initial_index = cap_string_length;
        exitif index (edt$x_not_alphabetic,
                substr (cap_string, initial_index, 1)) = 0;
        initial_index := initial_index + 1
endloop;

rest_of_string := substr (cap_string, initial_index + 1,
        cap_string_length);
change_case (initial_letter, upper);
change_case (rest_of_string, lower);
cap_string := initial_letter + rest_of_string;

ENDPROCEDURE;
```

```
!
!
! EDT2 - Set Status Line
!
!
PROCEDURE edt$set_status_line
local   mode_string,
        left_margin,
        right_margin,
        wrap_string,
        margin_string,
        direction_string;

if      (current_buffer = dcl_buffer) or
        (current_buffer = paste_buffer)
then
        this_filespec :=
            get_info (current_buffer, "name") + " Buffer";
        set (status_line, current_window, reverse,
            this_filespec);
        return;
else
        this_filespec :=
            get_info (current_buffer, "output_file");
        if      this_filespec = 0
        then
                this_filespec := edt$x_empty;
        endif;

        this_filespec := "File: " + this_filespec;
endif;

if      length (this_filespec) > 43
then
        this_buffer_label := substr (this_filespec, 1, 43);
else
        this_buffer_label := this_filespec +
            substr (edt$x_extra_spaces, 1,
                43 - length (this_filespec));
endif;
if      get_info (current_buffer, "mode") = INSERT
then
        mode_string := | INS |";
else
        mode_string := " | Ovstr |";
endif;

        !
```

```
                ! Find out if the user is in Overstrike or Insert Mode.
                !

if      (current_window = top_window) or
        (current_window = main_window)
then
        if      edt$x_first_window_wordwrap <> 0
        then
                wrap_string := " Wrap  |";
        else
                wrap_string := " No Wrap |";
        endif;
else
        if      edt$x_secd_window_wordwrap <> 0
        then
                wrap_string := " Wrap |";
        else
                wrap_string := " NoWrap |";
        endif;
endif;

if      get_info (current_buffer, "direction") = REVERSE
then
        direction_string := " Rev | ";
else
        direction_string := " Fwd | ";
endif;
        !
        ! Find out if the user is moving up or down the screen.
        !
 left_margin := str (get_info (current_buffer, "left_margin"));
 right_margin := str (get_info (current_buffer,
     "right_margin"));
 margin_string := "M[" + left_margin + ","
     + right_margin + "]";


        !
        ! Find out what the current margins settings are.
        !
set (status_line, current_window, reverse,
        this_buffer_label + mode_string + wrap_string +
                direction_string + margin_string;
        !
        ! Print out status line on screen for the associated
        ! window.
        !


ENDPROCEDURE;
```

Appendix E

File Protection

VMS provides two file protection mechanisms for all system objects (files, directories, and devices):

UIC (User Identification Code)

ACL (Access Control List)

E.1 *UIC-Based Protection*

Every VMS system object has a UIC-based protection mask. You can see your own UIC by typing

```
$ show process
```

VMS uses the UIC to identify users as well as groups of users. Table E.1 lists various forms of UICs.

Table E.1   Sample UICs

UIC	Interpretion
[100,6]	Group 100, member 6 (numeric form)
[MUSIC,MOZART]	Group MUSIC, member MOZART (alphanumeric)
[MOZART]	Group MUSIC, member MOZART is understood (alphanumeric)
[GROUP_100,YOU]	Group_100, member YOU (alphanumeric)

Table E.2   UIC Levels of Protection

Level Name	Short Form	Scope
SYSTEM	S	All system users
OWNER	O	User UIC
GROUP	G	All users in the same group
WORLD	W	All users

Every UIC has four levels of protection associated with it, as listed in Table E.2.

Each protection level can be allowed or denied any of the types of access listed in Table E.3.

For example, when you create a subdirectory, you can choose its protection as follows:

```
$ create/directory/protection = (s:rwed,o:rwed,g:re,w)
```

You can change the default UIC protection on your local system by inserting the following command line in your **LOGIN.COM** file:

```
$ set protection = (s:rwed,o:rwed,g,w)/default
```

E.2   ## Access Control Lists

An access control list is a list associated with a system object. The **SET FILE/ACL** command makes it possible to establish an ACL for a system object. This command has the following syntax:

set file/acl [= (*acl* [, . . .])] *filespec* [, . . .]

Suppose, for example, that you want users with the following UICs to have access to **COM** files in your **VMS.VMS2** subdirectory:

UIC = [GROUP_2006, JSBACH] (*not in your group*)
UIC = [WAMOZART] (*in your group*)

Table E.3 Types of Access for Each UIC Protection Level

Access Name	Short Form	Interpretation
READ	R	Allocate privilege to read from a file
WRITE	W	Allocate writing privilege
EXECUTE	E	Allocate privilege to execute an image
DELETE	D	Allocate privilege to delete a file

Then you would type

```
$ set file/acl = (id = [group_206, jsbach], access = r+w+e+d) -
_$ /log/confirm [.vms.vms2]*.com
```

You can display the ACL for an object by typing

```
$ show acl [.vms.vms2]catch.com
```

Appendix F

Programming Languages

This appendix gives an overview of some commonly used VMS programming languages: VAX Macro, Pascal, Ada, Lisp, and C. The aim of this appendix is to point out the bare essentials needed to compile and run a program in one of these languages. For all of them, with the exception of Lisp, here are the steps you need to follow to obtain an executable version of a program:

1. Use an editor to create a file containing the source for a program. For example, to begin the creation of a Pascal program, **SAMPLE.PAS**, you might type

```
(*
This is a sample Pascal program to print a message.
*)
program sample (output);
begin
     writeln('Hello, world!');
end.
<CTRL/Z>
[Exit]
```

2. Next you need to compile your source text. A compiler is a program that translates a source file into machine-readable form. In a VMS programming environment, a compiler typically produces a machine-readable file with an **OBJ** file type. For example, to compile the sample program in step 1, you would type

```
$ pascal sample
```

If the source file compiled correctly, the directory will have a **SAMPLE.OBJ** entry.

3. Next you need to link the **OBJ** file to obtain an executable image. The linker is a program that does a variety of things needed to prepare an executable version of a program. It resolves references you might have made to internal and external procedures as well as performing various housekeeping tasks needed to install the executable version in physical memory. For example, to use the linker to link the sample program, you would type

```
$ link sample
```

Now a **SAMPLE.EXE** file is listed in the directory.

4. The last step is to execute the file. For example, to execute the sample program, you would type

```
$ run sample
Hello, world!
```

If you get stuck and you are not sure how to use any of the compilers on your system, enter the **HELP** command followed by the programming language name. Help about that compiler appears. For example,

```
$ help pascal
PASCAL
VAX PASCAL is an extended implementation of the PASCAL
language that has been developed for use under the
VAX/VMS operating system.
The command, PASCAL, invokes the VAX PASCAL compiler
to compile one or more source programs.
Format:
PASCAL file-spec, . . .
Additional information available:
Parameters Qualifiers
/ANALYSIS_DATA[ = file-spec] D = /NOANALYSIS_DATA
Press RETURN to continue . . .
```

To look behind the scenes at the internal machine characteristics of the translated source file produced by the Pascal compiler, you would type

```
$ pascal/list sample ! creates sample.lis
$ !
$ type sample.lis
SAMPLE
2:06 VAX Pascal V3.6-225 Page 1
 . . . . . . . . .
```

```
00001 C 0 0 (*
00002 C 0 0 This is a sample Pascal program . . .
00003 C 0 0 *)
00004 0 0 program sample(output);
00005 0 1 begin
    .  .  .  .  .  .  .  .
```

Bug Clinic: Detecting Programming Errors

Each of the compilers supplied by Digital provides debugging facilities as well as helpful, verbose, contextual error messages. For example, with the SAMPLE.PAS file, you might have typed the following *incorrect* version of the program:

```
(*
This is a sample Pascal program (with a bug!).
*)
program sample (output);
begin
     writeln(Hello, world!');
end.
```

This version of SAMPLE.PAS (called BUGGY.PAS) has a missing apostrophe. To find bugs, you can compile the source file with the /LIST qualifier. For example, you could compile BUGGY.PAS by typing:

```
$ pascal/list buggy
00003 0 1 writeln(Hello, world!');
% PASCAL-E-UNDECLID, (1) Undeclared identifier HELLO
% PASCAL-E-UNDECLID, (2) Undeclared identifier WORLD
% PASCAL-E-SYNASCII, (3) Illegal ASCII character
% PASCAL-E-ENDDIAGS, Pascal completed with 3 diagnostics.
```

You can also use the /DEBUG qualifier to invoke a debugger program. For example, you could type

```
$ pascal/debug buggy.pas
```

The /DEBUG qualifier invokes the debugger after program execution has been interrupted by either a <CTRL/y>or <CTRL/c>. For more information about /DEBUG, type

```
$ help debug
```

VAX Macro: Assembly Language Programming

Assembly language gives you a way to write the symbolic forms of machine instructions. VAX Macro source programs have a **MAR** file type and the following syntax:

```
; introductory comments
;
; possible macro definitions, declarations of variables:
;
begin: .word ; begins program section
;
; assembly language instructions:
repeat:
movl #1, r6 ; puts 1 in register 6
clrl r7 ; clears register 7
jmp repeat ; jumps back to repeat
$exit_s ; ends program section
;
; optional subroutines
;
.end begin ; identifiers transfer address
```

If you are new to assembly language programming, having an infinite loop in your program is helpful so that you can interrupt the execution with a <CTRL/y>. Then it will be possible for you to examine the contents of main memory to see various forms of the machine code being used by the VAX to execute your program.

Here is a sample assembly language program, INF.MAR.

```
; sample VAXMacro program with an infinite loop
;
begin: .word ; begin program
movl #1, r6 ; moves a 1 into register 6
repeat:
jmp repeat ; jumps back to repeat forever
$exit_s
.end begin ; supplies transfer address
```

To compile, link, and run this sample program, you would type

```
$ macro inf
$ link inf
$ run inf
```

To interrupt the execution of INF.EXE, you would type

```
<CTRL/y>
[Interrupt]
$
```

To examine the contents of the virtual memory used for **INF.EXE**, you would type

```
$ examine 200:21c
00000200: 01D00000 1757D456 01DF8AF 409F01FB . . . .
0000021c: 00000000
$
```

The **EXAMINE** command displays the contents of specified memory addresses. In the example, you display the base 16 machine codes for **INF.EXE**, which you were executing before you typed <CTRL/y>, as well as the virtual memory addresses used by the run-time system to store **INF.EXE**. You can create a **LIS** file containing lots of information about the compiled program by typing

```
$ macro/list inf.mar
```

INF.LIS appears in the current directory. This file cross-references the machine code, virtual memory addresses, and your assembly language source text. It also provides the symbol table set up VAX Macro for any labels used in the program. In addition, it shows how the compiled program (the **OBJ** version) has been organized. To see this, you would type

```
$ type inf.lis
```

F.3   ## VAX Ada

Digital Equipment Corporation supplies a certified Ada compiler as specified by the Department of Defense. It conforms to the complete specification given in ANSI/MIL-STD-1815A-1983. It is called VAX Ada.

If you are learning VAX Ada for the first time, you might want to read the help information about it. Type the following to get help:

```
$ help ada
```

VAX Ada has its own library management utility called ACS. It is ACS that provides an interface between the Ada source file, the VAX Ada compiler, and the VAX/VMS linker. To find out about the ACS system, type

```
$ acs
ACS>
```

After the **ACS>** system prompt appears, you can access help by typing

```
ACS> help
```

This will provide the full range of information needed to work inside the VAX Ada ACS environment. You will probably find the Getting_Started information especially helpful. To see this information, enter the following line at the **ACS>** prompt:

```
ACS> Getting_Started
```

VAX Ada programs are compiled and linked in the context of an ADA program library, which is managed by the VAX Ada program library manager (ACS). To start using VAX Ada, execute the following ACS commands to create, initialize, and define your current program library. This series of commands ensures that your program library is a subdirectory of your current VMS working directory.

```
$ acs create library [.adalib]
$ acs set library [.adalib]
    .
    .
    .
```

After executing these ACS commands, you should find that you have an **ADALIB.DIR** entry in your current directory.

You can then use an editor to create an Ada source file and then enter the following command lines to compile, link, and run the program:

```
$ ada/list/dir = [.adalib] sample.ada
$ acs link sample
$ run sample
```

The following is a complete ADA program called **OVERWRITE.ADA** that illustrates the use of Ada text input/output.

```
with text_in; use text_in;
procedure overwrite is
inout_line: string(1 . . 10) := "tenletters";
last_char: natural;
begin
loop
put_line("enter line of text: ");
get_line(inout_line, last_char);
put_line(inout_line);
end loop;
end overwrite;
```

This Ada overwrite procedure will take up ten characters you enter from a keyboard and overwrite the "tenletters" string. For example, you can compile, link, and then run the program as follows:

```
$ ada/list/directory-[.adalib] overwrite.ada
$ acs link overwrite
$ run overwrite
Enter a line of text: cpu
cpuletters
Enter a line of text: It rains in springtime . . .
It rains i
Enter a line of text:
n springti
Enter a line of text:
me . . . ingti
Enter a line of text:
sing
sing.ingti
Enter a line of text:
<CTRL/z>
[Interrupt]
$
```

If you enter a <CTRL/y> instead of a <CTRL/z>, you receive a host of complaints from the Ada run-time system about your bad input (an entered string that exceeds the specified string length).

F.4

VAX Lisp

VAX Lisp is a powerful Lisp system that includes both a compiler and an interpreter. You should start off in the interpreter environment. To do so, type

```
$ lisp
Welcome to VAX LISP, version V2.2
Lisp>
```

To get help when working in this Lisp interpreter environment, you can type

```
Lisp> (help)
VAX LISP is an implementation of the Common LISP
language specification. The language is described in
detail in "Common LISP: The Language" by Guy L. Steele Jr.
Bedford, Mass.: Digital Press, 1984.
    .
    .
    .
Lisp>
```

To get a feeling for what can be done in this environment, enter the following command lines after the **Lisp>** prompt:

```
Lisp> ( )
NIL
Lisp> (+ 2 3)
5
Lisp> (* 2 3333)
6666
Lisp> (car '(Time flows easily in May.))
TIME
Lisp> (cdr '(Time flows easily in May.))
FLOWS EASILY IN MAY.
Lisp> (cons '(Time) '(and the river))
((TIME) AND THE RIVER)
Lisp> (exit)
$
```

Notice that you need to type **(exit)** to return to VMS and the DCL **$** prompt.

VAX C

The VAX C compiler makes it possible to write C programs in a VMS environment. C programs have a **c** file type. To compile, link, and run a C program, type

```
$ cc filename
$ link filename
$ run filename
```

If you are used to working with C in a UNIX environment, you will find that VAX C is subtly different syntactically. For example, instead of using

```
#include<stdio.h>
```

VAX C requires

```
#include stdio
```

to invoke the standard input/output C library functions. In addition, you do not use the VAX C Curses Screen Management package. Instead, you must define the following logical name:

```
define lnk$library sys$library:vaxctrl
```

F.6   *References*

Peters, J. F. *The Art of Assembly Language Programming VAX-11*. Englewood Cliffs, N.J.: Prentice-Hall, 1985.

Peters, J. F. *Pascal with Program Design*. New York: Holt, Rinehart, and Winston, 1986.

Order from Digital Equipment Corporation, POB CS2008, Nashua, NH 03061:

Guide to VAX C. Order no. AI-L370C-TE

VAX Ada Programmer's Run-Time Reference Manual. Order no. AA-EF88A-TE.

VAX LISP/VMS User's Guide. Order no. Y921B-TE.

ANSI Mode Control Sequences

This appendix describes each control sequence recognized by a VT200 or VT100 terminal in ANSI mode. Many of the sequences described in this appendix conform to the basic format, as specified by the ANSI X3.64 standard.

G.1   **Syntax for Control Sequences**

The syntax for control sequences is

```
ESC [Ps/Pn  F.
```

ESC [is the lead-in sequence as specified by the ANSI standard. Sometimes it is referred to as the Control Sequence Indicator. Ps refers to a selective parameter; Pn refers to a numeric parameter. Some sequences use selective parameters, and others use numeric parameters. The same control sequence is never used together. If the Ps or Pn value is not specified, the default value is assumed. F is the termination character of the sequence. It specifies the function to be performed. This character varies with each function.

G.2   **Define the Scrolling Region**

The command syntax is

```
ESC [x;y r
```

This command is used to set the top and bottom lines of the screen scrolling region. The lines on the screen are numbered 1 through 24. The first numeric parameter, **x**, sets the top boundary. The second numeric parameter, **y**, sets the bottom boundary of the scrolling region. The default values are the entire screen (that is, x = 1 and y = 24).

G.3 Move a Single Character

The command syntax is

```
ESC [Pn F
```

By using a single control sequence, the cursor can be moved any number of increments up, down, right, or left. The numeric parameter specifies how many increments the cursor is to move; the default value is 1. The value of the termination character, **F**, determines the direction of movement, as specified in Table G.1.

G.4 Absolute Cursor Positioning

The command syntax is

```
ESC [x;y H
```

or

```
ESC [x;y f
```

Either of these control sequences can be used for positioning the cursor on an absolute basis. These sequences will position the cursor to the line specified by **x** and the column specified by **y**. The default value for both **x** and **y** is 1.

G.5 Index

The command syntax is

```
ESC D
```

This sequence causes the cursor to move down one position. If the cursor is positioned on the bottom line of the screen or the bottom of the screen scrolling region, the contents of the screen or scrolling region will scroll up one line.

Table G.1   Cursor Control Commands

Command Name	F Value	Control Sequence
Cursor up	A	`ESC [Pn A`
Cursor down	B	`ESC [Pn B`
Cursor right	C	`ESC [Pn C`
Cursor left	D	`ESC [Pn D`

G.6   Reverse Index

The command syntax is

`ESC M`

This sequence causes the cursor to move up one position. If the cursor is positioned on the top of the screen or the top of the scrolling region, the contents of the screen or scrolling region will scroll down one line.

G.7   Next Line

The command syntax is

`ESC E`

This sequence causes the cursor to move to the beginning of the next line. If the cursor is positioned on the bottom line of the screen or the bottom of the screen scrolling region, the contents of the screen or scrolling region will scroll up one line.

G.8   Erasure Commands

The command syntax is

`ESC [Ps F`

The same control sequence format is used for all erasure commands. The termination character, `F`, determines whether erasure will occur on a line or screen basis. The selective parameter, `Ps`, determines the portion of the line or screen to be erased, as seen in Table G.2. In all cases, erasure commands do not cause the cursor to move.

Table G.2 Erasure Commands

Command Name	F Value	Ps Value	Control Sequence
From the cursor to the end of the line	K	0 or none	ESC [0 K
From the beginning of the line to the cursor	K	1	ESC [1 K
The entire line containing the cursor	K	2	ESC [2 K
From the cursor to the end of the screen	J	0 or none	ESC [0 J
From the beginning of the screen to the cursor	J	1	ESC [1 J
The entire screen	J	2	ESC [2 J

G.9 Change the Line to Single Height and Single Width

The command syntax is

ESC #5

This command causes all characters displayed on the line marked by the cursor to be single height and single width.

G.10 Change the Line to Single Height and Double Width

The command syntax is

ESC #6

This command causes all characters displayed on the line marked by the cursor to be single height and double width. If the line was previously single height and single width, all characters from the middle of the line to the end of the line are lost. The cursor remains at the same character position unless the character position is lost, in which case, the cursor is moved to the right margin.

**Change the Line to Double Height
and Double Width**

The command syntax is

`ESC #3`

and

`ESC #4`

These two commands are used as a pair, on adjacent lines, from double-height and double-width characters. The same character must be sent to the same column of both lines to form each character. If the line was previously single height and single width, all characters from the middle of the line to the end of the line are lost. The cursor remains at the same character position unless the character position is lost, in which case, the cursor is moved to the right margin.

Video Attribute Commands

Data on the screen can be displayed in any combination of the following video attributes: High Intensity, Underline, Blink, or Reverse Video.

The attributes are cumulative. Data received will be displayed according to all attributes that are enabled. The control sequence format for enabling video attributes is

`ESC [Ps;Ps;  . . . Ps m`

where `Ps;Ps;  . . . Ps` is the parameter string defining which video attributes to enable. If multiple video attributes are to be enabled with one control sequence, use a semicolon to separate each selective parameter in the sequence.

Table G.3 summarizes all the video attributes and their associated selective parameters.

Table G.3   Video Attribute Commands

Attribute	Selective Parameter	Control Sequence
Attributes OFF	0 (default)	`ESC [m`
High intensity	1	`ESC [1m`
Underline	4	`ESC [4m`
Blink	5	`ESC [5m`
Reverse video	7	`ESC [7m`

Appendix H

Terminal Characteristics

To display the current characteristics of a specific terminal, type the following command sequence:

```
$ show terminal
```

If you display characteristic information for a terminal allocated to another user, the input, output, LFfill, CRfill, width, page, and parity characteristics will not be displayed.

The following is an example of the information VMS returns. Each characteristic corresponds to an option of the **SET TERMINAL** command. Table H.1 provides a brief explanation of each terminal characteristic.

```
Terminal: _TXB4:      Device_Type: VT200_Series    Owner: PJ_Holmay

   Input:    9600      LFfill: 0       Width: 80     Parity: None
   Output:   9600      CRfill: 0       Page:   24

Terminal Characteristics:
   Interactive        Echo              Type_ahead       No Escape
   Hostsync           TTsync            Lowercase        Tab
   No Wrap            Scope             Remote           No Eightbit
   No Broadcast       No Readsync       No Form          Fulldup
```

Modem	No Local_echo	Autobaud	Hangup
Brdcstmbx	DMA	No Altypeahd	Set_speed
Line Editing	Overstrike editing	No Fallback	No Dialup
No Secure serve	No Disconnect	No Pasthru	No Sys-password
No SIXEL Graphics	No Soft Characters	Printer Port	Numeric Keypad
ANSI_CRT	No Regis	No Block_mode	Advanced _video
No Edit_mode	DEC_CRT	No DEC_CRT2	No DEC_CRT3

Table H.1 Terminal Characteristics

Characteristic	Description
[NO] Advanced_video	Specifies whether the terminal has advanced video attributes and is capable of 132-column mode.
[NO] Altypeahd	Controls the size of the type-ahead buffer.
[NO] ANSI_CRT	Specifies whether the terminal conforms to ANSI CRT programming standards. The default of all VT100-family terminals is ANSI_CRT.
Application Keypad	Enables the use of the DEFINE/KEY facility. The default is NUMERIC KEYPAD.
[NO] Autobaud	Controls whether to enable automatic baud rate detection for a terminal.
[NO] Block_mode	Specifies whether the terminal is capable of performing block mode transmission, local editing, and field protection.
[NO] Brdcstmbx	Controls whether broadcast messages are sent to an associated mailbox if one exists.
[NO] Broadcast	Controls the display of MAIL notifications and REPLY messages. NOBROADCAST is specified when special output should not be interrupted by messages. The default is BROADCAST.
CRfill: #	Prevents the system from sending out data before the terminal is ready to accept it. A number between 0 and 9 indicates the number of null fill characters to be generated after a return. The default is CRFILL: 0.
[NO] DEC_CRT	Specifies whether the terminal conforms to DEC VT100-family standards and supports the minimum VT100 standards including DEC escape sequences.

Characteristic	Description
Device_Type: type	Specifies the default terminal type for which characteristics will be set.
[NO] Dialup	Specifies that the terminal is a dial-up terminal. The default is NO DIALUP.
[NO] Disconnect	Specifies that the process connected to this terminal not be discontinued if the line detects a hangup. The default is NO DISCONNECT.
[NO] DMA	Controls the use of direct memory access (DMA) mode on a controller that supports this feature. The default is hardware-dependent.
[NO] Echo	Controls whether the terminal will display any input lines it receives. The default is ECHO.
[NO] Edit_mode	Specifies whether the terminal will be capable of performing ANSI defined editing functions. The default is hardware-dependent.
[NO] Eight_bit	Indicates whether the terminal uses an eight-bit ASCII character code. The default is NO EIGHT_BIT for all terminals except VT200 series.
[NO] Escape	Controls whether the terminal driver checks an escape sequence for syntax before passing it to an application program. The default is NO ESCAPE.
[NO] Fallback	Specifies that eight-bit DEC Multinational Character Set characters be displayed as their seven-bit representation. The default depends on if the EIGHT_BIT characteristic is set.
[NO] Form	Controls whether form-feed characters translate into one or more line feeds or are left alone.
Fulldup	Specifies that the terminal will operate in full duplex.
Halfdup	Specifies that the terminal will operate in half duplex. The default is HALFDUP.

Table H.1 Terminal Characteristics *(continued)*

Characteristic	Description
[NO] Hangup	Controls whether the terminal mode is hung up when you log out. To use this feature, you may be required to have certain privileges.
Hardcopy	Indicates that the terminal is a hard-copy (i.e., keyboard printer) device.
[NO] Hostsync	Controls whether the computer system will generate ctrl-s and ctrl-q to enable or disable the reception of input. The default is NO HOSTSYNC.
Input: ####	Specifies the rate at which the terminal will receive characters. The default is installation-dependent.
Insert Editing	Controls whether characters will be inserted when editing command lines. The default is OVERSTRIKE.
LFfill: #	Specifies whether the system must generate fill characters following a line-feed on the terminal. This characteristic prevents the system from sending out data before the terminal is ready to accept them.
[NO] Line Editing	Enables or disables the advanced editing features for editing command lines.
[NO] Local_echo	Controls whether the terminal echoes characters locally rather than relying on the host to echo them. The default is NO LOCAL_ECHO.
Lowercase	Controls whether characters input to the terminal will be displayed as lowercase letters.
[NO] Modem	Indicates whether the terminal is connected to a modem or standard EIA cable arrangement.
Numeric Keypad	Specifies that the numeric keypad can be used to type numbers and punctuation marks. The default is NUMERIC KEYPAD.
Output: ####	Specifies the rate at which the terminal will transmit characters. The default is installation-dependent.
Overstrike	Indicates that the current character can be overwritten when editing a command line. The default is OVERSTRIKE.
Page: ##	Specifies the page length of a terminal or printer.
Parity: xxxx	Specifies the parity currently set for the terminal. The default is EVEN.

Characteristic	Description
[NO] Pasthru	Controls whether the system interprets special characters or passes all data to an application program as binary data. The default is NO PASTHRU.
[NO] Printer Port	Specifies whether the terminal has a printer port available. The default is installation-dependent.
[NO] Readsync	Controls whether the system will solicit read data from a terminal using ctrl-q and ctrl-s sequences. The default is NO READSYNC.
[NO] Regis	Specifies whether the terminal understands ReGIS graphic commands.
[NO] Scope	Indicates that the terminal is a video device.
[NO] Set_speed	Controls whether the /SPEED qualifier can be used to change the terminal speed. Requires specific privileges.
[NO] Secure Server	Determines if the use of the Break key on the terminal will log out the current process. The default is NO SECURE SERVER.
[NO] SIXEL Graphics	Controls whether the terminal is capable of displaying graphics using the ReGIS-defined SIXEL graphics protocol. The default is device-dependent.
[NO] Soft Characters	Controls whether the terminal can load a user-defined character set. The default is device-dependent.
[NO] Tab	Controls whether tab characters are expanded to spaces or are left alone.
[NO] TTsync	Controls whether the system responds to ctrl-s and ctrl-q issued from the terminal in order to synchronize output. The default is TTSYNC.
[NO] Type_ahead	Controls whether the terminal will accept unsolicited input. The default is TYPE_AHEAD.
Uppercase	Specifies that the terminal will translate all input lowercase letters to uppercase.
Width: ##	Specifies the number of characters that will be accepted on each input or output line. The width value n must be in the range of 1 to 511.
[NO] Wrap	Controls whether the terminal generates a carriage return/line feed when it reaches the end of the line. The default is WRAP.

Index

Commands (*cont.*)

Commands (*cont.*)

USER MODE qualifier, 246, 249
Username parameters, 4

VAX Macro programming language, 275, 278, 279
VAXTPU, 122, 267
VERSION LIMIT qualifier, 256
Video attribute commands, 288

Wildcards
  hyphen, 63, 70
  using, to specify files, 40, 44, 45, 46, 47, 55, 70,
     71, 175
Windows
  EVE, 122, 147, 148, 155
  in Phone utility, 160
Word, 117
WORD command, 94, 99, 115
WRITE command
  Command procedure, 218, 221, 222, 223, 239
WRITE qualifier, 221